SELECTED FOR A TOP-SECRET GOVERNMENT PROGRAM THAT GAVE HIM A HYPERACTIVE HEALING FACTOR, WADE WILSON USES HIS TALENTS TO BE THE WORLD'S MOST SKILLED MERCENARY— AND CERTAINLY ITS MOST ANNOYING. LOVED AND LOATHED AS THE MERC WITH THE MOUTH, WADE MAKES HIS MONEY AS A GUN FOR HIRE. FOR ALL YOUR HOMICIDAL NEEDS, NO QUESTIONS ASKED BUT PLENTY OF TASTELESS QUIPS DELIVERED WITH MAXIMUM POSSIBLE TRAUMA, CALL...

DEADPOOL Assassin

CULLEN BUNN
writer

MARK BAGLEY
penciler

JOHN DELL (#1-6)
WITH ROBERTO POGGI (#4), JP MAYER (#5),
SCOTT HANNA (#6) & CAM SMITH (#6)
inkers

**EDGAR DELGADO (#1-6) &
DONO SÁNCHEZ-ALMARA (#3-5) WITH REX LOKUS (#5)**
color artists

VC's JOE SABINO
letterer

**MARK BAGLEY, JOHN DELL
& VAL STAPLES**
cover artists

DEADPOOL created by **FABIAN NICIEZA & ROB LIEFELD**

LAUREN AMARO assistant editor   **DEVIN LEWIS** editor

MARK D. BEAZLEY   **CAITLIN O'CONNELL**   **KATERI WOODY**
collection editor   assistant editor   associate managing editor

JOE HOCHSTEIN   **JENNIFER GRÜNWALD**   **JEFF YOUNGQUIST**
associate manager, digital assets   senior editor, special projects   vp production & special projects

C.B. CEBULSKI   **JOE QUESADA**   **DAN BUCKLEY**   **ALAN FINE**
editor in chief   chief creative officer   president   executive producer

DEADPOOL: ASSASSIN. Contains material originally published in magazine form as DEADPOOL: ASSASSIN #1-6. First printing 2018. ISBN 978-1-302-91171-3. Published by MARVEL WORLDWIDE, INC., a subsidiary of MARVEL ENTERTAINMENT, LLC. OFFICE OF PUBLICATION: 135 West 50th Street, New York, NY 10020. Copyright © 2018 MARVEL No similarity between any of the names, characters, persons, and/or institutions in this magazine with those of any living or dead person or institution is intended, and any such similarity which may exist is purely coincidental. **Printed in the U.S.A.** DAN BUCKLEY, President, Marvel Entertainment; JOHN NEE, Publisher; JOE QUESADA, Chief Creative Officer; TOM BREVOORT, SVP of Publishing; DAVID BOGART, SVP of Business Affairs & Operations, Publishing & Partnership; DAVID GABRIEL, SVP of Sales & Marketing, Publishing; JEFF YOUNGQUIST, VP of Production & Special Projects; DAN CARR, Executive Director of Publishing Technology; ALEX MORALES, Director of Publishing Operations; DAN EDINGTON, Managing Editor; SUSAN CRESPI, Production Manager; STAN LEE, Chairman Emeritus. For information regarding advertising in Marvel Comics or on Marvel.com, please contact Vit DeBellis, Custom Solutions & Integrated Advertising Manager, at vdebellis@marvel.com. For Marvel subscription inquiries, please call 888-511-5480. **Manufactured between 8/31/2018 and 10/2/2018 by LSC COMMUNICATIONS INC., KENDALLVILLE, IN, USA.**

10 9 8 7 6 5 4 3 2 1

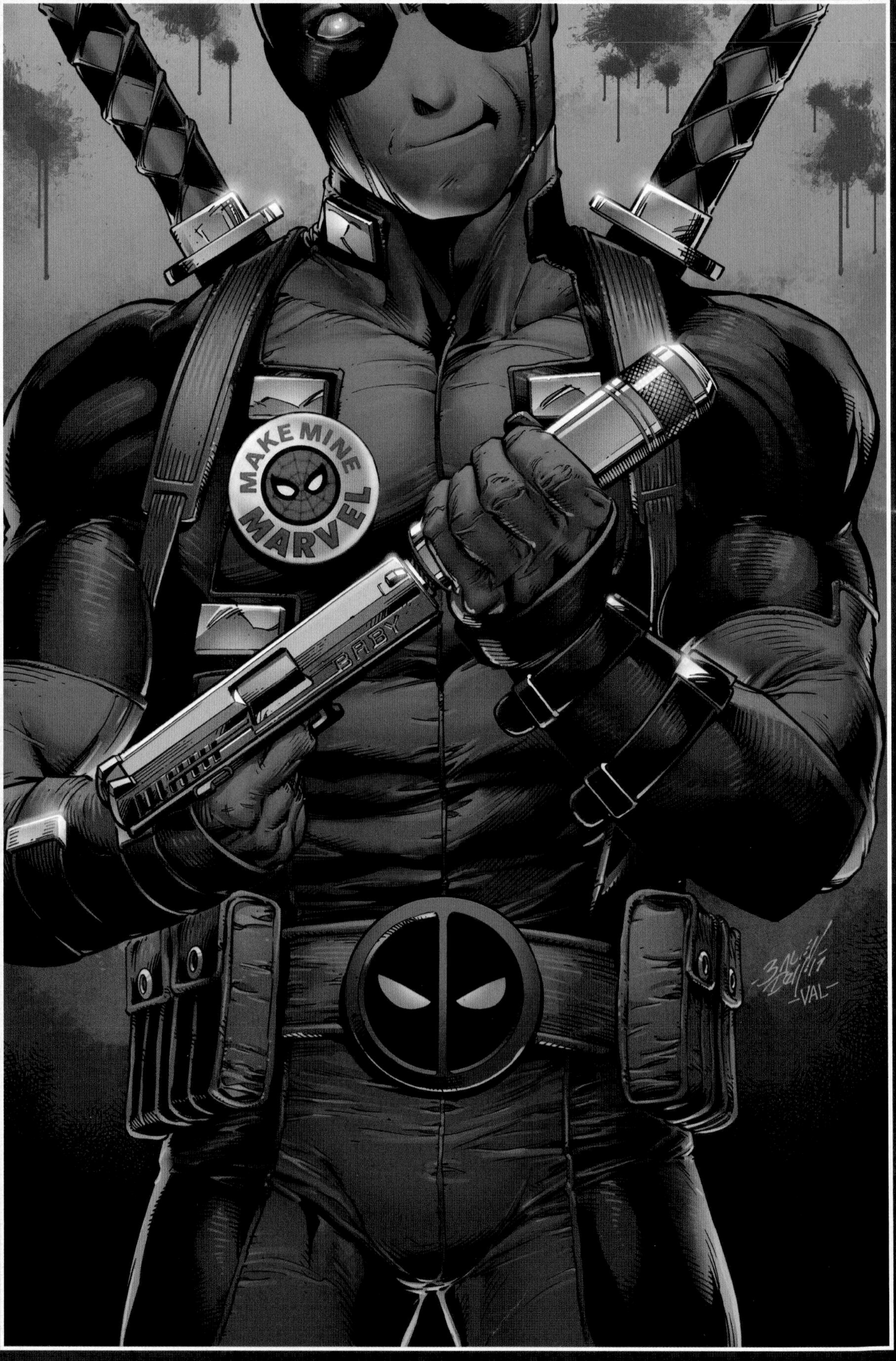
MAKE MINE
MARVEL
BABY
VAL

1

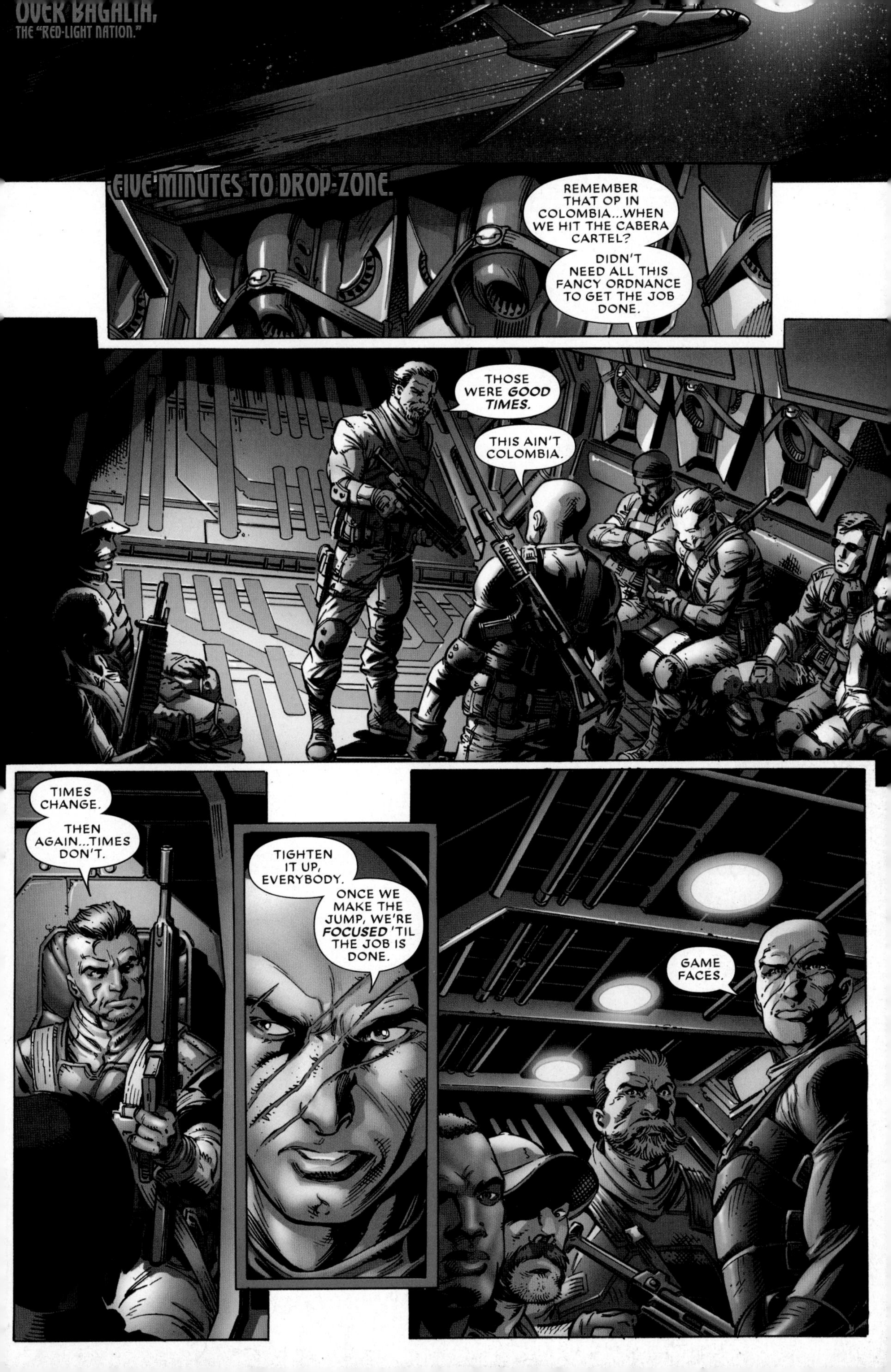
OVER BAGALIA, THE "RED-LIGHT NATION."
FIVE MINUTES TO DROP-ZONE.
REMEMBER THAT OP IN COLOMBIA...WHEN WE HIT THE CABERA CARTEL?
DIDN'T NEED ALL THIS FANCY ORDNANCE TO GET THE JOB DONE.
THOSE WERE GOOD TIMES.
THIS AIN'T COLOMBIA.
TIMES CHANGE.
THEN AGAIN...TIMES DON'T.
TIGHTEN IT UP, EVERYBODY.
ONCE WE MAKE THE JUMP, WE'RE FOCUSED 'TIL THE JOB IS DONE.
GAME FACES.

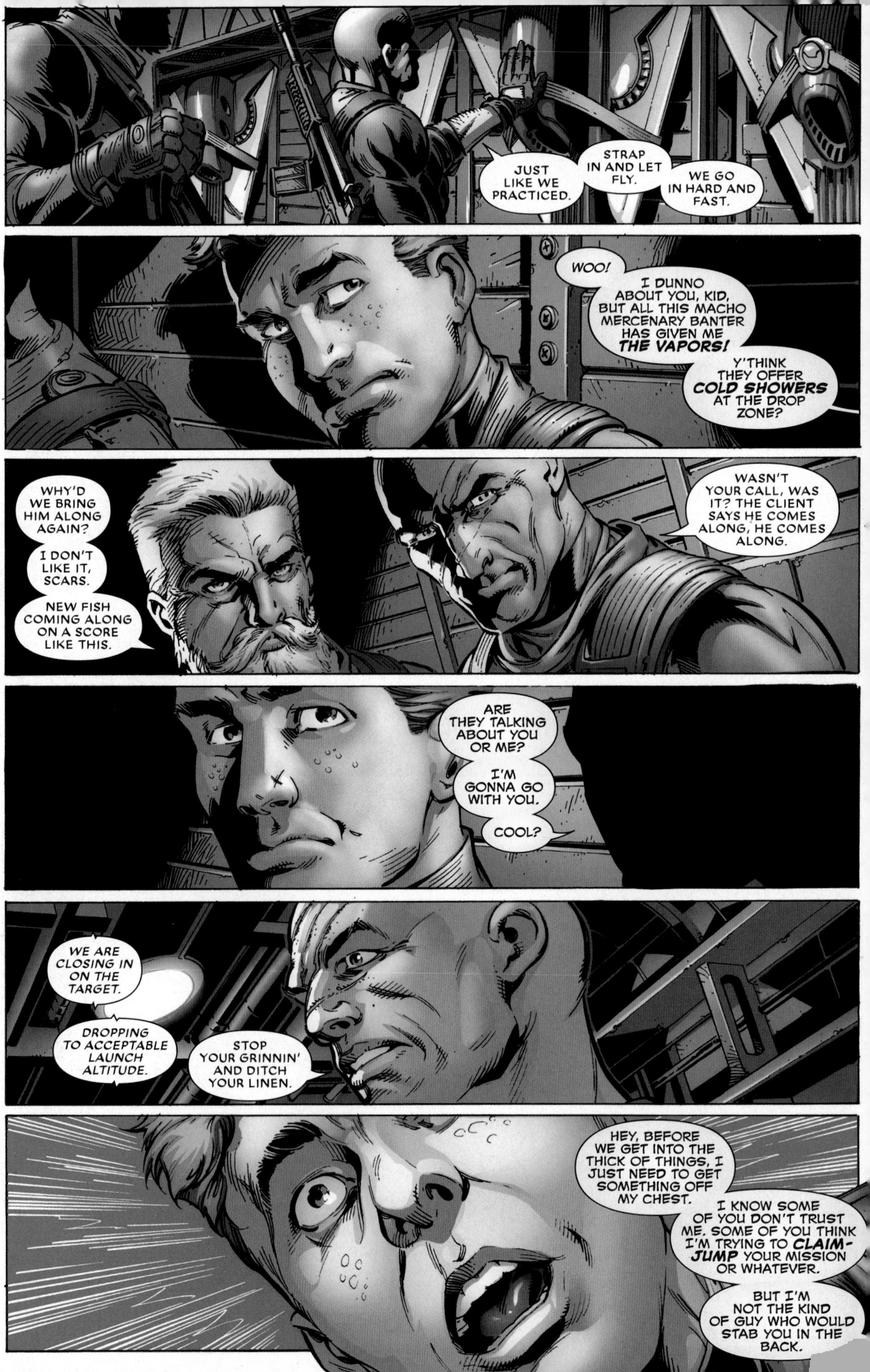
JUST LIKE WE PRACTICED.
STRAP IN AND LET FLY.
WE GO IN HARD AND FAST.
WOO!
I DUNNO ABOUT YOU, KID, BUT ALL THIS MACHO MERCENARY BANTER HAS GIVEN ME THE VAPORS!
Y'THINK THEY OFFER COLD SHOWERS AT THE DROP ZONE?
WHY'D WE BRING HIM ALONG AGAIN?
I DON'T LIKE IT, SCARS.
NEW FISH COMING ALONG ON A SCORE LIKE THIS.
WASN'T YOUR CALL, WAS IT? THE CLIENT SAYS HE COMES ALONG, HE COMES ALONG.
ARE THEY TALKING ABOUT YOU OR ME?
I'M GONNA GO WITH YOU.
COOL?
WE ARE CLOSING IN ON THE TARGET.
DROPPING TO ACCEPTABLE LAUNCH ALTITUDE.
STOP YOUR GRINNIN' AND DITCH YOUR LINEN.
HEY, BEFORE WE GET INTO THE THICK OF THINGS, I JUST NEED TO GET SOMETHING OFF MY CHEST.
I KNOW SOME OF YOU DON'T TRUST ME. SOME OF YOU THINK I'M TRYING TO CLAIM-JUMP YOUR MISSION OR WHATEVER.
BUT I'M NOT THE KIND OF GUY WHO WOULD STAB YOU IN THE BACK.

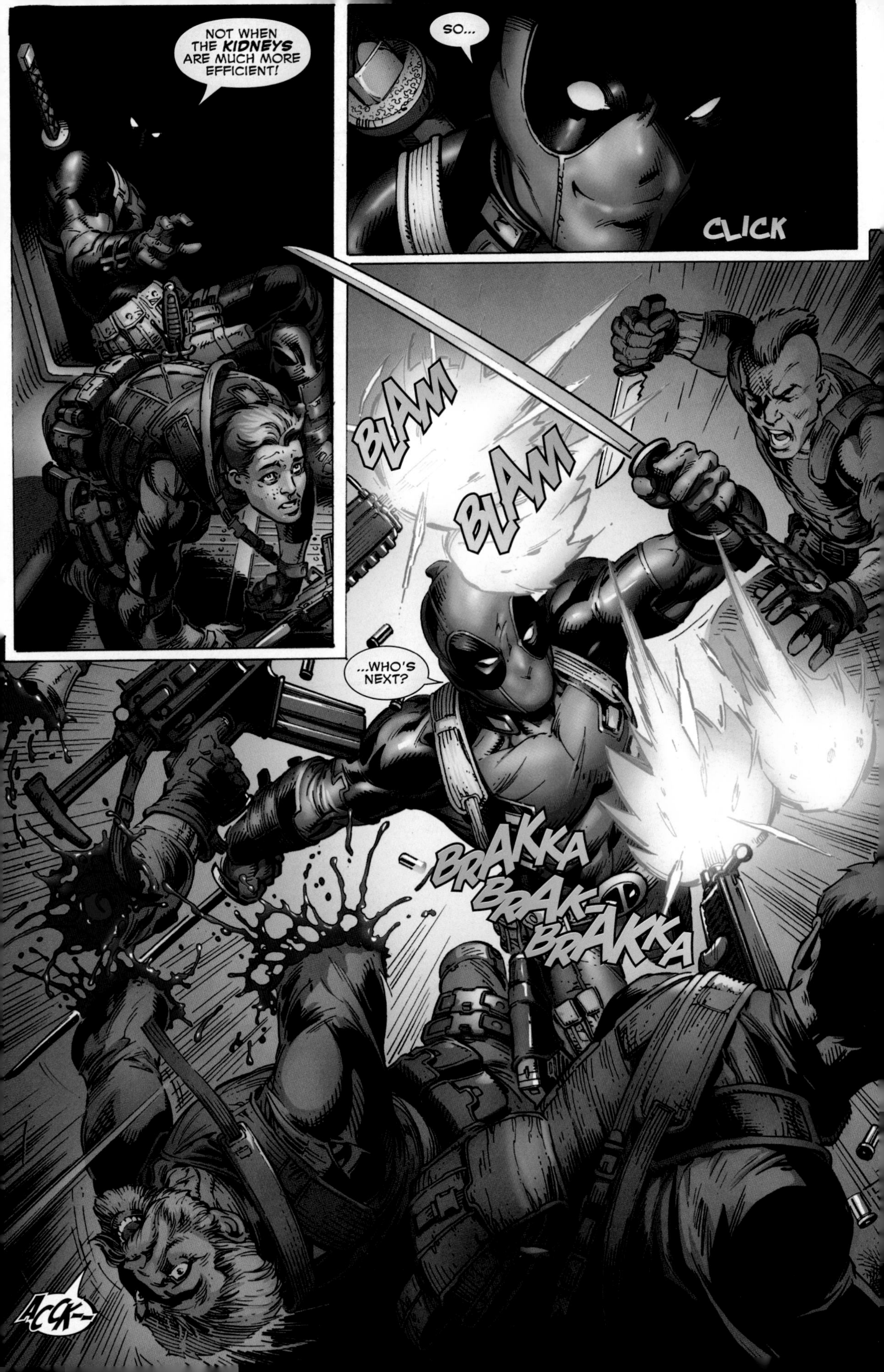
NOT WHEN THE KIDNEYS ARE MUCH MORE EFFICIENT!
SO...
CLICK
BLAM
BLAM
...WHO'S NEXT?
BRAKKA
BRAK-
BRAKKA
ACCK--

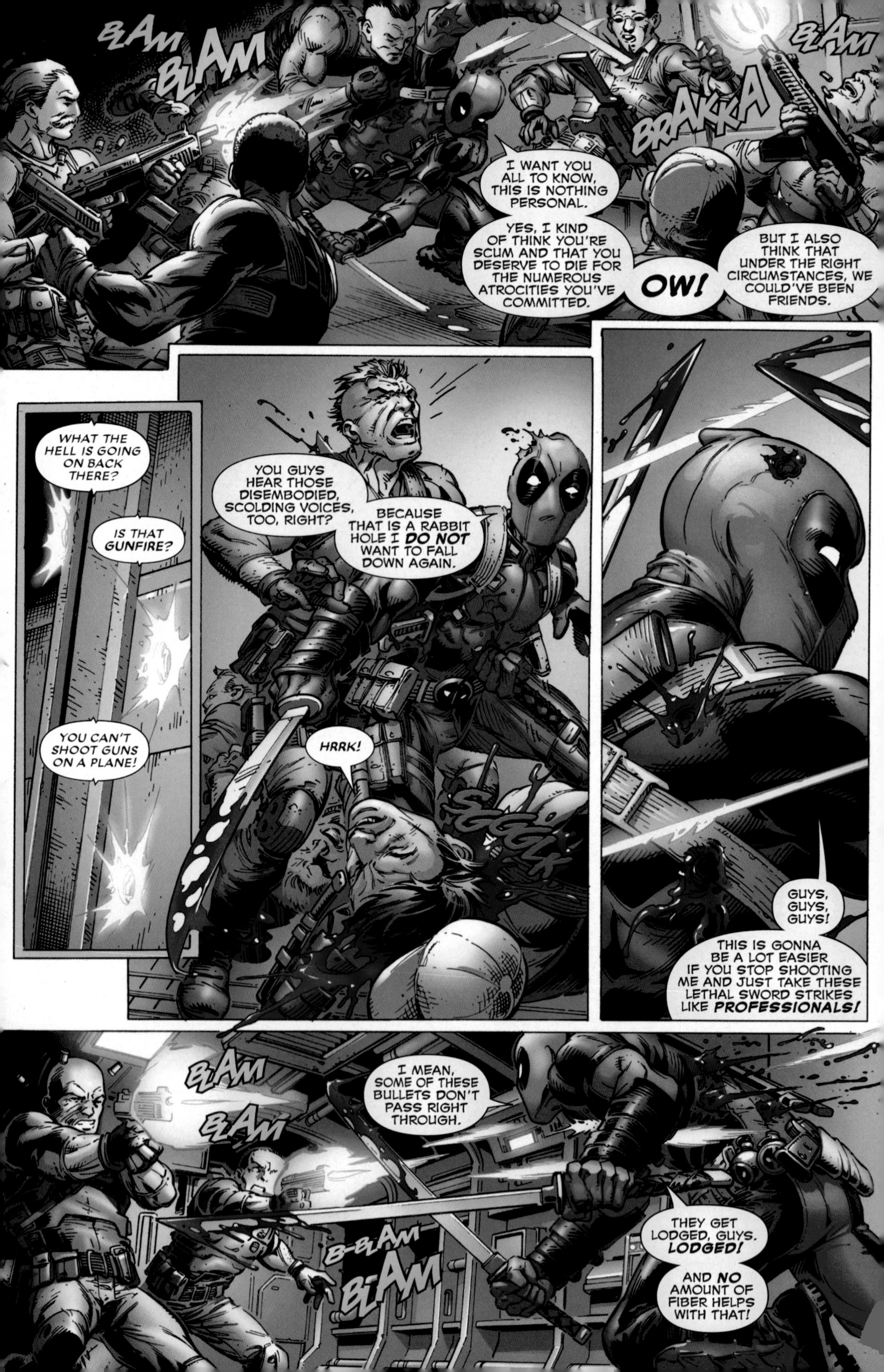
BLAM
BLAM
BRAKKA
BLAM
I WANT YOU ALL TO KNOW, THIS IS NOTHING PERSONAL.
YES, I KIND OF THINK YOU'RE SCUM AND THAT YOU DESERVE TO DIE FOR THE NUMEROUS ATROCITIES YOU'VE COMMITTED.
OW!
BUT I ALSO THINK THAT UNDER THE RIGHT CIRCUMSTANCES, WE COULD'VE BEEN FRIENDS.
WHAT THE HELL IS GOING ON BACK THERE?
IS THAT GUNFIRE?
YOU CAN'T SHOOT GUNS ON A PLANE!
YOU GUYS HEAR THOSE DISEMBODIED, SCOLDING VOICES, TOO, RIGHT?
BECAUSE THAT IS A RABBIT HOLE I DO NOT WANT TO FALL DOWN AGAIN.
HRRK!
SKGGGLK
GUYS, GUYS, GUYS!
THIS IS GONNA BE A LOT EASIER IF YOU STOP SHOOTING ME AND JUST TAKE THESE LETHAL SWORD STRIKES LIKE PROFESSIONALS!
BLAM
BLAM
I MEAN, SOME OF THESE BULLETS DON'T PASS RIGHT THROUGH.
B-BLAM
BLAM
THEY GET LODGED, GUYS. LODGED!
AND NO AMOUNT OF FIBER HELPS WITH THAT!

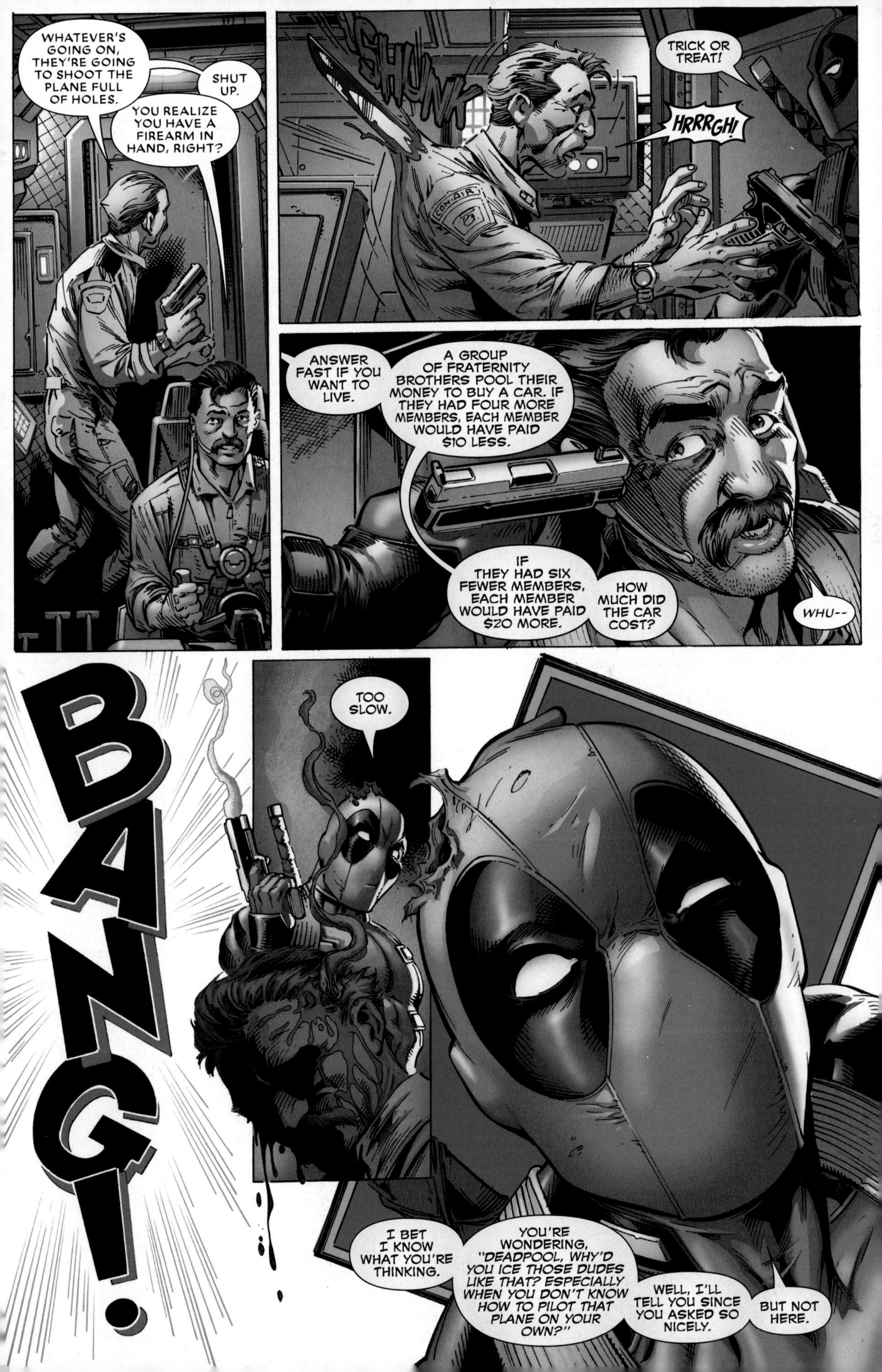
WHATEVER'S GOING ON, THEY'RE GOING TO SHOOT THE PLANE FULL OF HOLES.
SHUT UP.
YOU REALIZE YOU HAVE A FIREARM IN HAND, RIGHT?
SHUNK
TRICK OR TREAT!
HRRRGH!
CON-AIR
ANSWER FAST IF YOU WANT TO LIVE.
A GROUP OF FRATERNITY BROTHERS POOL THEIR MONEY TO BUY A CAR. IF THEY HAD FOUR MORE MEMBERS, EACH MEMBER WOULD HAVE PAID $10 LESS.
IF THEY HAD SIX FEWER MEMBERS, EACH MEMBER WOULD HAVE PAID $20 MORE.
HOW MUCH DID THE CAR COST?
WHU--
BANG!
TOO SLOW.
I BET I KNOW WHAT YOU'RE THINKING.
YOU'RE WONDERING, "DEADPOOL, WHY'D YOU ICE THOSE DUDES LIKE THAT? ESPECIALLY WHEN YOU DON'T KNOW HOW TO PILOT THAT PLANE ON YOUR OWN?"
WELL, I'LL TELL YOU SINCE YOU ASKED SO NICELY.
BUT NOT HERE.

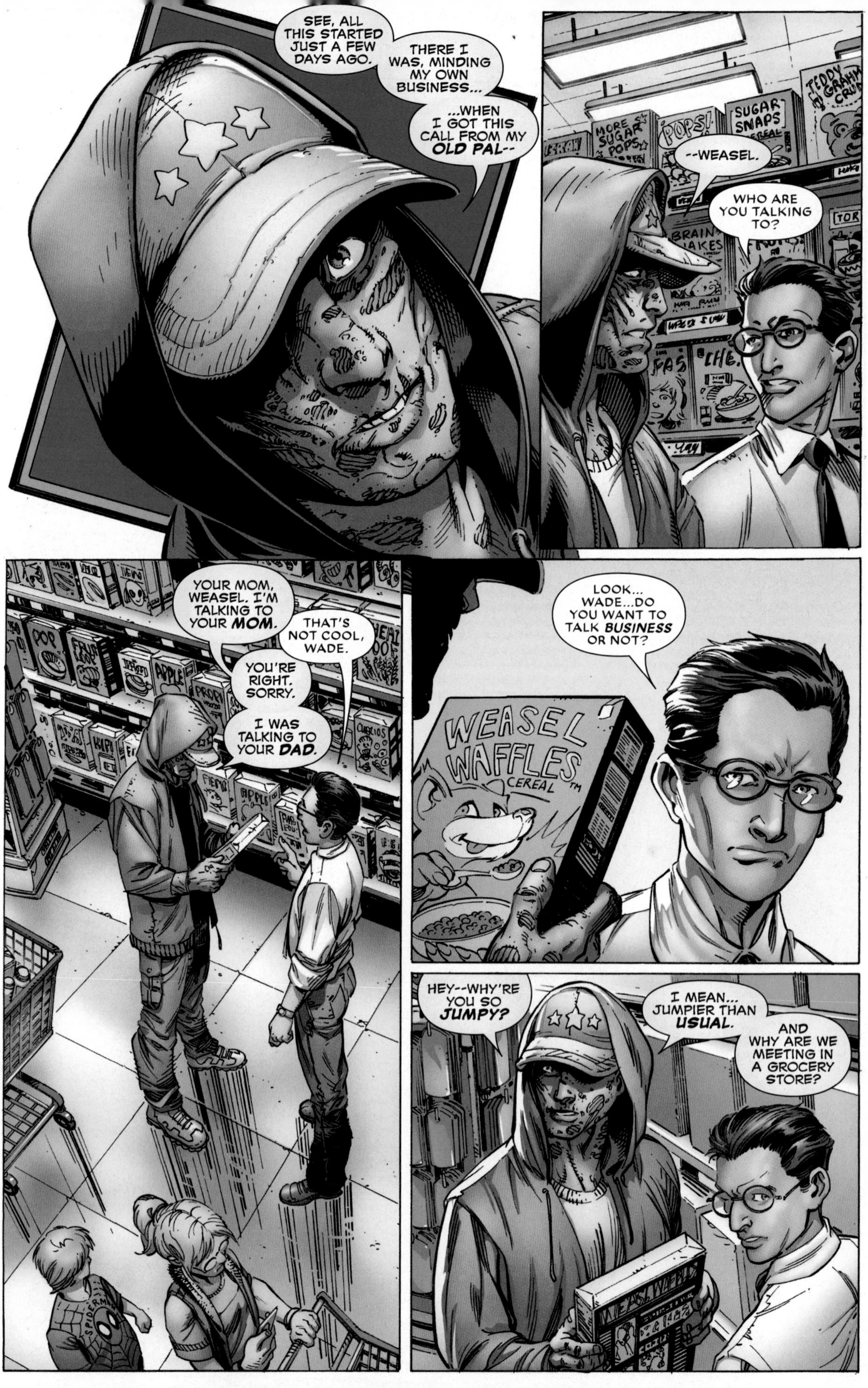
SEE, ALL THIS STARTED JUST A FEW DAYS AGO.
THERE I WAS, MINDING MY OWN BUSINESS...
...WHEN I GOT THIS CALL FROM MY ***OLD PAL***--
--WEASEL.
WHO ARE YOU TALKING TO?
YOUR MOM, WEASEL. I'M TALKING TO YOUR ***MOM***.
THAT'S NOT COOL, WADE.
YOU'RE RIGHT. SORRY.
I WAS TALKING TO YOUR ***DAD***.
LOOK... WADE...DO YOU WANT TO TALK ***BUSINESS*** OR NOT?
WEASEL WAFFLES CEREAL
HEY--WHY'RE YOU SO ***JUMPY?***
I MEAN... JUMPIER THAN ***USUAL***.
AND WHY ARE WE MEETING IN A GROCERY STORE?

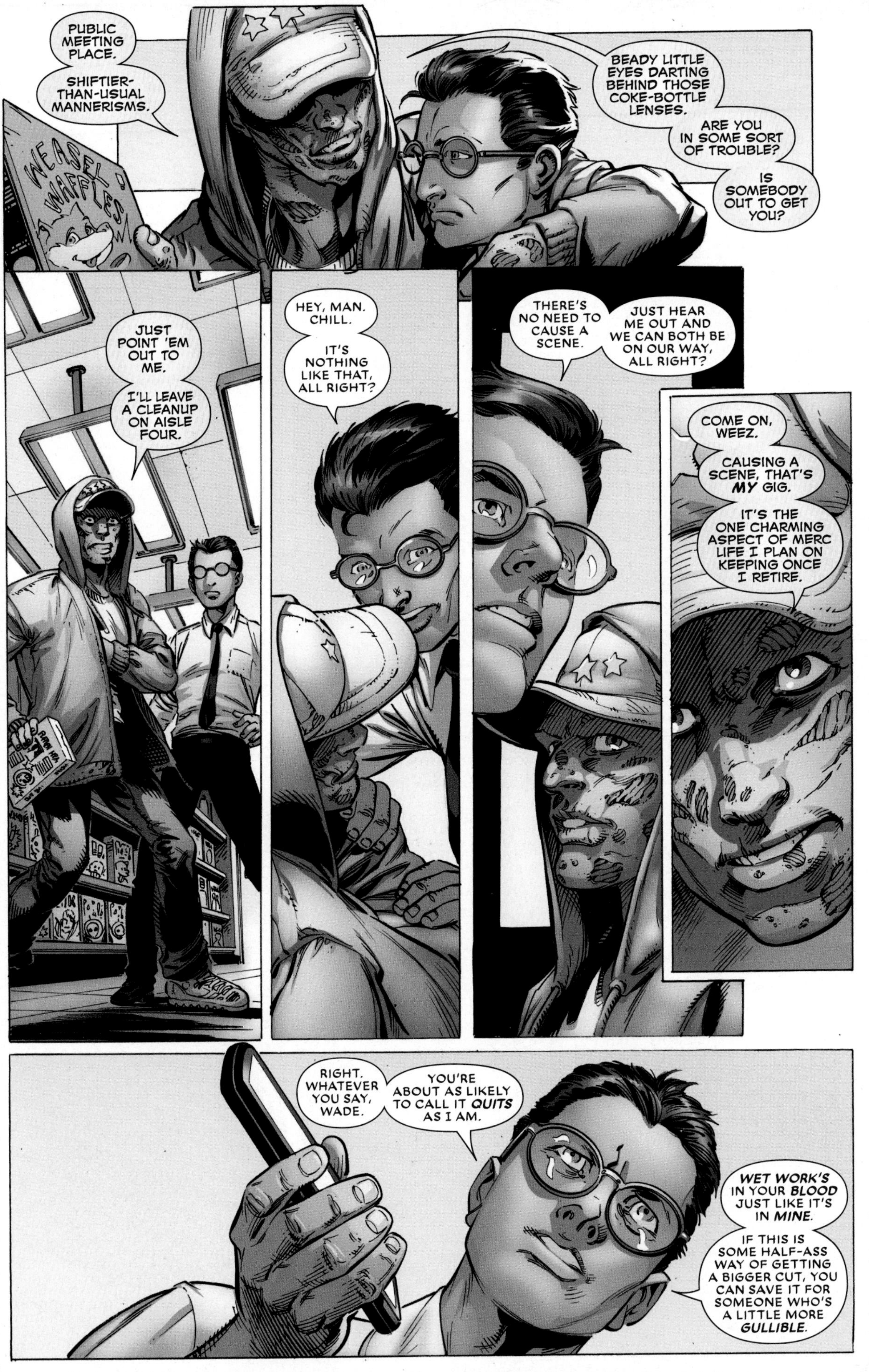
PUBLIC MEETING PLACE.
SHIFTIER-THAN-USUAL MANNERISMS.
BEADY LITTLE EYES DARTING BEHIND THOSE COKE-BOTTLE LENSES.
ARE YOU IN SOME SORT OF TROUBLE?
IS SOMEBODY OUT TO GET YOU?
WEASEL WAFFLES
JUST POINT 'EM OUT TO ME.
I'LL LEAVE A CLEANUP ON AISLE FOUR.
HEY, MAN. CHILL.
IT'S NOTHING LIKE THAT, ALL RIGHT?
THERE'S NO NEED TO CAUSE A SCENE.
JUST HEAR ME OUT AND WE CAN BOTH BE ON OUR WAY, ALL RIGHT?
COME ON, WEEZ.
CAUSING A SCENE, THAT'S *MY* GIG.
IT'S THE ONE CHARMING ASPECT OF MERC LIFE I PLAN ON KEEPING ONCE I RETIRE.
RIGHT. WHATEVER YOU SAY, WADE.
YOU'RE ABOUT AS LIKELY TO CALL IT *QUITS* AS I AM.
WET WORK'S IN YOUR *BLOOD* JUST LIKE IT'S IN *MINE*.
IF THIS IS SOME HALF-ASS WAY OF GETTING A BIGGER CUT, YOU CAN SAVE IT FOR SOMEONE WHO'S A LITTLE MORE *GULLIBLE*.

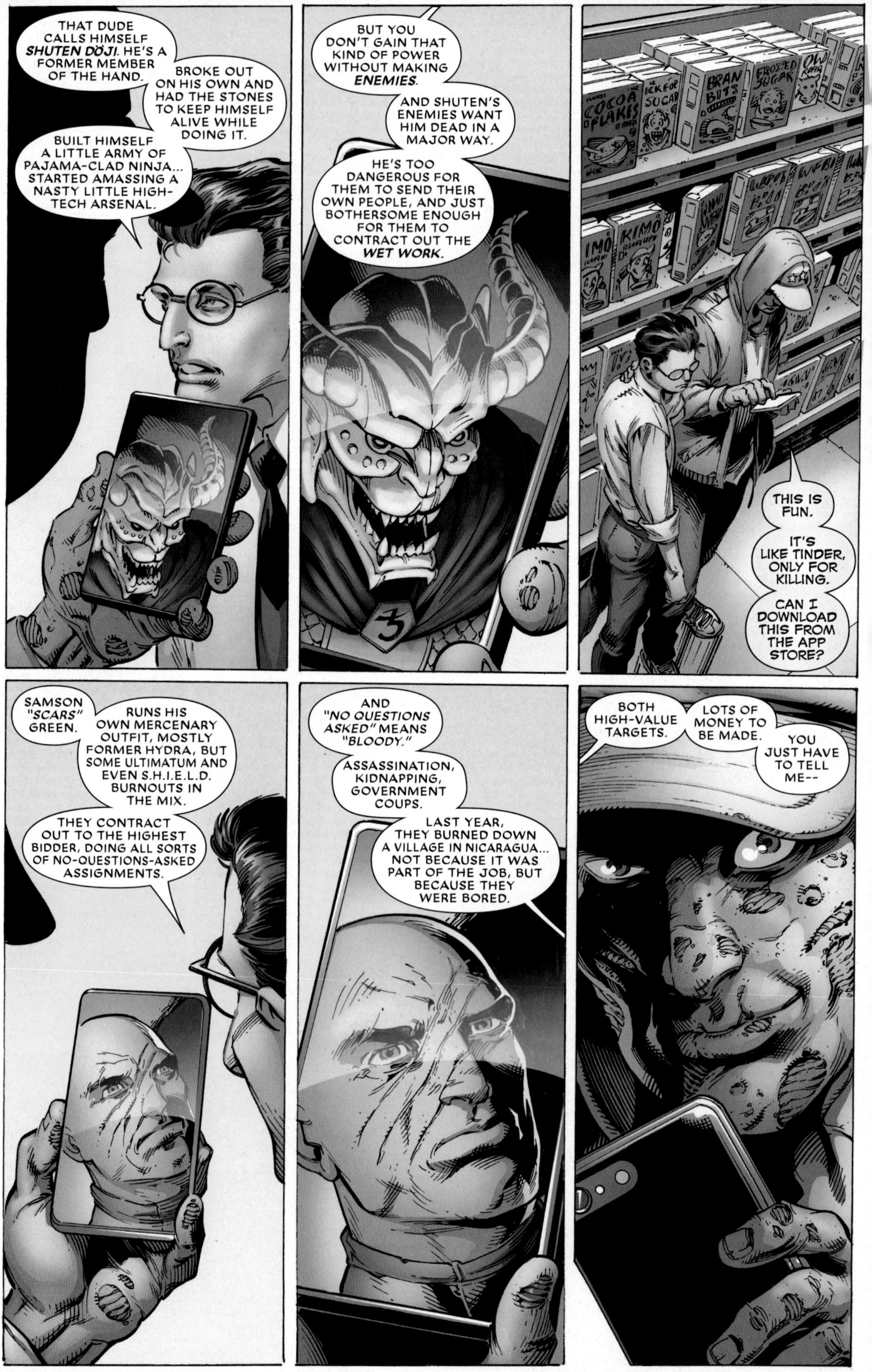
THAT DUDE CALLS HIMSELF SHUTEN DŌJI. HE'S A FORMER MEMBER OF THE HAND.
BROKE OUT ON HIS OWN AND HAD THE STONES TO KEEP HIMSELF ALIVE WHILE DOING IT.
BUILT HIMSELF A LITTLE ARMY OF PAJAMA-CLAD NINJA... STARTED AMASSING A NASTY LITTLE HIGH-TECH ARSENAL.
BUT YOU DON'T GAIN THAT KIND OF POWER WITHOUT MAKING ENEMIES.
AND SHUTEN'S ENEMIES WANT HIM DEAD IN A MAJOR WAY.
HE'S TOO DANGEROUS FOR THEM TO SEND THEIR OWN PEOPLE, AND JUST BOTHERSOME ENOUGH FOR THEM TO CONTRACT OUT THE WET WORK.
COCOA FLAKES
BRAN BITS
FROSTED SUGAR
THIS IS FUN.
IT'S LIKE TINDER, ONLY FOR KILLING.
CAN I DOWNLOAD THIS FROM THE APP STORE?
SAMSON "SCARS" GREEN.
RUNS HIS OWN MERCENARY OUTFIT, MOSTLY FORMER HYDRA, BUT SOME ULTIMATUM AND EVEN S.H.I.E.L.D. BURNOUTS IN THE MIX.
THEY CONTRACT OUT TO THE HIGHEST BIDDER, DOING ALL SORTS OF NO-QUESTIONS-ASKED ASSIGNMENTS.
AND "NO QUESTIONS ASKED" MEANS "BLOODY."
ASSASSINATION, KIDNAPPING, GOVERNMENT COUPS.
LAST YEAR, THEY BURNED DOWN A VILLAGE IN NICARAGUA... NOT BECAUSE IT WAS PART OF THE JOB, BUT BECAUSE THEY WERE BORED.
BOTH HIGH-VALUE TARGETS.
LOTS OF MONEY TO BE MADE.
YOU JUST HAVE TO TELL ME--

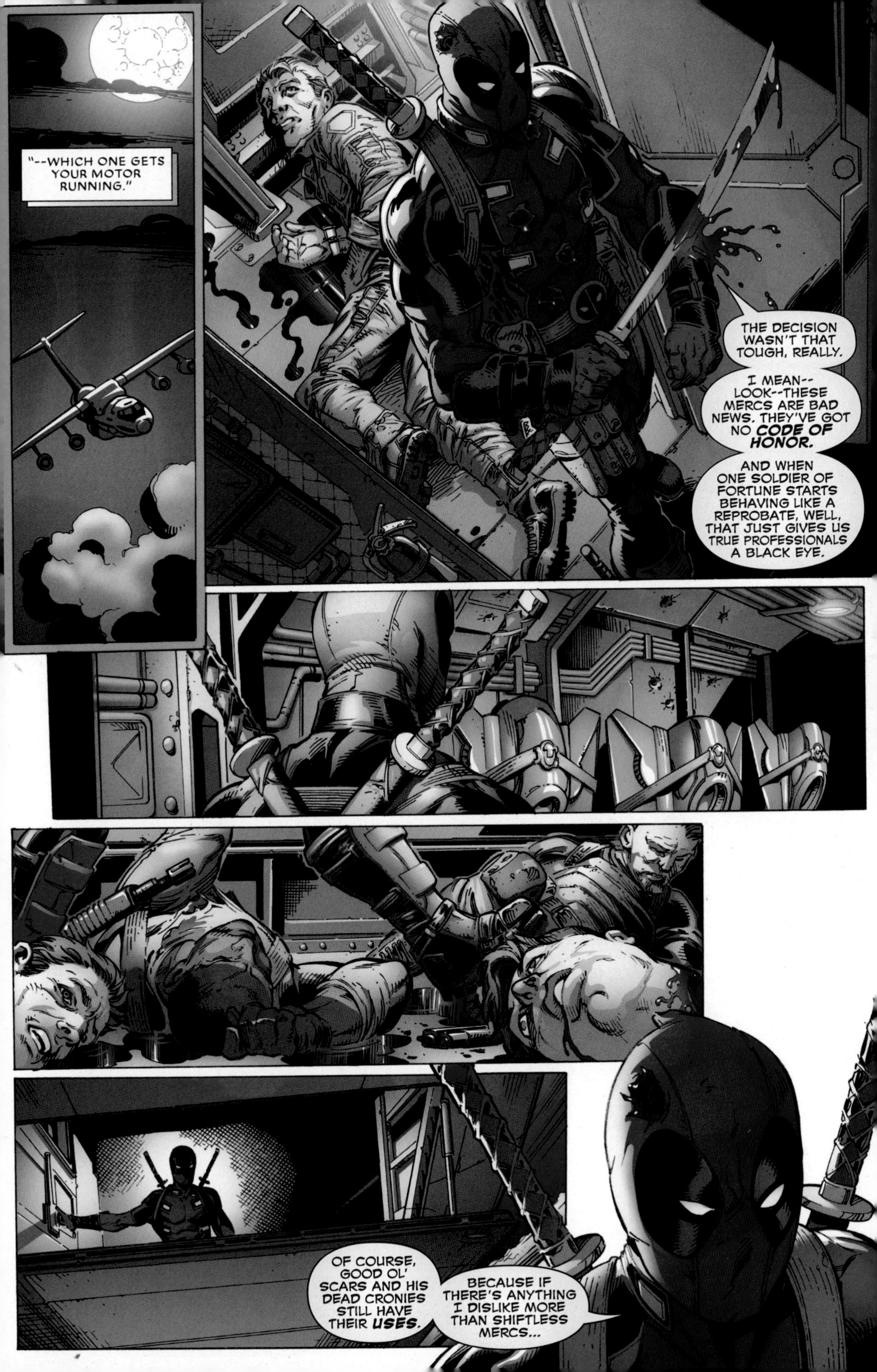
"--WHICH ONE GETS YOUR MOTOR RUNNING."
THE DECISION WASN'T THAT TOUGH, REALLY.
I MEAN-- LOOK--THESE MERCS ARE BAD NEWS. THEY'VE GOT NO CODE OF HONOR.
AND WHEN ONE SOLDIER OF FORTUNE STARTS BEHAVING LIKE A REPROBATE, WELL, THAT JUST GIVES US TRUE PROFESSIONALS A BLACK EYE.
OF COURSE, GOOD OL' SCARS AND HIS DEAD CRONIES STILL HAVE THEIR USES.
BECAUSE IF THERE'S ANYTHING I DISLIKE MORE THAN SHIFTLESS MERCS...

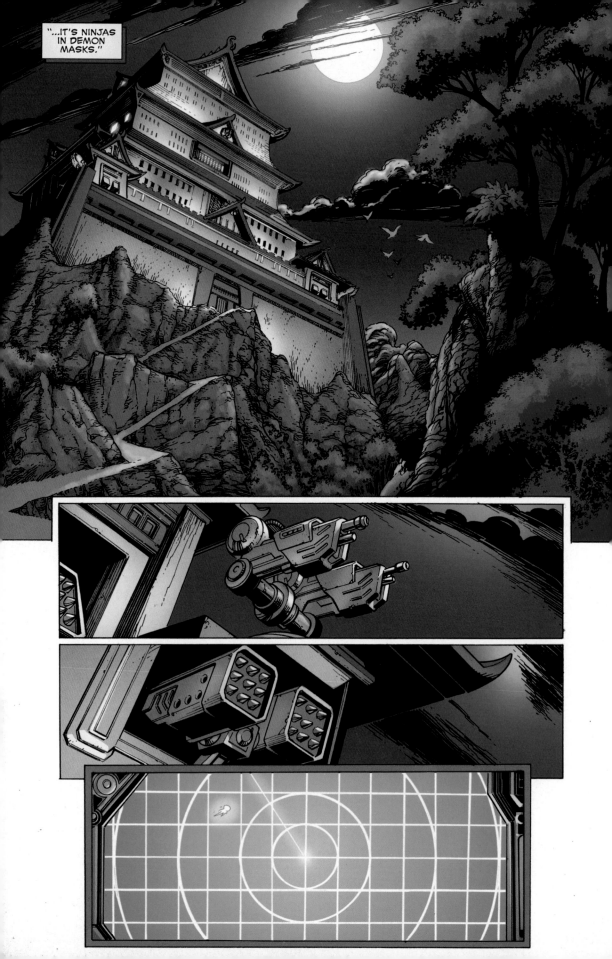

"...IT'S NINJAS IN DEMON MASKS."

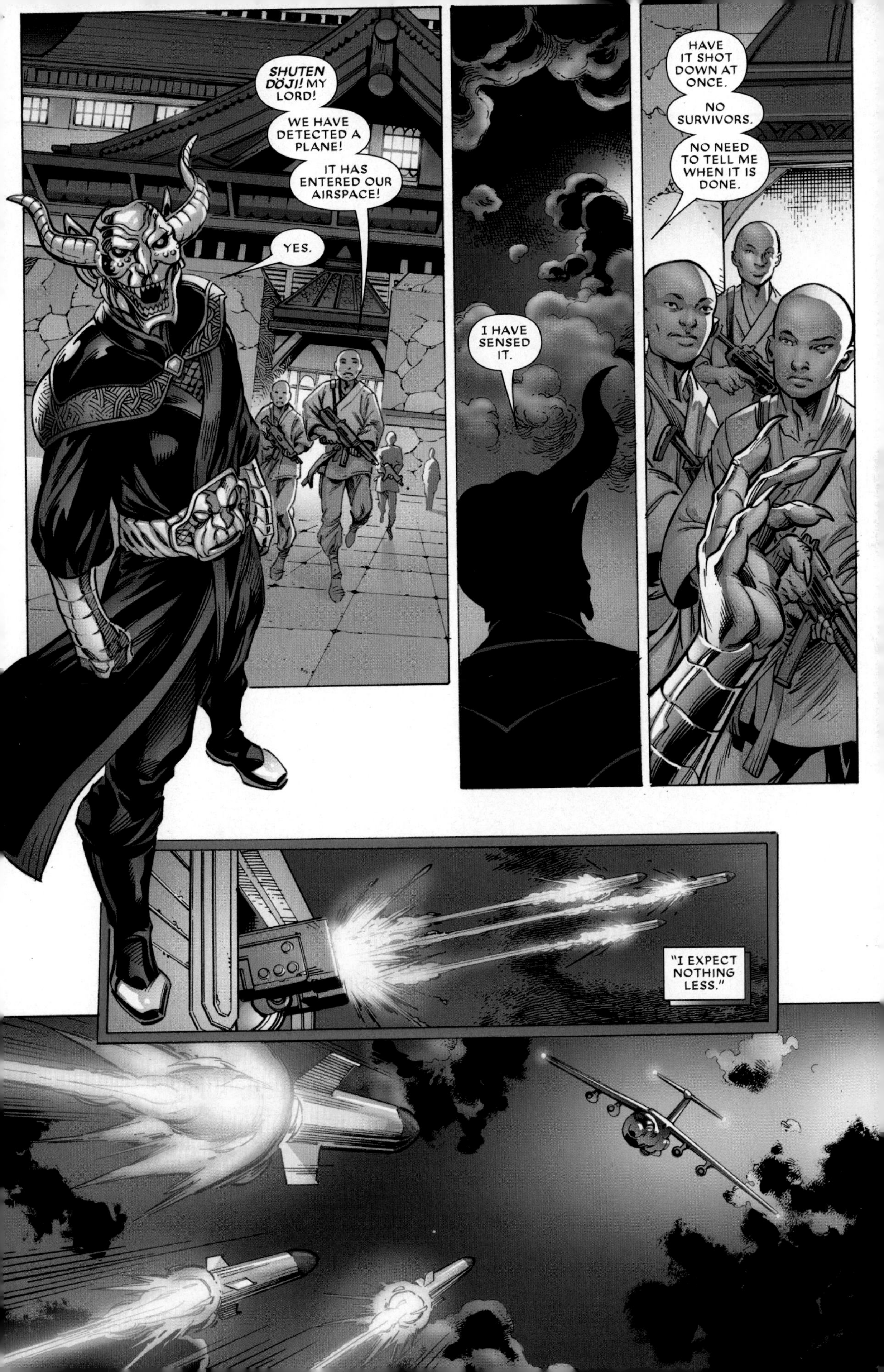

SHUTEN DŌJI! MY LORD!
WE HAVE DETECTED A PLANE!
IT HAS ENTERED OUR AIRSPACE!
YES.
I HAVE SENSED IT.
HAVE IT SHOT DOWN AT ONCE.
NO SURVIVORS.
NO NEED TO TELL ME WHEN IT IS DONE.
"I EXPECT NOTHING LESS."

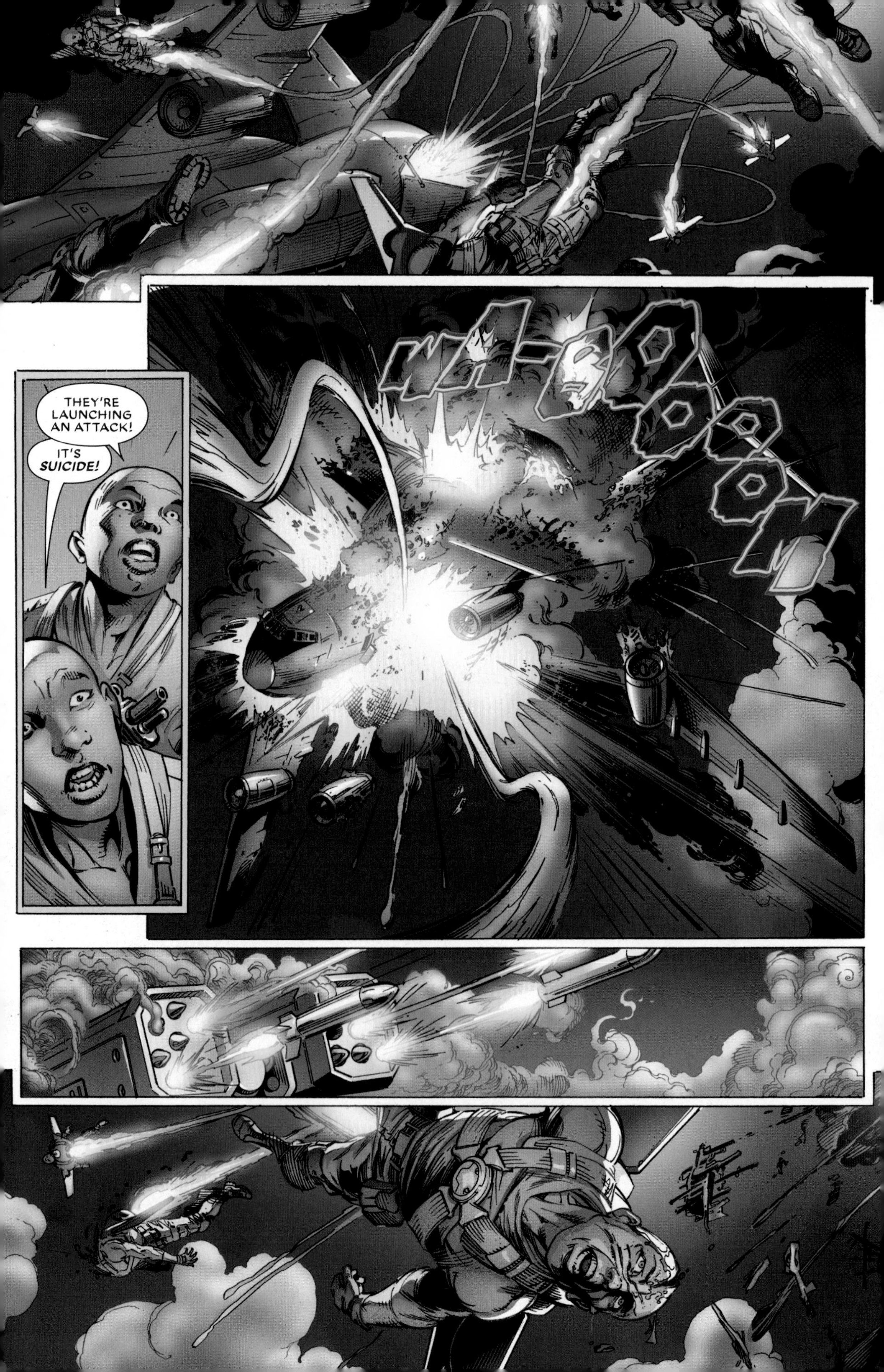
THEY'RE LAUNCHING AN ATTACK!
IT'S SUICIDE!

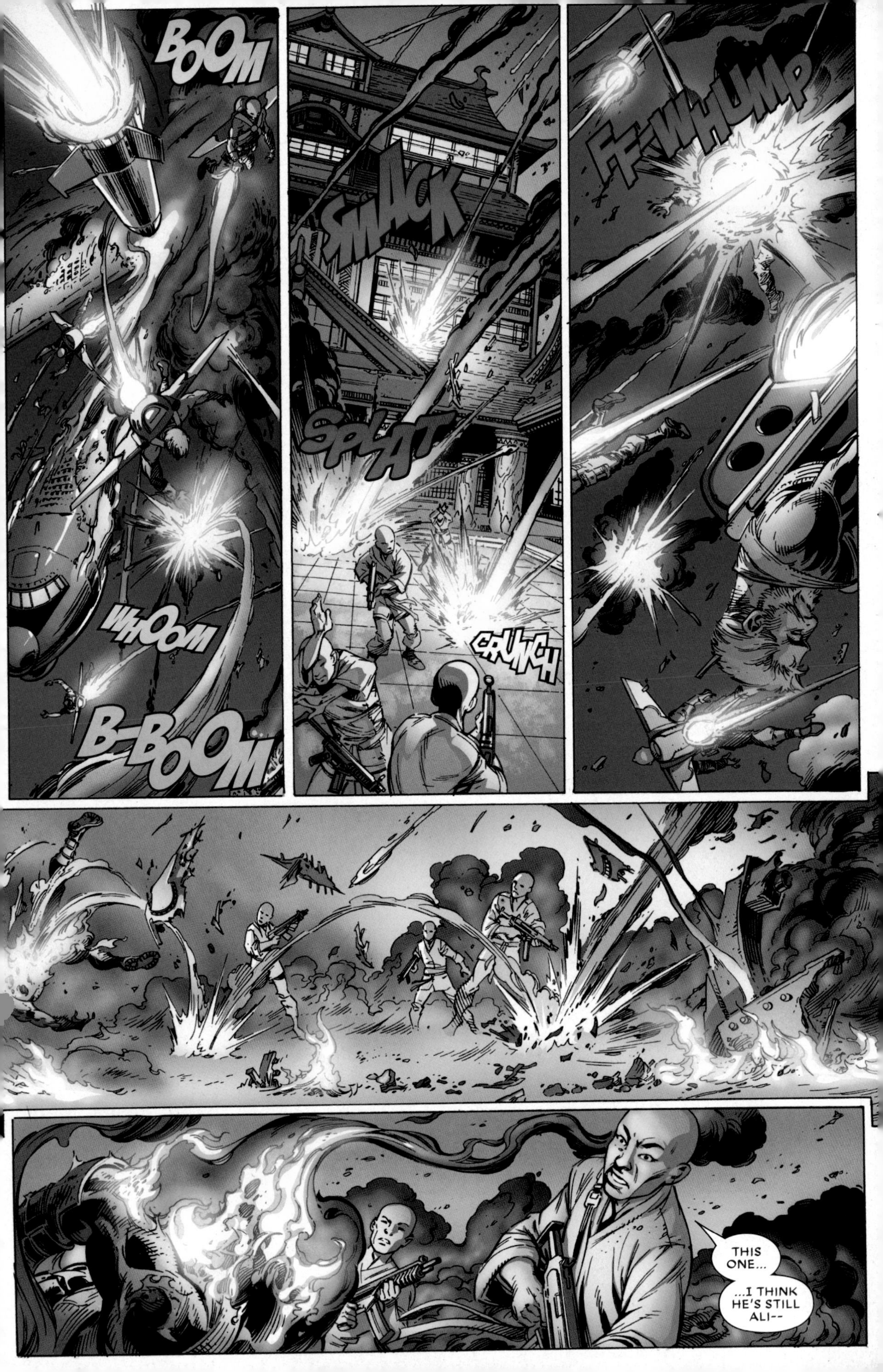
BOOM
WHOOM
B-BOOM
SMACK
SPLAT
CRUNCH
FF-WHUMP
THIS ONE...
...I THINK HE'S STILL ALI--

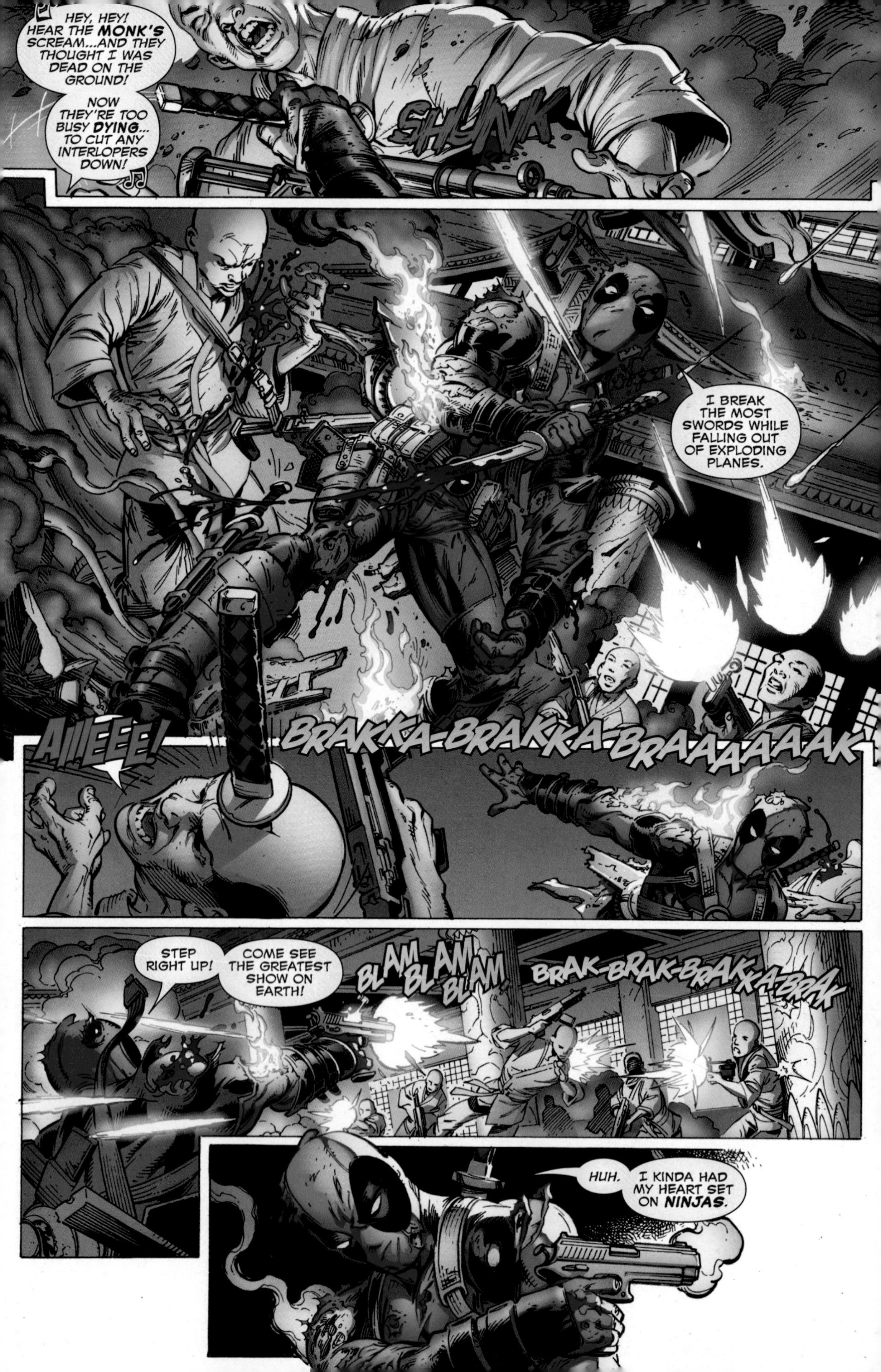
HEY, HEY! HEAR THE MONK'S SCREAM...AND THEY THOUGHT I WAS DEAD ON THE GROUND!
NOW THEY'RE TOO BUSY DYING... TO CUT ANY INTERLOPERS DOWN!
SHUNK
I BREAK THE MOST SWORDS WHILE FALLING OUT OF EXPLODING PLANES.
AIIEEE!
BRAKKA-BRAKKA-BRAAAAAAAK
STEP RIGHT UP!
COME SEE THE GREATEST SHOW ON EARTH!
BLAM BLAM BLAM BLAM
BRAK-BRAK-BRAK-KA-BRAK
HUH.
I KINDA HAD MY HEART SET ON NINJAS.

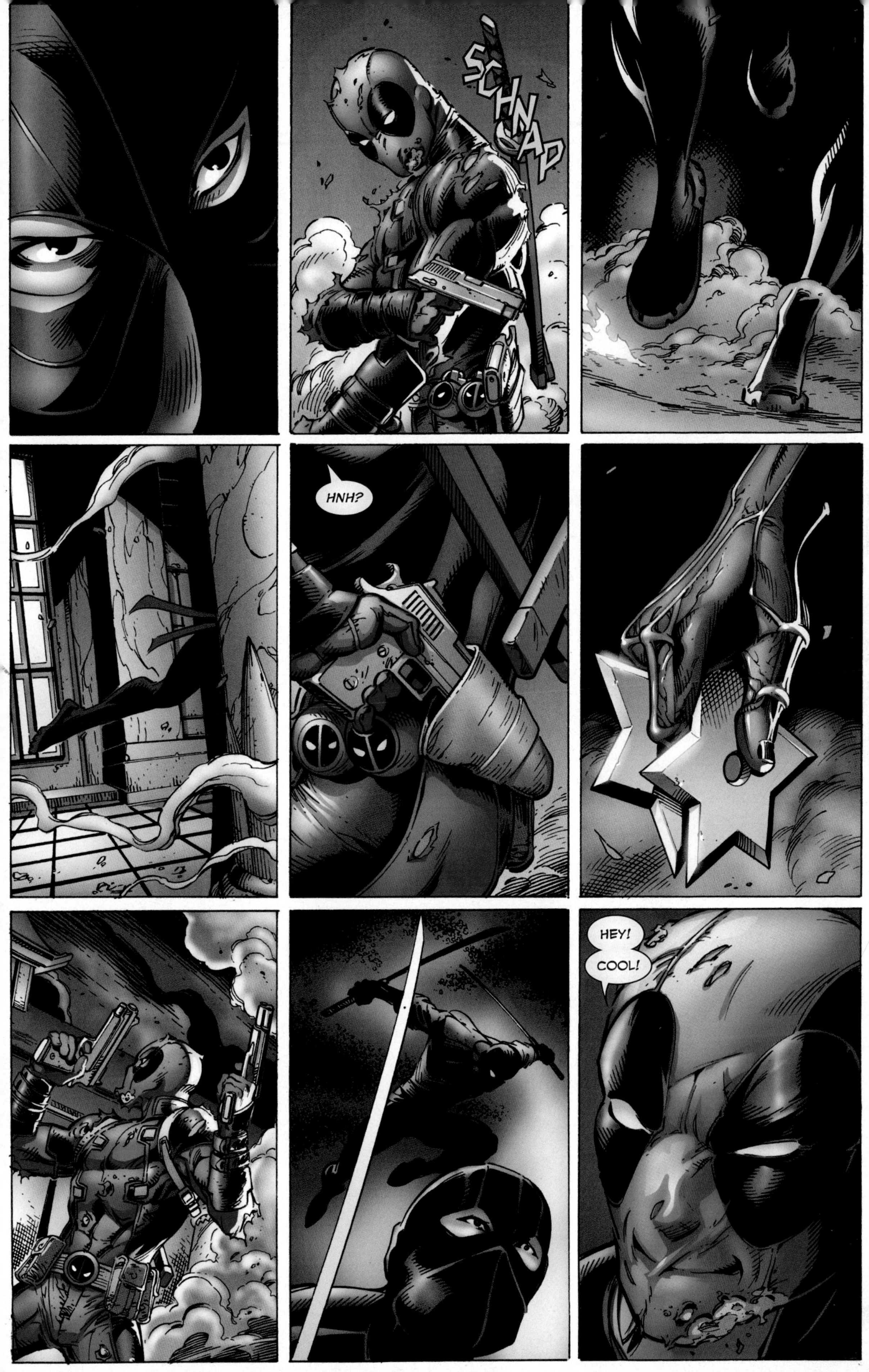
SCHNAP
HNH?
HEY!
COOL!

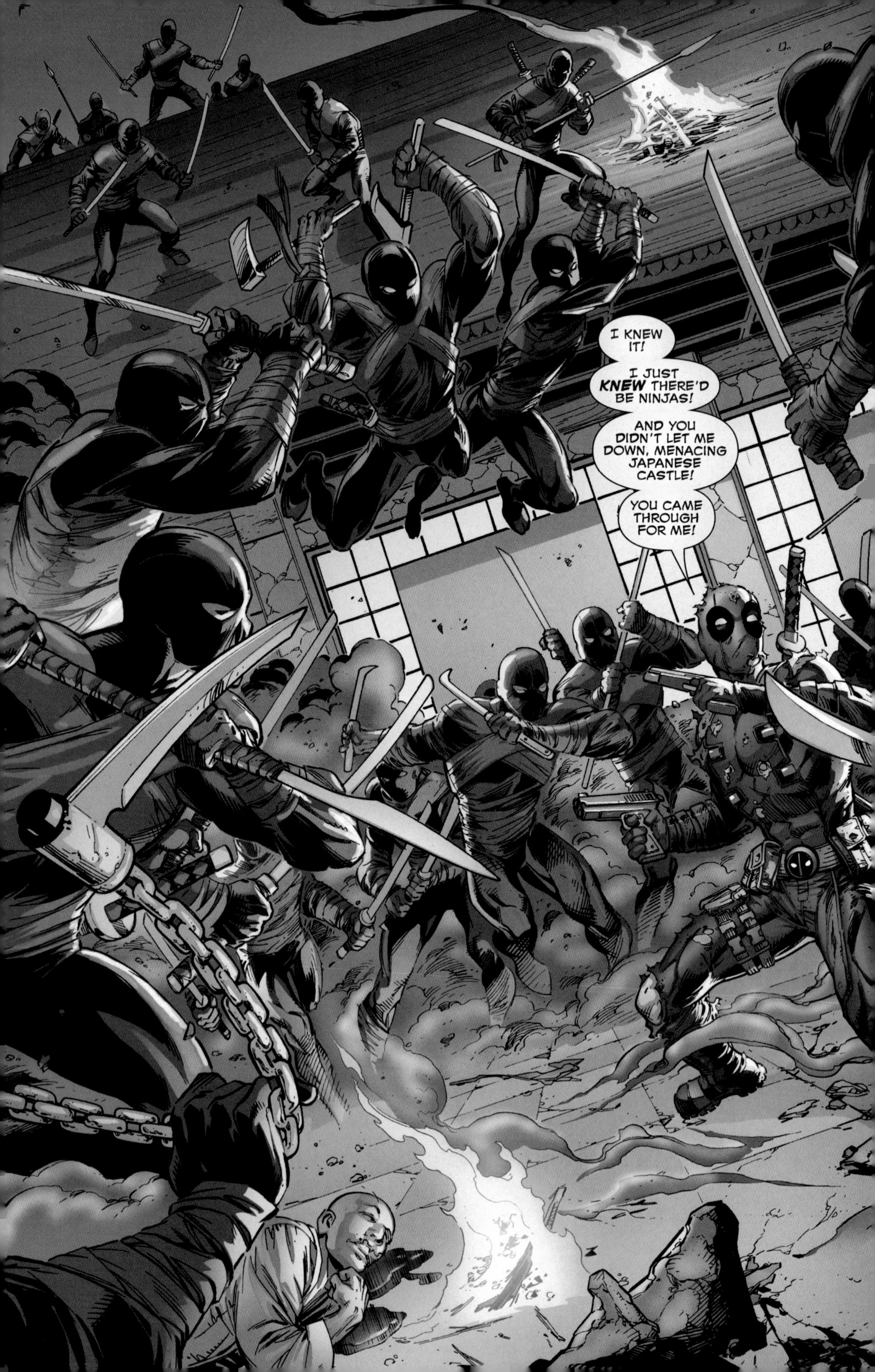
I KNEW IT!
I JUST **KNEW** THERE'D BE NINJAS!
AND YOU DIDN'T LET ME DOWN, MENACING JAPANESE CASTLE!
YOU CAME THROUGH FOR ME!

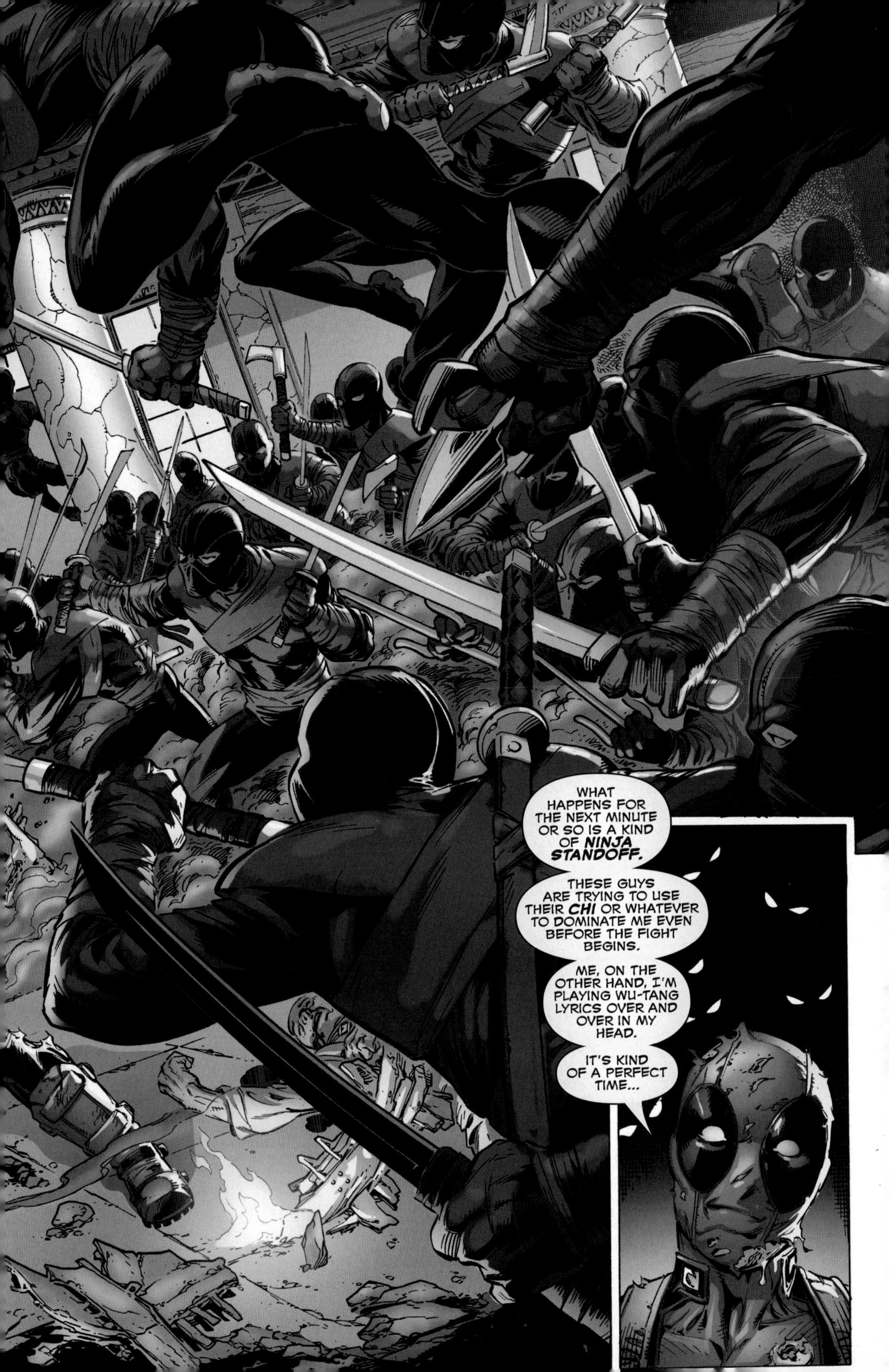
WHAT HAPPENS FOR THE NEXT MINUTE OR SO IS A KIND OF NINJA STANDOFF.
THESE GUYS ARE TRYING TO USE THEIR CHI OR WHATEVER TO DOMINATE ME EVEN BEFORE THE FIGHT BEGINS.
ME, ON THE OTHER HAND, I'M PLAYING WU-TANG LYRICS OVER AND OVER IN MY HEAD.
IT'S KIND OF A PERFECT TIME...

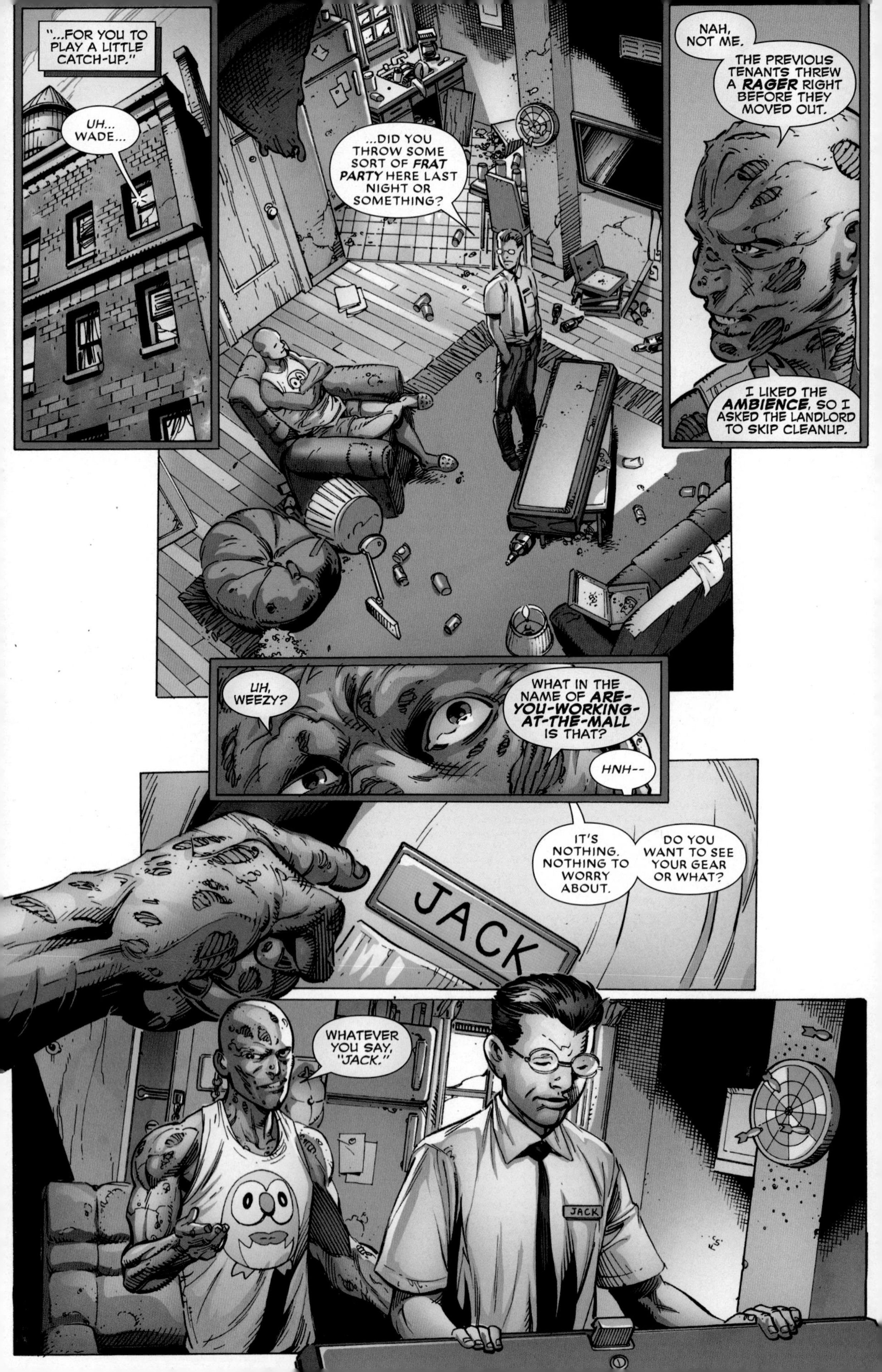
"...FOR YOU TO PLAY A LITTLE CATCH-UP."
UH... WADE...
...DID YOU THROW SOME SORT OF FRAT PARTY HERE LAST NIGHT OR SOMETHING?
NAH, NOT ME.
THE PREVIOUS TENANTS THREW A RAGER RIGHT BEFORE THEY MOVED OUT.
I LIKED THE AMBIENCE, SO I ASKED THE LANDLORD TO SKIP CLEANUP.
UH, WEEZY?
WHAT IN THE NAME OF ARE-YOU-WORKING-AT-THE-MALL IS THAT?
HNH--
IT'S NOTHING. NOTHING TO WORRY ABOUT.
DO YOU WANT TO SEE YOUR GEAR OR WHAT?
JACK
WHATEVER YOU SAY, "JACK."
JACK

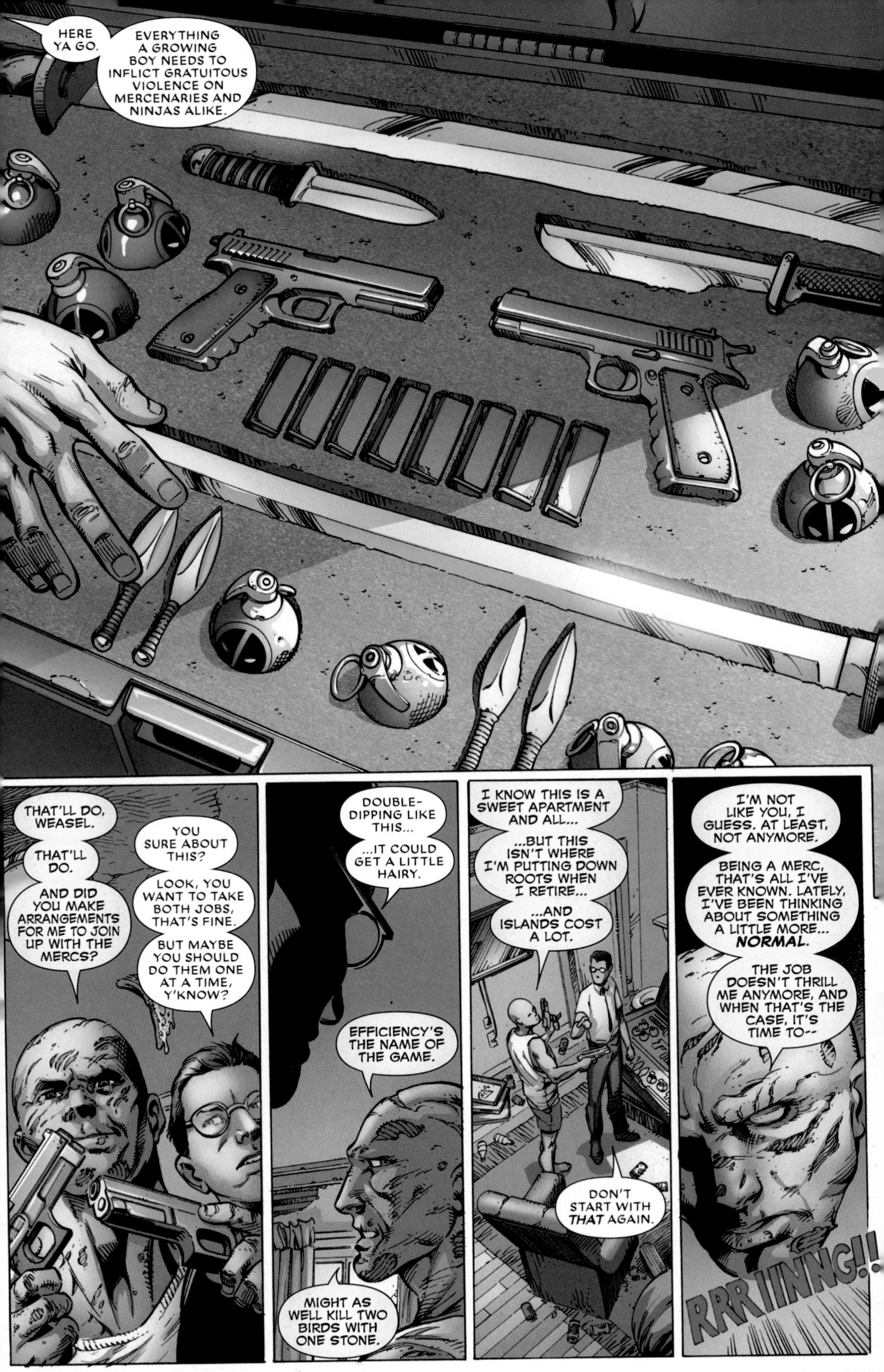
HERE YA GO.
EVERYTHING A GROWING BOY NEEDS TO INFLICT GRATUITOUS VIOLENCE ON MERCENARIES AND NINJAS ALIKE.
THAT'LL DO, WEASEL.
THAT'LL DO.
AND DID YOU MAKE ARRANGEMENTS FOR ME TO JOIN UP WITH THE MERCS?
YOU SURE ABOUT THIS?
LOOK, YOU WANT TO TAKE BOTH JOBS, THAT'S FINE.
BUT MAYBE YOU SHOULD DO THEM ONE AT A TIME, Y'KNOW?
DOUBLE-DIPPING LIKE THIS...
...IT COULD GET A LITTLE HAIRY.
EFFICIENCY'S THE NAME OF THE GAME.
MIGHT AS WELL KILL TWO BIRDS WITH ONE STONE.
I KNOW THIS IS A SWEET APARTMENT AND ALL...
...BUT THIS ISN'T WHERE I'M PUTTING DOWN ROOTS WHEN I RETIRE...
...AND ISLANDS COST A LOT.
DON'T START WITH *THAT* AGAIN.
I'M NOT LIKE YOU, I GUESS. AT LEAST, NOT ANYMORE.
BEING A MERC, THAT'S ALL I'VE EVER KNOWN. LATELY, I'VE BEEN THINKING ABOUT SOMETHING A LITTLE MORE... ***NORMAL.***
THE JOB DOESN'T THRILL ME ANYMORE, AND WHEN THAT'S THE CASE, IT'S TIME TO--
RRRIINNG!!

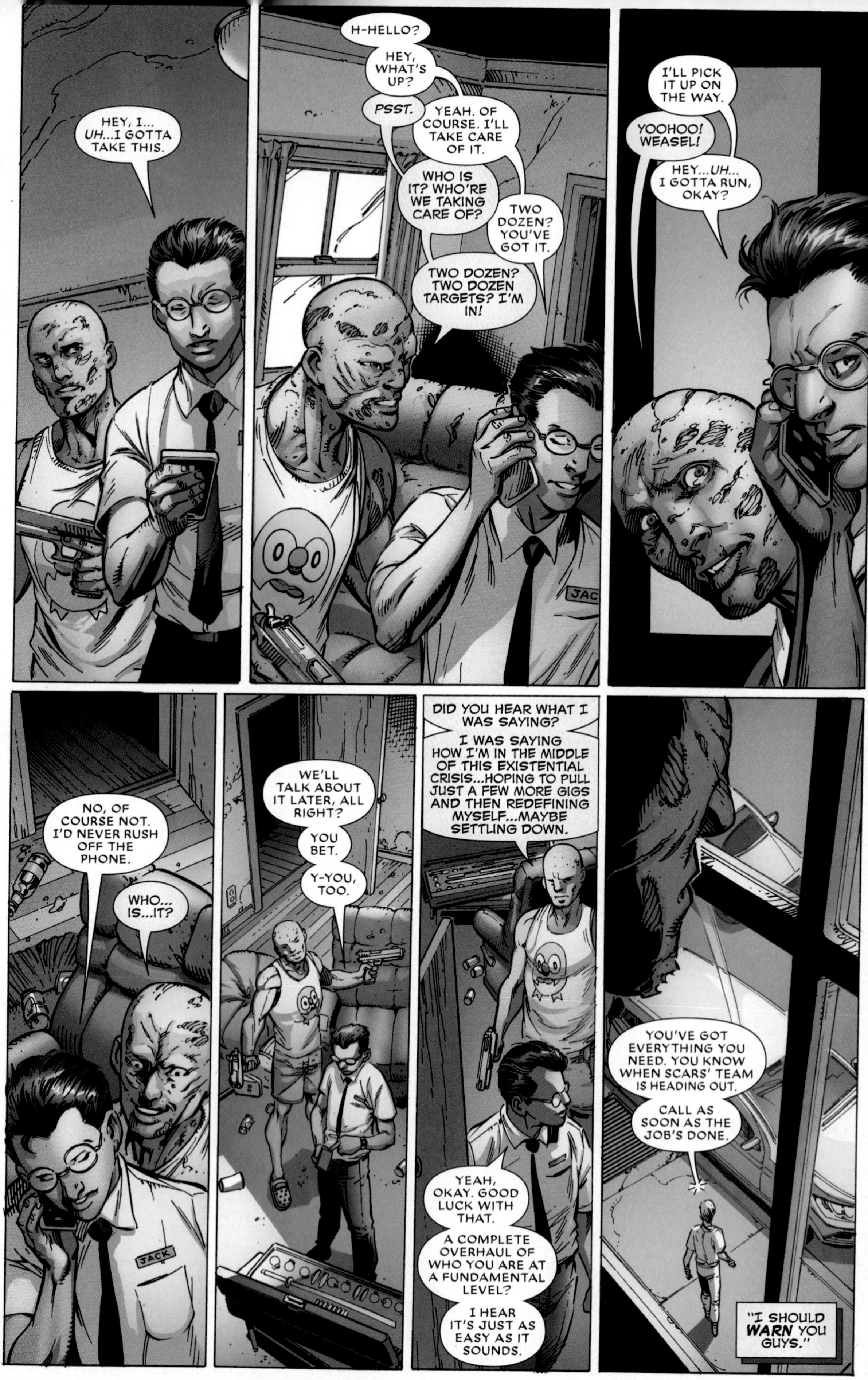
HEY, I... *UH*...I GOTTA TAKE THIS.
H-HELLO?
HEY, WHAT'S UP?
PSST.
YEAH. OF COURSE. I'LL TAKE CARE OF IT.
WHO IS IT? WHO'RE WE TAKING CARE OF?
TWO DOZEN? YOU'VE GOT IT.
TWO DOZEN? TWO DOZEN TARGETS? I'M IN!
I'LL PICK IT UP ON THE WAY.
YOOHOO! WEASEL!
HEY...*UH*... I GOTTA RUN, OKAY?
NO, OF COURSE NOT. I'D NEVER RUSH OFF THE PHONE.
WHO... IS...IT?
JACK
WE'LL TALK ABOUT IT LATER, ALL RIGHT?
YOU BET.
Y-YOU, TOO.
DID YOU HEAR WHAT I WAS SAYING?
I WAS SAYING HOW I'M IN THE MIDDLE OF THIS EXISTENTIAL CRISIS...HOPING TO PULL JUST A FEW MORE GIGS AND THEN REDEFINING MYSELF...MAYBE SETTLING DOWN.
YEAH, OKAY. GOOD LUCK WITH THAT.
A COMPLETE OVERHAUL OF WHO YOU ARE AT A FUNDAMENTAL LEVEL?
I HEAR IT'S JUST AS EASY AS IT SOUNDS.
YOU'VE GOT EVERYTHING YOU NEED. YOU KNOW WHEN SCARS' TEAM IS HEADING OUT.
CALL AS SOON AS THE JOB'S DONE.
"I SHOULD **WARN** YOU GUYS."

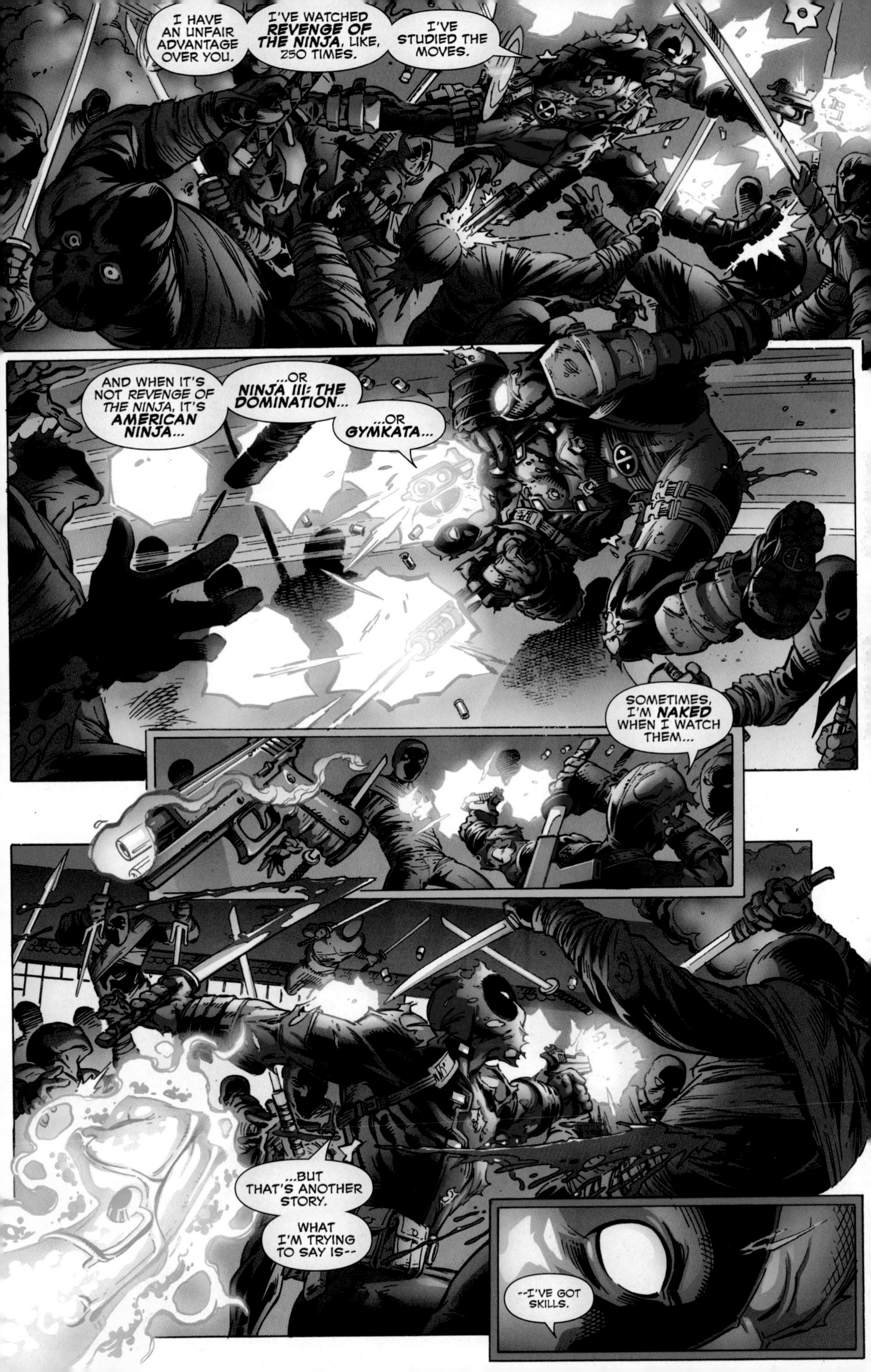
I HAVE AN UNFAIR ADVANTAGE OVER YOU.
I'VE WATCHED ***REVENGE OF THE NINJA***, LIKE, 250 TIMES.
I'VE STUDIED THE MOVES.
AND WHEN IT'S NOT *REVENGE OF THE NINJA*, IT'S ***AMERICAN NINJA***...
...OR ***NINJA III: THE DOMINATION***...
...OR ***GYMKATA***...
SOMETIMES, I'M ***NAKED*** WHEN I WATCH THEM...
...BUT THAT'S ANOTHER STORY.
WHAT I'M TRYING TO SAY IS--
--I'VE GOT SKILLS.

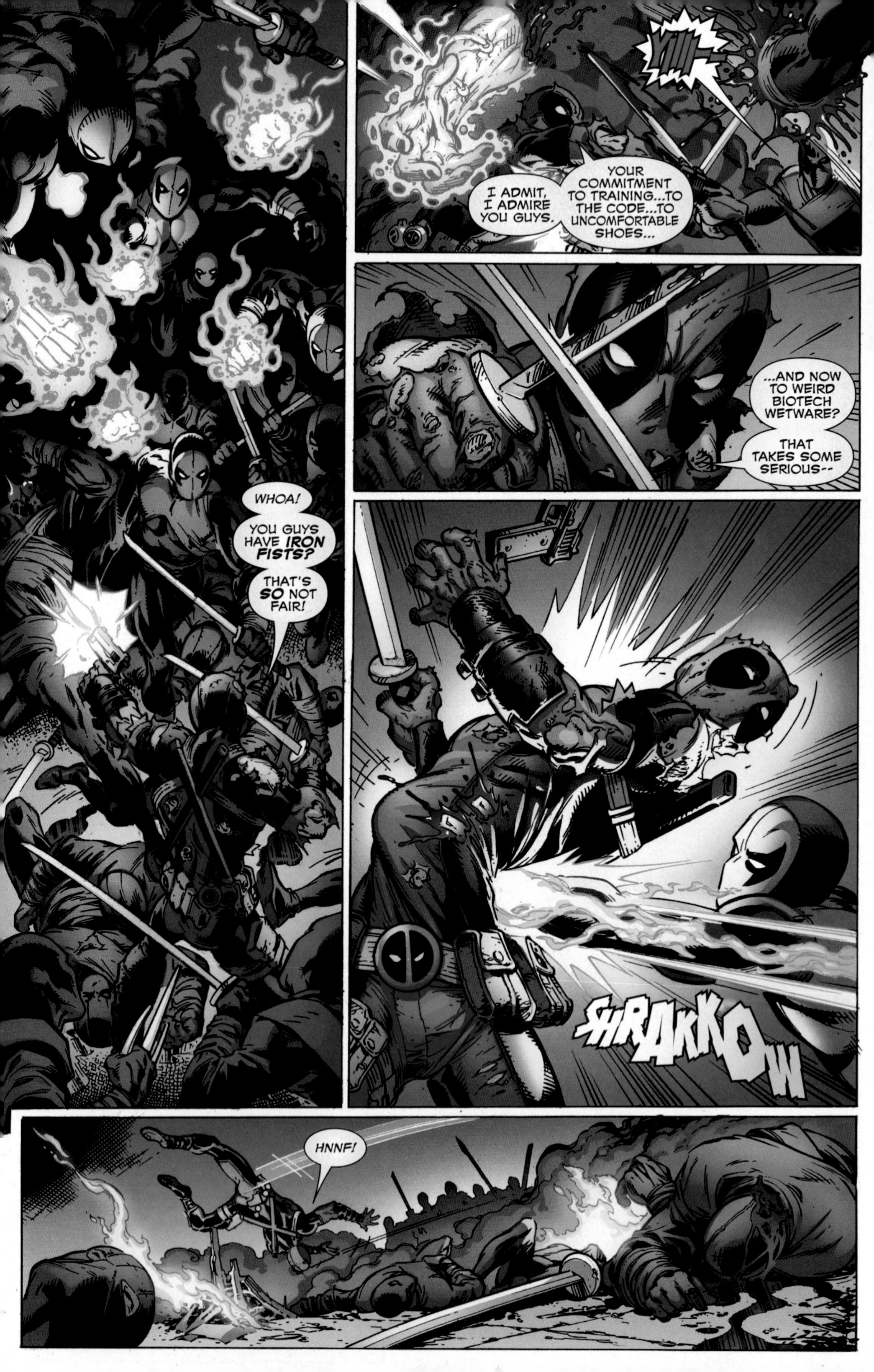
WHOA!
YOU GUYS HAVE IRON FISTS?
THAT'S SO NOT FAIR!
I ADMIT, I ADMIRE YOU GUYS.
YOUR COMMITMENT TO TRAINING...TO THE CODE...TO UNCOMFORTABLE SHOES...
...AND NOW TO WEIRD BIOTECH WETWARE?
THAT TAKES SOME SERIOUS--
SHRAKKOW
HNNF!

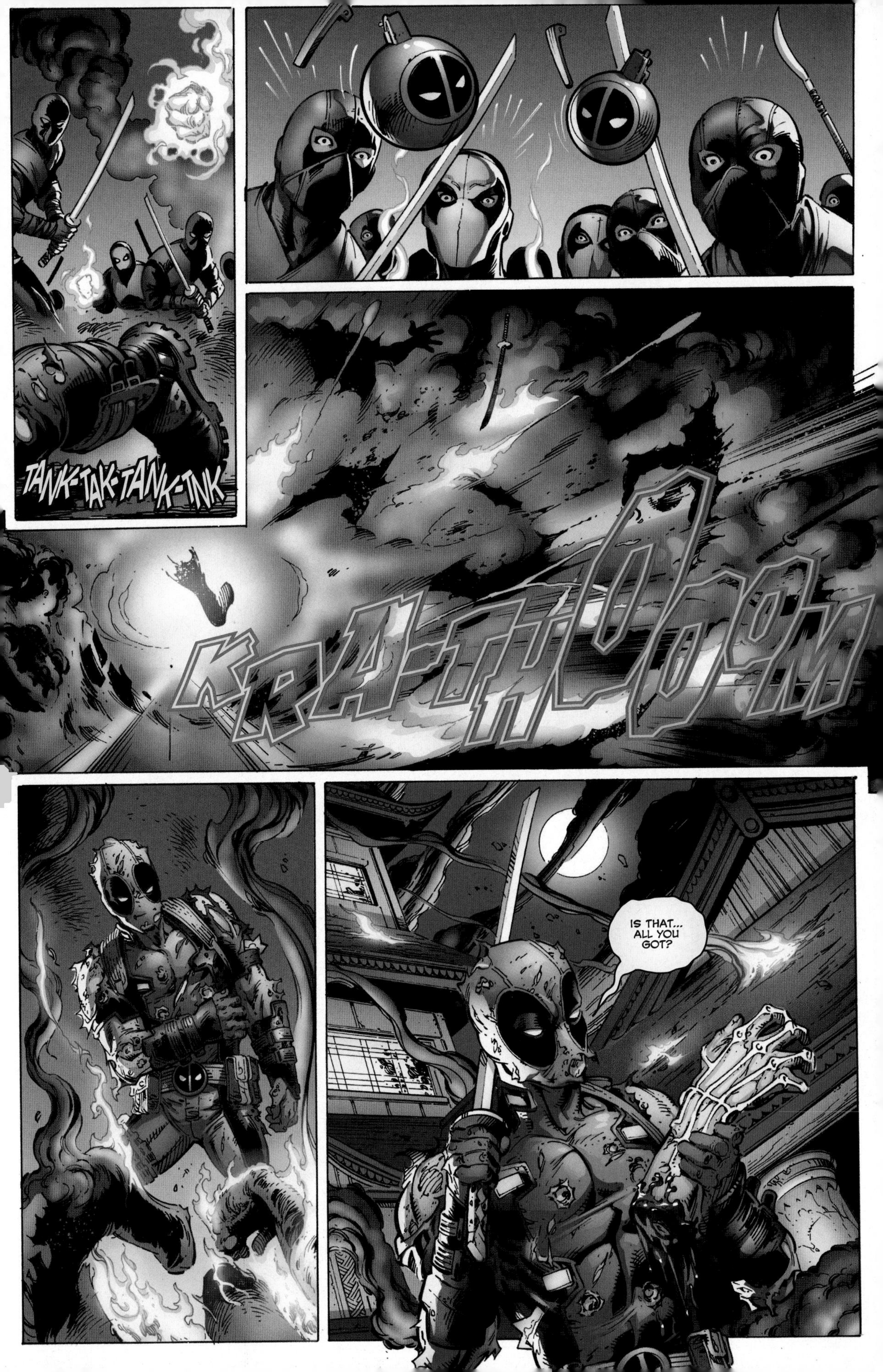
TANK-TAK-TANK-TNK
KRA-THOOOM
IS THAT... ALL YOU GOT?

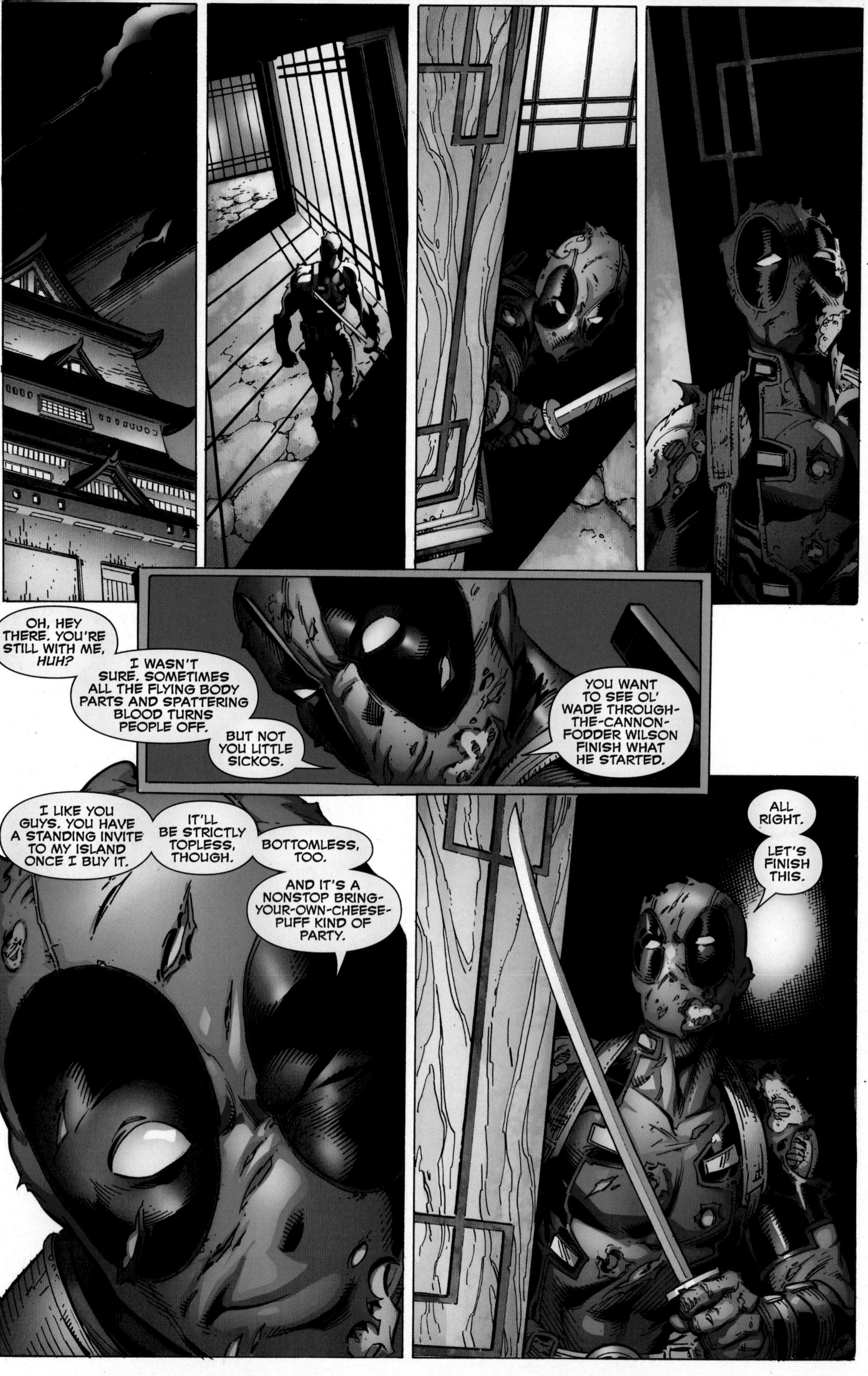
OH, HEY THERE. YOU'RE STILL WITH ME, HUH?
I WASN'T SURE. SOMETIMES ALL THE FLYING BODY PARTS AND SPATTERING BLOOD TURNS PEOPLE OFF.
BUT NOT YOU LITTLE SICKOS.
YOU WANT TO SEE OL' WADE THROUGH-THE-CANNON-FODDER WILSON FINISH WHAT HE STARTED.
I LIKE YOU GUYS. YOU HAVE A STANDING INVITE TO MY ISLAND ONCE I BUY IT.
IT'LL BE STRICTLY TOPLESS, THOUGH.
BOTTOMLESS, TOO.
AND IT'S A NONSTOP BRING-YOUR-OWN-CHEESE-PUFF KIND OF PARTY.
ALL RIGHT.
LET'S FINISH THIS.

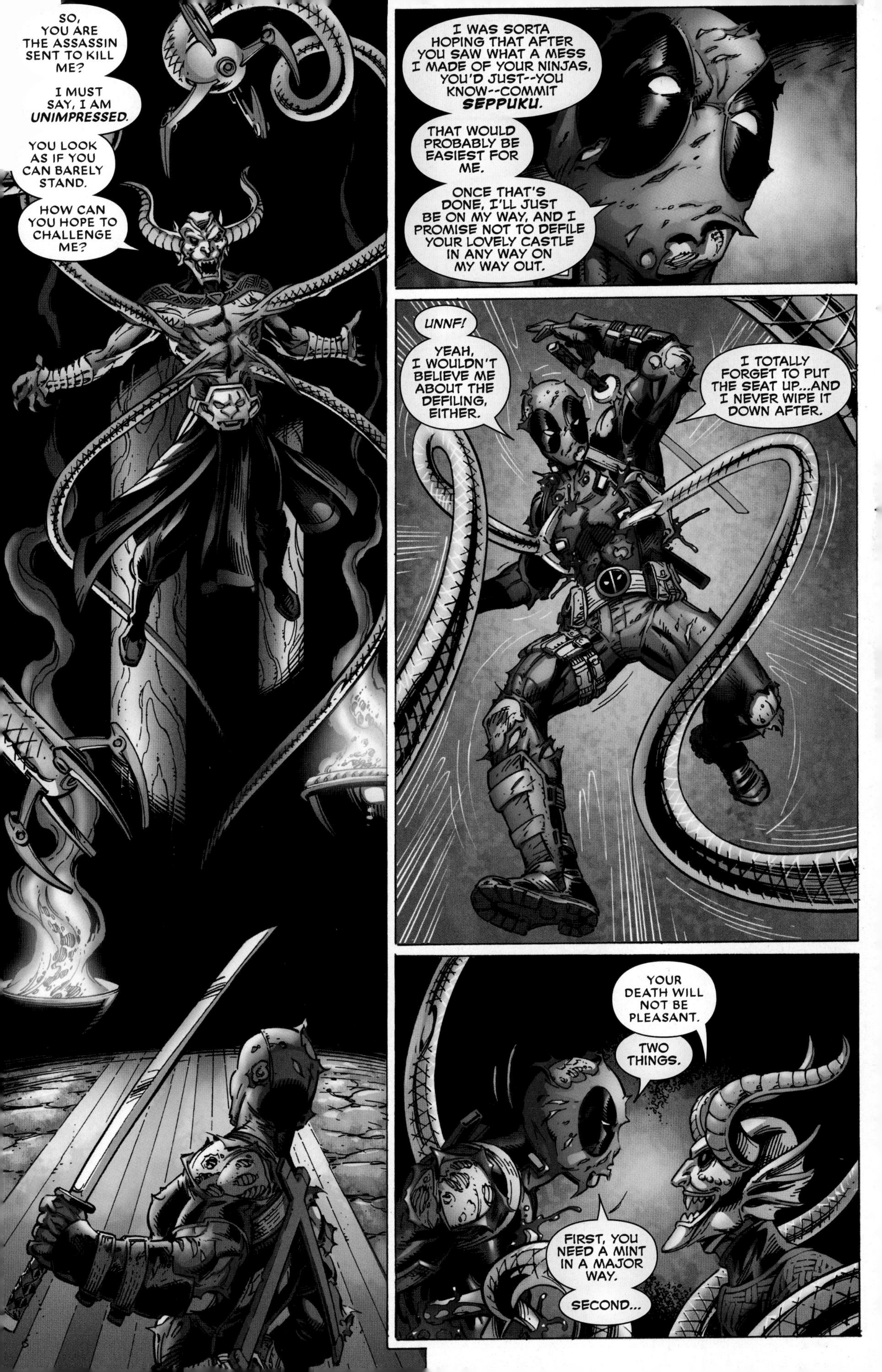

SO, YOU ARE THE ASSASSIN SENT TO KILL ME?
I MUST SAY, I AM *UNIMPRESSED.*
YOU LOOK AS IF YOU CAN BARELY STAND.
HOW CAN YOU HOPE TO CHALLENGE ME?
I WAS SORTA HOPING THAT AFTER YOU SAW WHAT A MESS I MADE OF YOUR NINJAS, YOU'D JUST--YOU KNOW--COMMIT *SEPPUKU.*
THAT WOULD PROBABLY BE EASIEST FOR ME.
ONCE THAT'S DONE, I'LL JUST BE ON MY WAY, AND I PROMISE NOT TO DEFILE YOUR LOVELY CASTLE IN ANY WAY ON MY WAY OUT.
UNNF!
YEAH, I WOULDN'T BELIEVE ME ABOUT THE DEFILING, EITHER.
I TOTALLY FORGET TO PUT THE SEAT UP...AND I NEVER WIPE IT DOWN AFTER.
YOUR DEATH WILL NOT BE PLEASANT.
TWO THINGS.
FIRST, YOU NEED A MINT IN A MAJOR WAY.
SECOND...

...YOU REALLY SHOULDN'T HAVE PULLED ME IN THIS CLOSE.

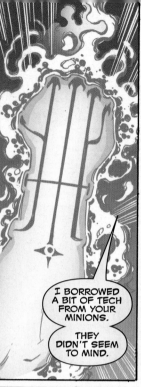

I BORROWED A BIT OF TECH FROM YOUR MINIONS.

THEY DIDN'T SEEM TO MIND.

N-NO--

WRRRRR-THOOOOM

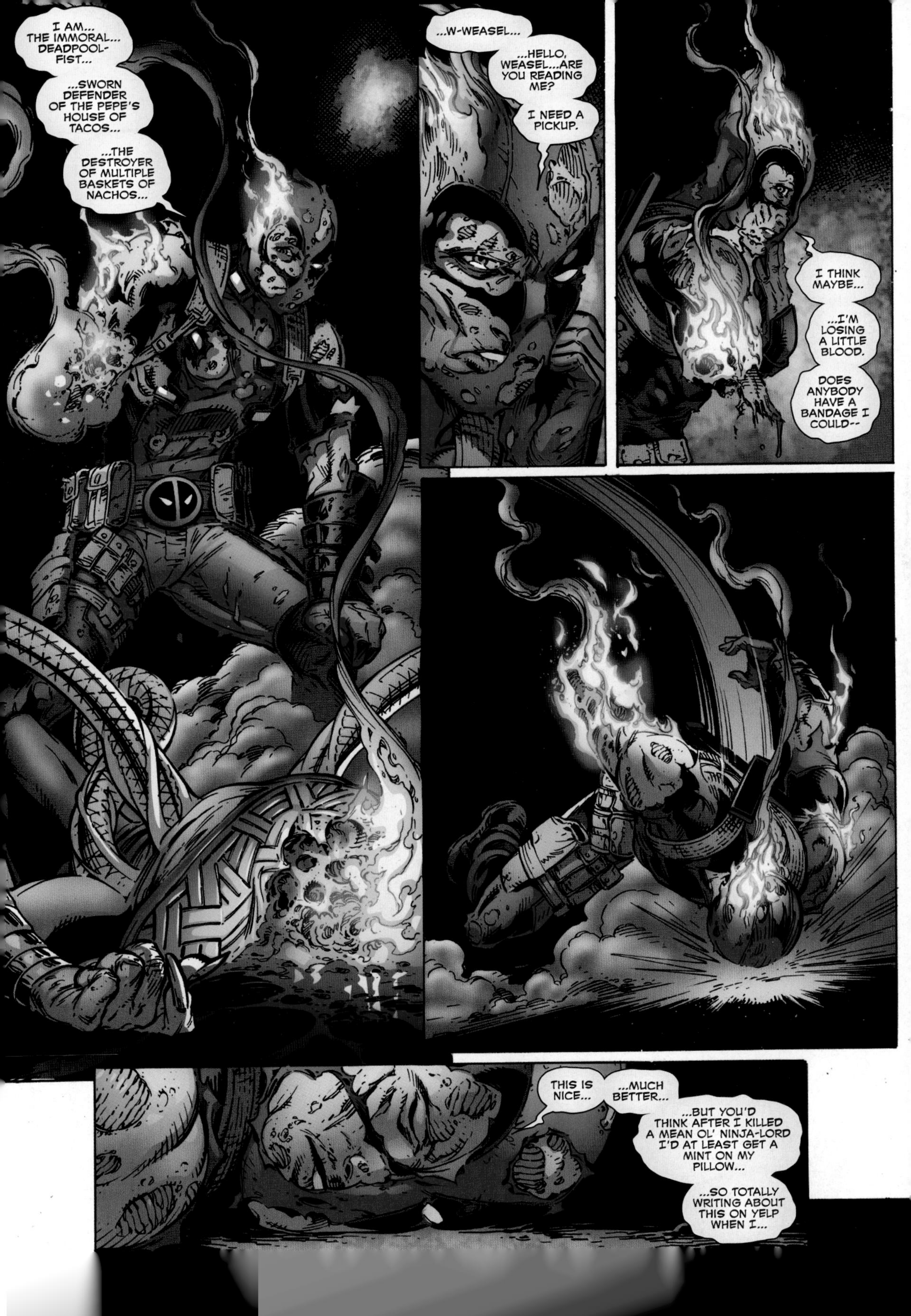
I AM... THE IMMORAL... DEADPOOL-FIST...
...SWORN DEFENDER OF THE PEPE'S HOUSE OF TACOS...
...THE DESTROYER OF MULTIPLE BASKETS OF NACHOS...
...W-WEASEL...
...HELLO, WEASEL...ARE YOU READING ME?
I NEED A PICKUP.
I THINK MAYBE...
...I'M LOSING A LITTLE BLOOD.
DOES ANYBODY HAVE A BANDAGE I COULD--
THIS IS NICE...
...MUCH BETTER...
...BUT YOU'D THINK AFTER I KILLED A MEAN OL' NINJA-LORD I'D AT LEAST GET A MINT ON MY PILLOW...
...SO TOTALLY WRITING ABOUT THIS ON YELP WHEN I...

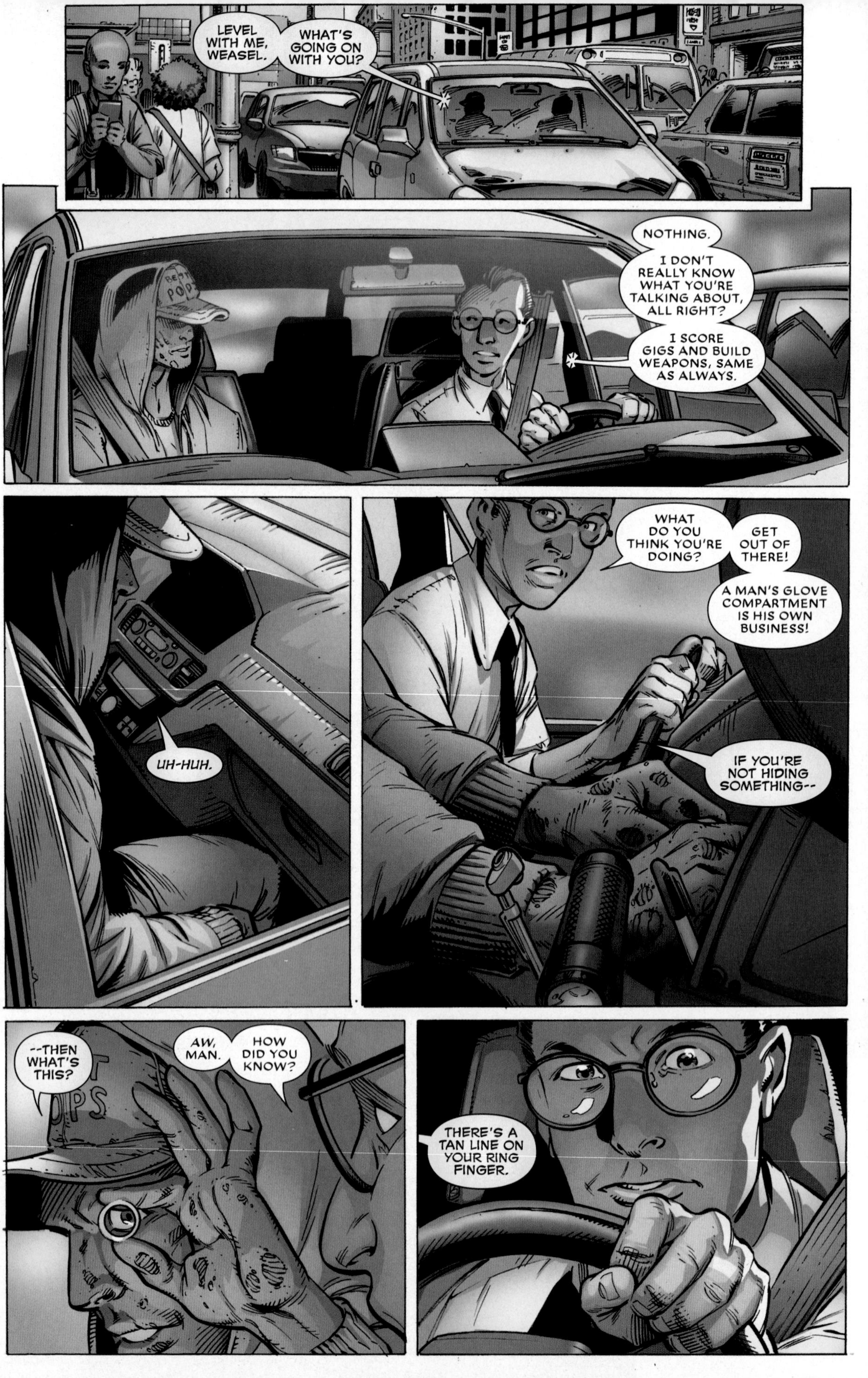
LEVEL WITH ME, WEASEL.
WHAT'S GOING ON WITH YOU?
NOTHING.
I DON'T REALLY KNOW WHAT YOU'RE TALKING ABOUT, ALL RIGHT?
I SCORE GIGS AND BUILD WEAPONS, SAME AS ALWAYS.
UH-HUH.
WHAT DO YOU THINK YOU'RE DOING?
GET OUT OF THERE!
A MAN'S GLOVE COMPARTMENT IS HIS OWN BUSINESS!
IF YOU'RE NOT HIDING SOMETHING--
--THEN WHAT'S THIS?
AW, MAN.
HOW DID YOU KNOW?
THERE'S A TAN LINE ON YOUR RING FINGER.

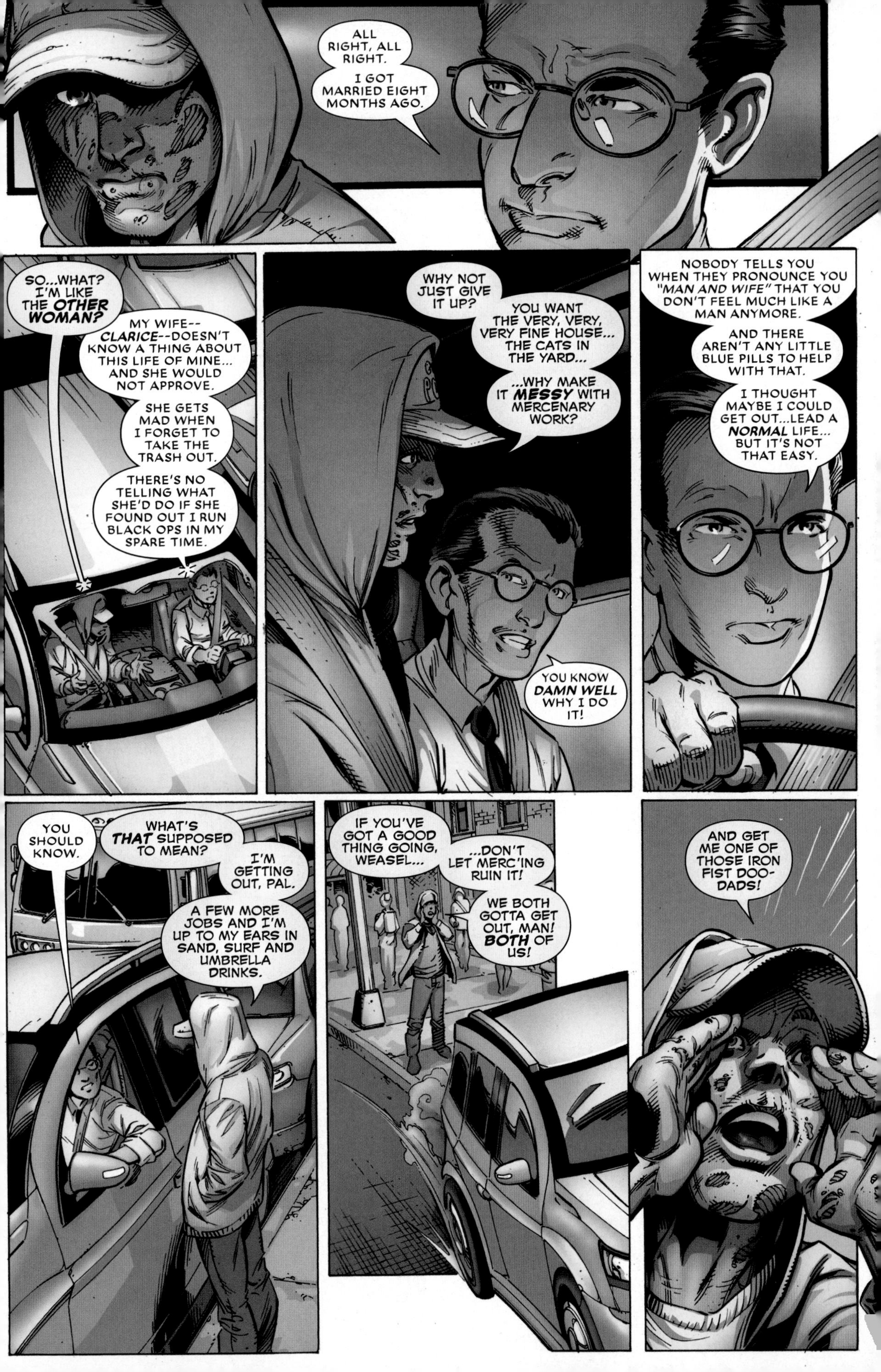

ALL RIGHT, ALL RIGHT.
I GOT MARRIED EIGHT MONTHS AGO.
SO...WHAT? I'M LIKE THE **OTHER WOMAN?**
MY WIFE-- ***CLARICE***--DOESN'T KNOW A THING ABOUT THIS LIFE OF MINE... AND SHE WOULD NOT APPROVE.
SHE GETS MAD WHEN I FORGET TO TAKE THE TRASH OUT.
THERE'S NO TELLING WHAT SHE'D DO IF SHE FOUND OUT I RUN BLACK OPS IN MY SPARE TIME.
WHY NOT JUST GIVE IT UP?
YOU WANT THE VERY, VERY, VERY FINE HOUSE... THE CATS IN THE YARD...
...WHY MAKE IT ***MESSY*** WITH MERCENARY WORK?
YOU KNOW ***DAMN WELL*** WHY I DO IT!
NOBODY TELLS YOU WHEN THEY PRONOUNCE YOU "*MAN AND WIFE*" THAT YOU DON'T FEEL MUCH LIKE A MAN ANYMORE.
AND THERE AREN'T ANY LITTLE BLUE PILLS TO HELP WITH THAT.
I THOUGHT MAYBE I COULD GET OUT...LEAD A ***NORMAL*** LIFE... BUT IT'S NOT THAT EASY.
YOU SHOULD KNOW.
WHAT'S ***THAT*** SUPPOSED TO MEAN?
I'M GETTING OUT, PAL.
A FEW MORE JOBS AND I'M UP TO MY EARS IN SAND, SURF AND UMBRELLA DRINKS.
IF YOU'VE GOT A GOOD THING GOING, WEASEL...
...DON'T LET MERC'ING RUIN IT!
WE BOTH GOTTA GET OUT, MAN! ***BOTH*** OF US!
AND GET ME ONE OF THOSE IRON FIST DOO-DADS!

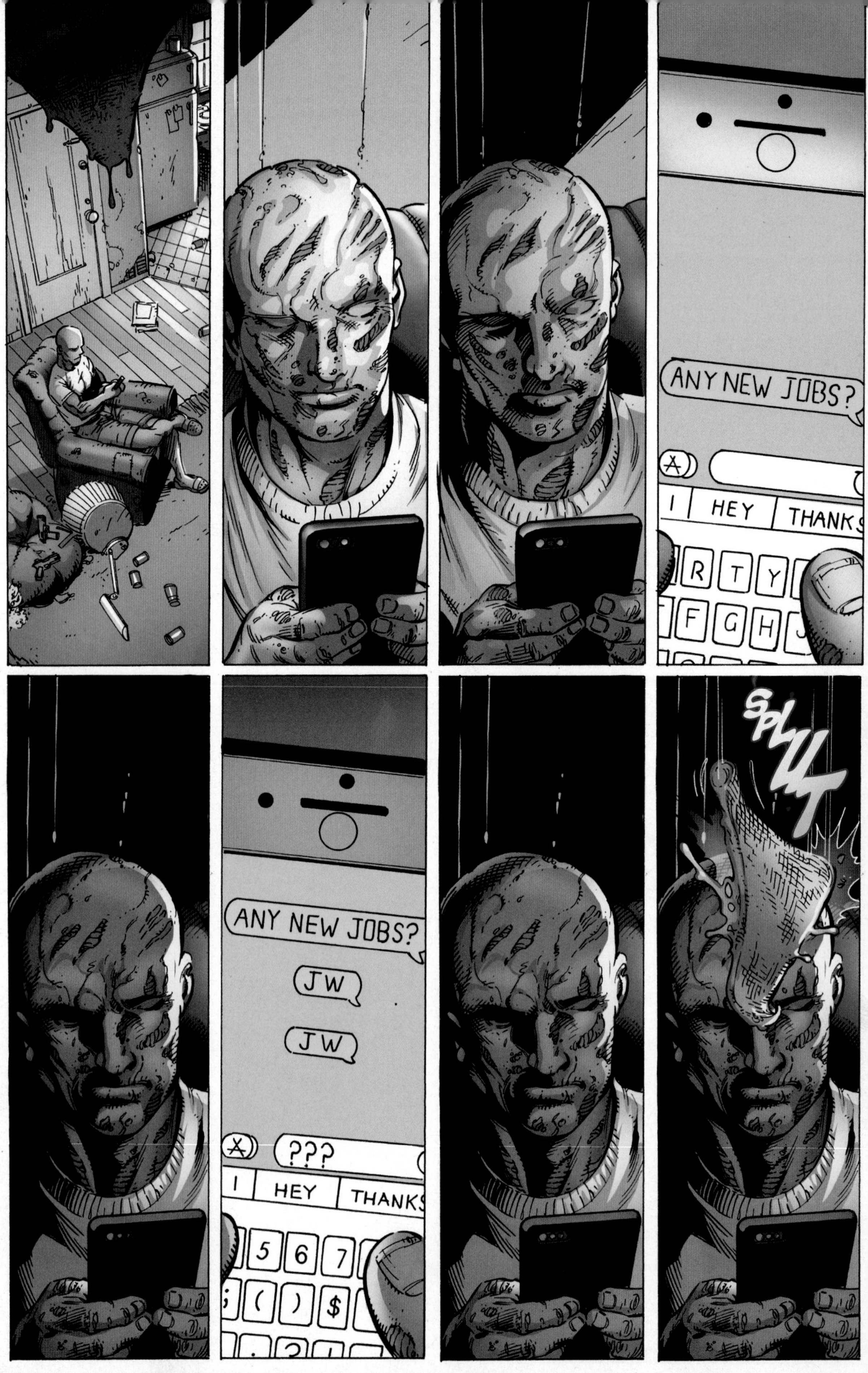
ANY NEW JOBS?
I
HEY
THANKS
R T Y
F G H
ANY NEW JOBS?
JW
JW
???
I
HEY
THANKS
5 6 7
; ( ) $
SPLUT

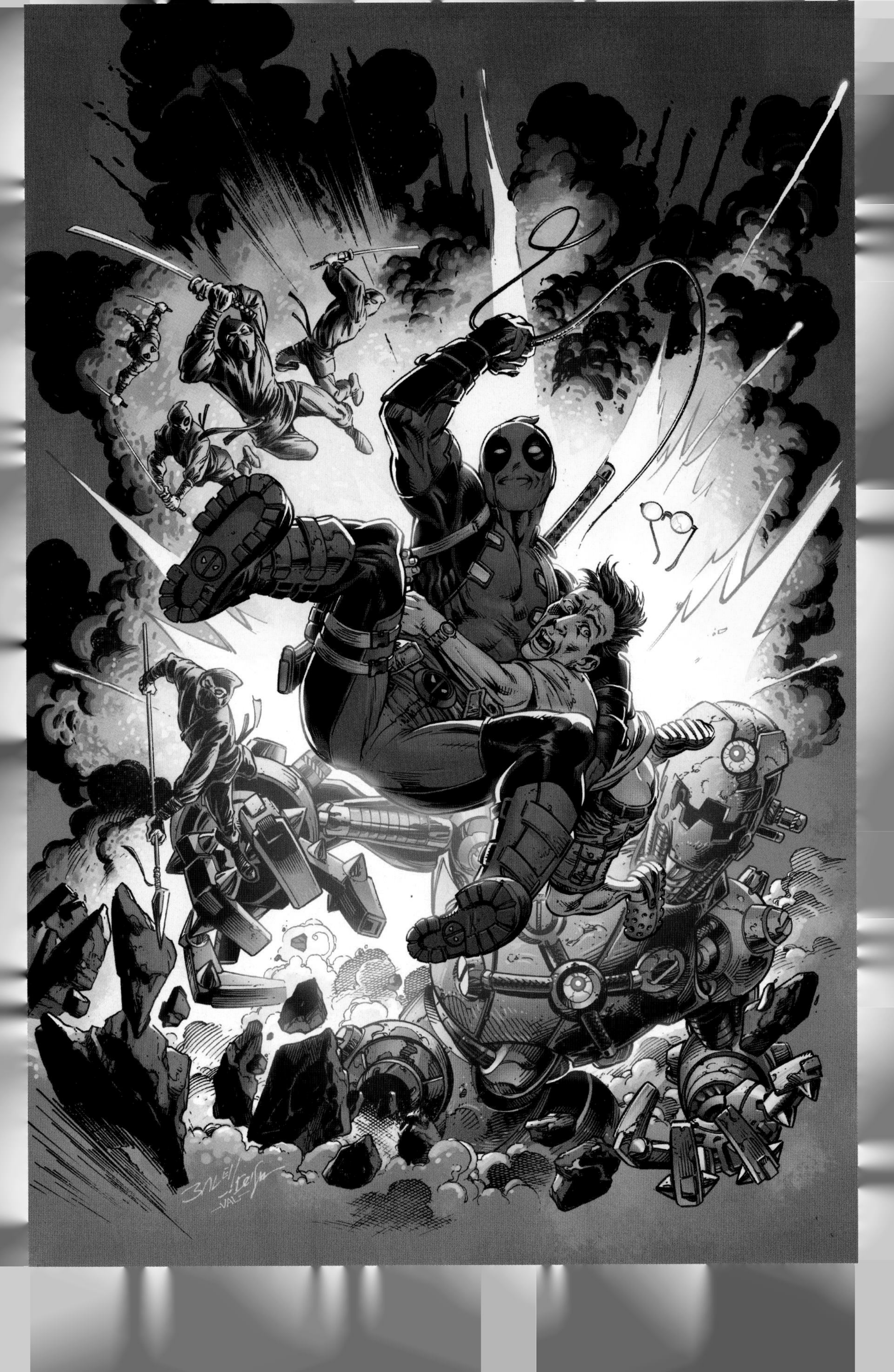

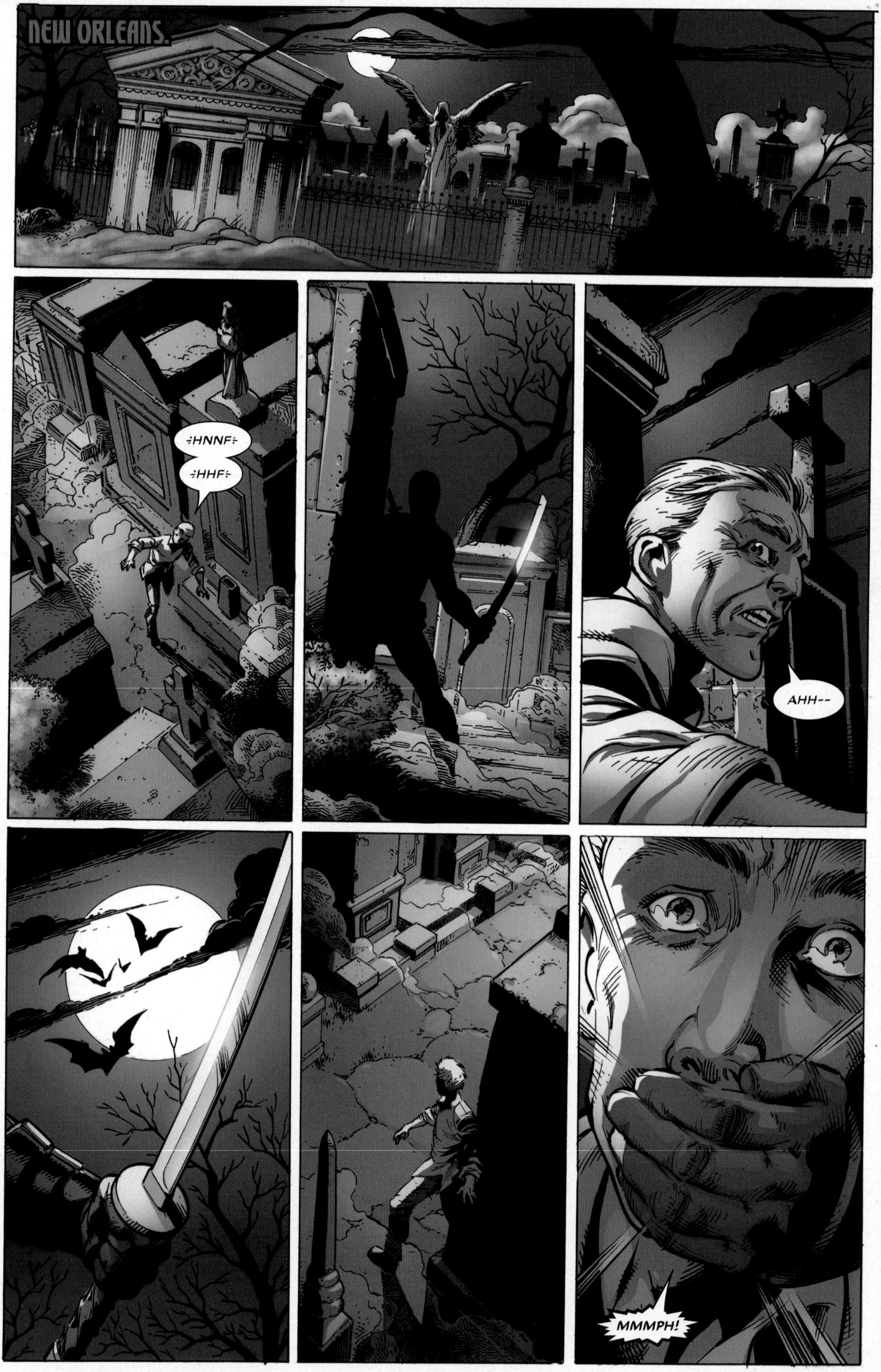
NEW ORLEANS.
HNNF
HHF
AHH--
MMMPH!

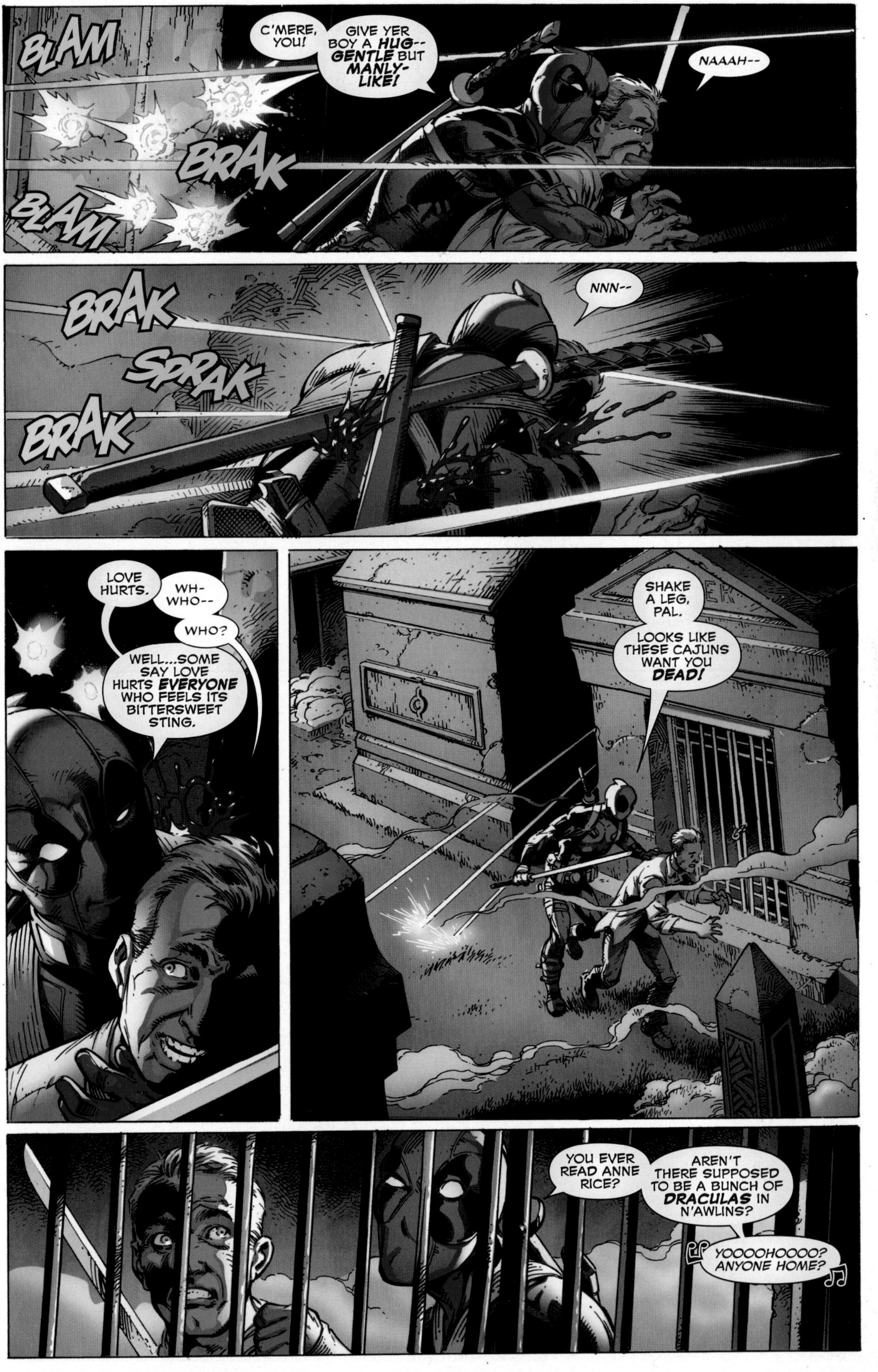
BLAM
C'MERE, YOU!
GIVE YER BOY A HUG-- GENTLE BUT MANLY-LIKE!
NAAAH--
BRAK
BLAM
BRAK
NNN--
SPRAK
BRAK
LOVE HURTS.
WH-WHO--
WHO?
WELL...SOME SAY LOVE HURTS EVERYONE WHO FEELS ITS BITTERSWEET STING.
SHAKE A LEG, PAL.
LOOKS LIKE THESE CAJUNS WANT YOU DEAD!
YOU EVER READ ANNE RICE?
AREN'T THERE SUPPOSED TO BE A BUNCH OF DRACULAS IN N'AWLINS?
YOOOOHOOOO? ANYONE HOME?

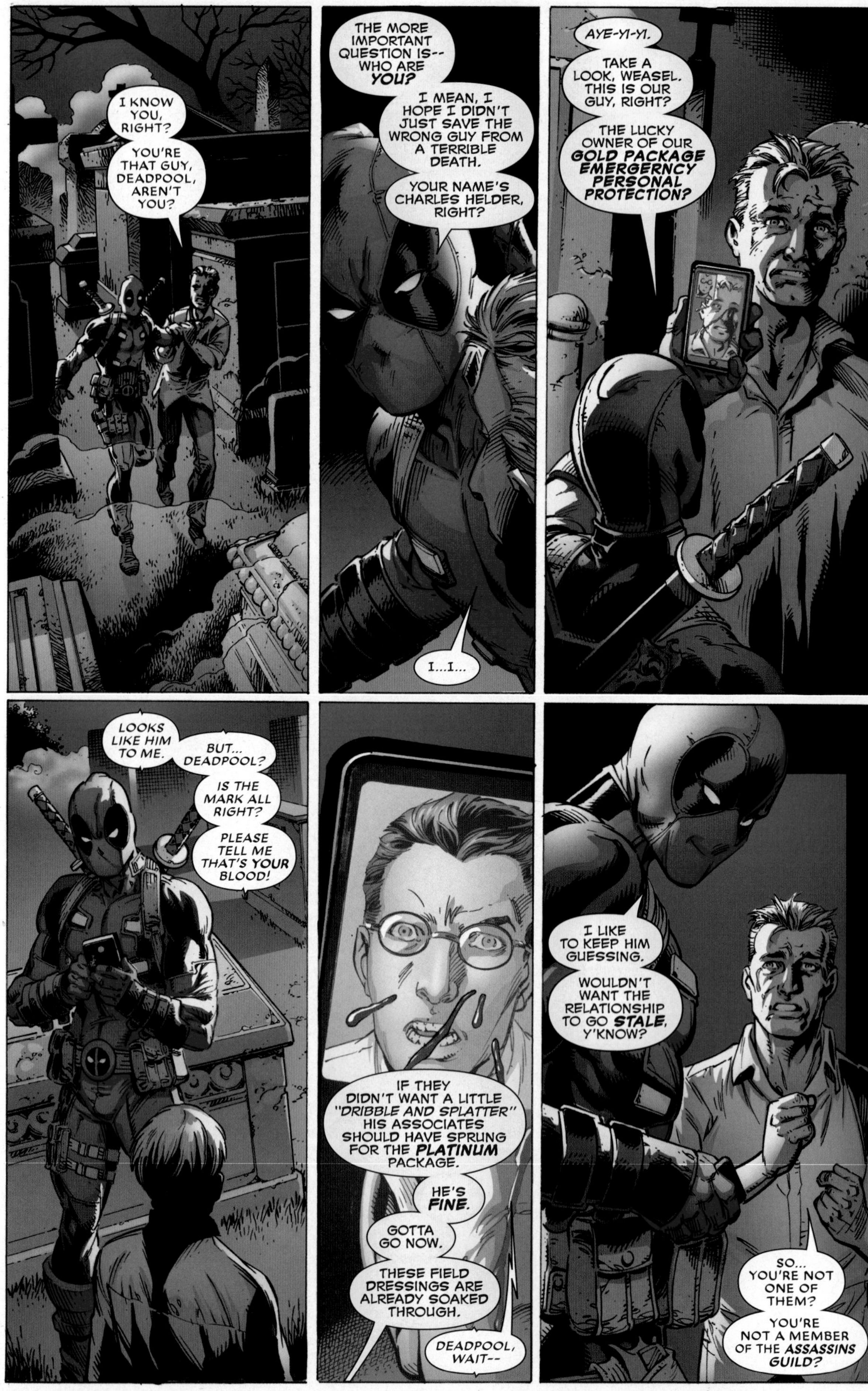
I KNOW YOU, RIGHT?
YOU'RE THAT GUY, DEADPOOL, AREN'T YOU?
THE MORE IMPORTANT QUESTION IS-- WHO ARE *YOU?*
I MEAN, I HOPE I DIDN'T JUST SAVE THE WRONG GUY FROM A TERRIBLE DEATH.
YOUR NAME'S CHARLES HELDER, RIGHT?
I...I...
AYE-YI-YI.
TAKE A LOOK, WEASEL. THIS IS OUR GUY, RIGHT?
THE LUCKY OWNER OF OUR **GOLD PACKAGE EMERGERNCY PERSONAL PROTECTION?**
LOOKS LIKE HIM TO ME.
BUT... DEADPOOL?
IS THE MARK ALL RIGHT?
PLEASE TELL ME THAT'S **YOUR** BLOOD!
IF THEY DIDN'T WANT A LITTLE *"DRIBBLE AND SPLATTER"* HIS ASSOCIATES SHOULD HAVE SPRUNG FOR THE **PLATINUM** PACKAGE.
HE'S **FINE.**
GOTTA GO NOW.
THESE FIELD DRESSINGS ARE ALREADY SOAKED THROUGH.
DEADPOOL, WAIT--
I LIKE TO KEEP HIM GUESSING.
WOULDN'T WANT THE RELATIONSHIP TO GO **STALE**, Y'KNOW?
SO... YOU'RE NOT ONE OF THEM?
YOU'RE NOT A MEMBER OF THE **ASSASSINS GUILD?**

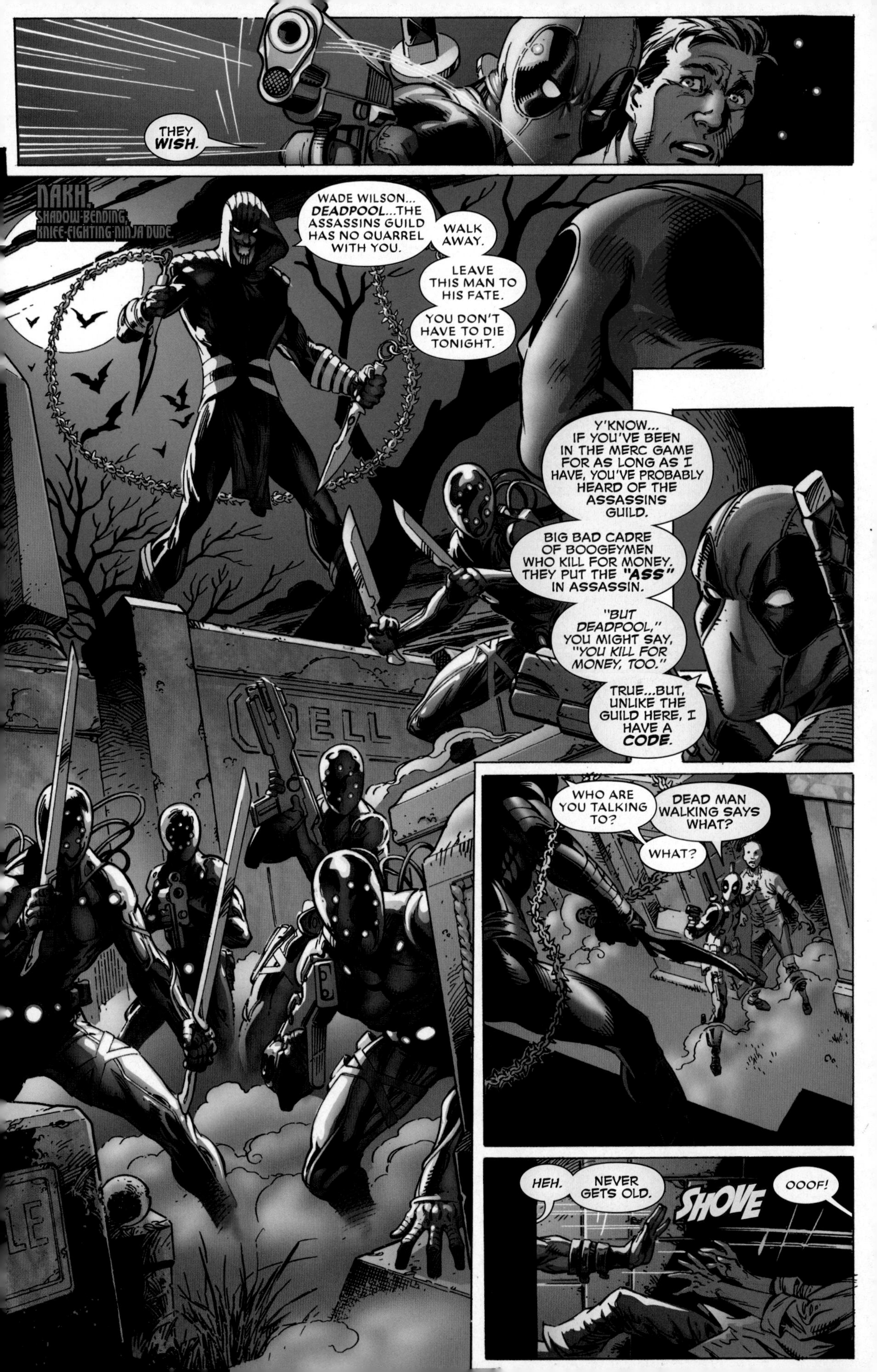
THEY WISH.
NAKH. SHADOW-BENDING, KNIFE-FIGHTING NINJA DUDE.
WADE WILSON... DEADPOOL...THE ASSASSINS GUILD HAS NO QUARREL WITH YOU.
WALK AWAY.
LEAVE THIS MAN TO HIS FATE.
YOU DON'T HAVE TO DIE TONIGHT.
Y'KNOW... IF YOU'VE BEEN IN THE MERC GAME FOR AS LONG AS I HAVE, YOU'VE PROBABLY HEARD OF THE ASSASSINS GUILD.
BIG BAD CADRE OF BOOGEYMEN WHO KILL FOR MONEY. THEY PUT THE "ASS" IN ASSASSIN.
"BUT DEADPOOL," YOU MIGHT SAY, "YOU KILL FOR MONEY, TOO."
TRUE...BUT, UNLIKE THE GUILD HERE, I HAVE A CODE.
WHO ARE YOU TALKING TO?
DEAD MAN WALKING SAYS WHAT?
WHAT?
HEH.
NEVER GETS OLD.
SHOVE
OOOF!

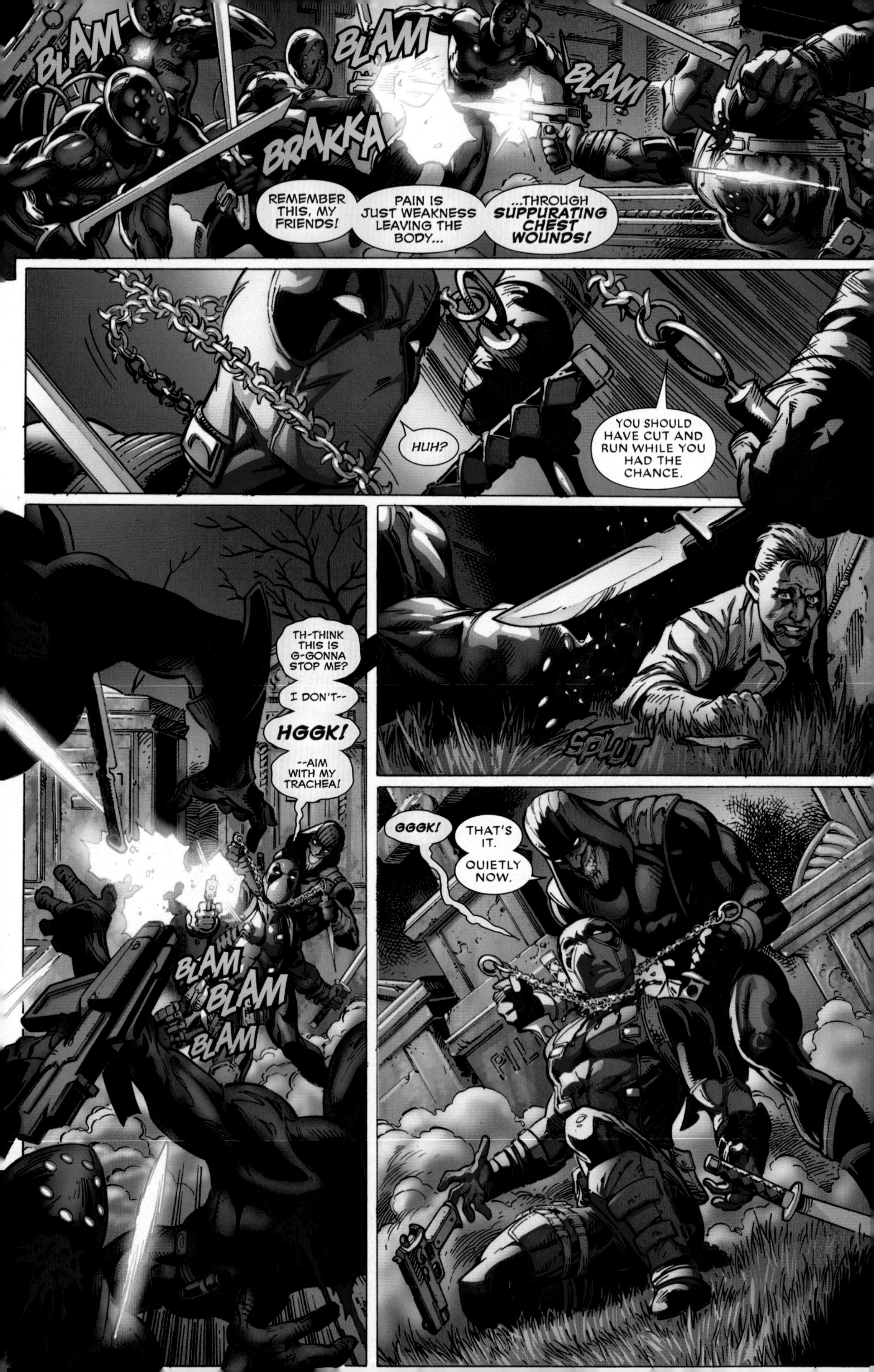
BLAM
BLAM
BLAM
BRAKKA
REMEMBER THIS, MY FRIENDS!
PAIN IS JUST WEAKNESS LEAVING THE BODY...
...THROUGH SUPPURATING CHEST WOUNDS!
HUH?
YOU SHOULD HAVE CUT AND RUN WHILE YOU HAD THE CHANCE.
SPLUT
TH-THINK THIS IS G-GONNA STOP ME?
I DON'T--
HGGK!
--AIM WITH MY TRACHEA!
BLAM
BLAM
BLAM
GGGK!
THAT'S IT.
QUIETLY NOW.

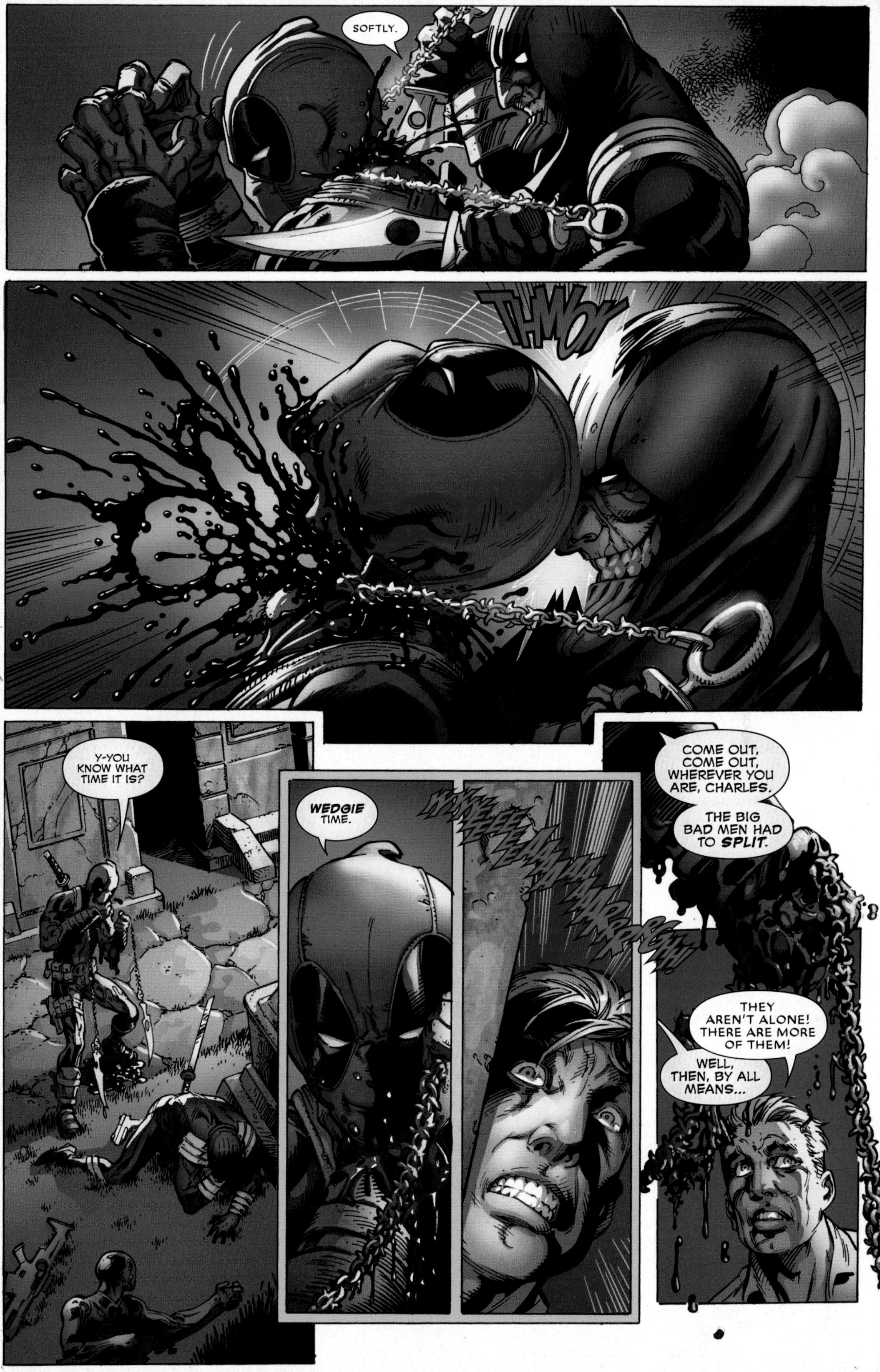
SOFTLY.
THWOK
Y-YOU KNOW WHAT TIME IT IS?
WEDGIE TIME.
COME OUT, COME OUT, WHEREVER YOU ARE, CHARLES.
THE BIG BAD MEN HAD TO SPLIT.
THEY AREN'T ALONE! THERE ARE MORE OF THEM!
WELL, THEN, BY ALL MEANS...

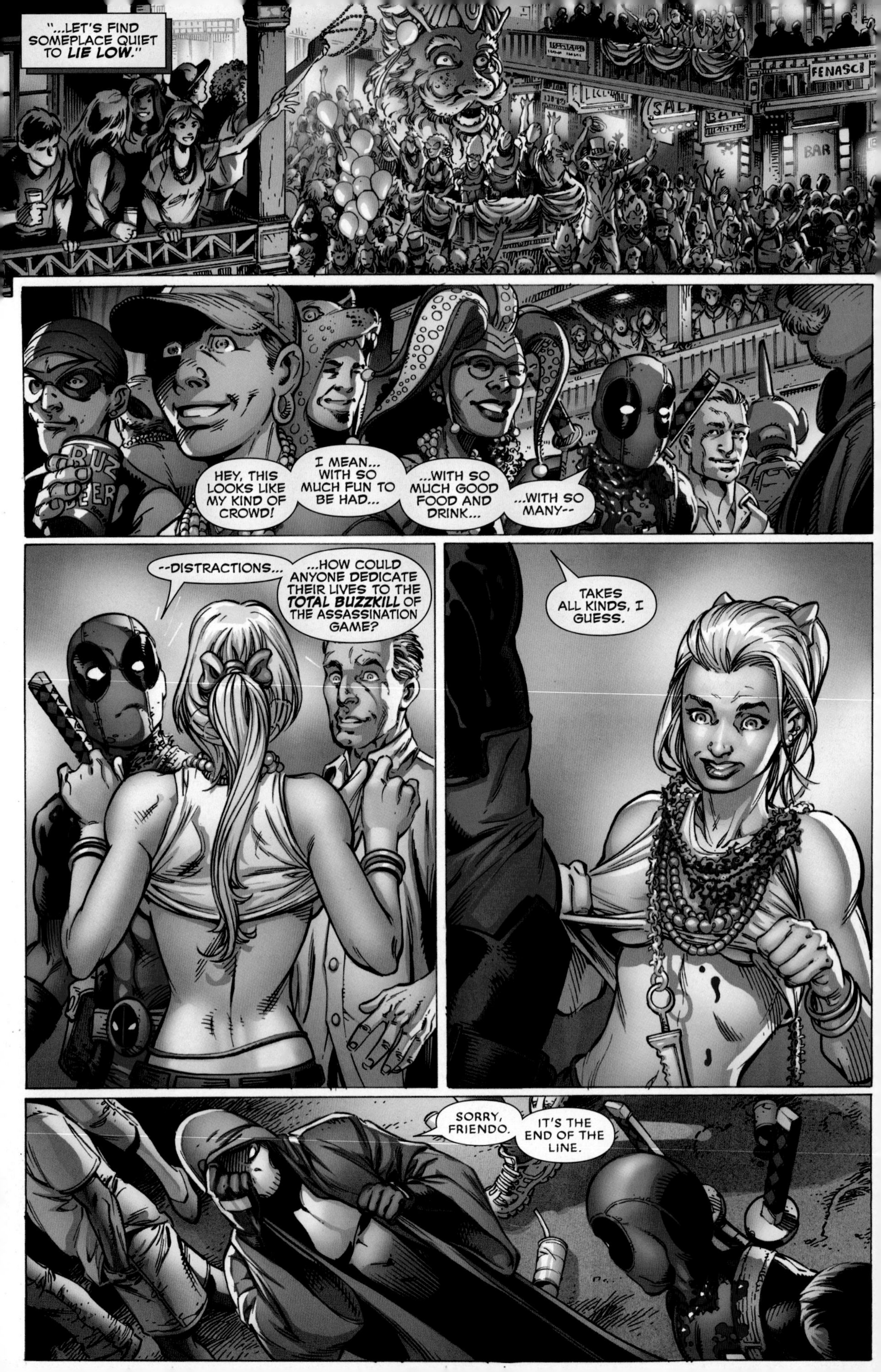
"...LET'S FIND SOMEPLACE QUIET TO LIE LOW."
HEY, THIS LOOKS LIKE MY KIND OF CROWD!
I MEAN... WITH SO MUCH FUN TO BE HAD...
...WITH SO MUCH GOOD FOOD AND DRINK...
...WITH SO MANY--
--DISTRACTIONS...
...HOW COULD ANYONE DEDICATE THEIR LIVES TO THE TOTAL BUZZKILL OF THE ASSASSINATION GAME?
TAKES ALL KINDS, I GUESS.
SORRY, FRIENDO.
IT'S THE END OF THE LINE.
BAR
FENASCI

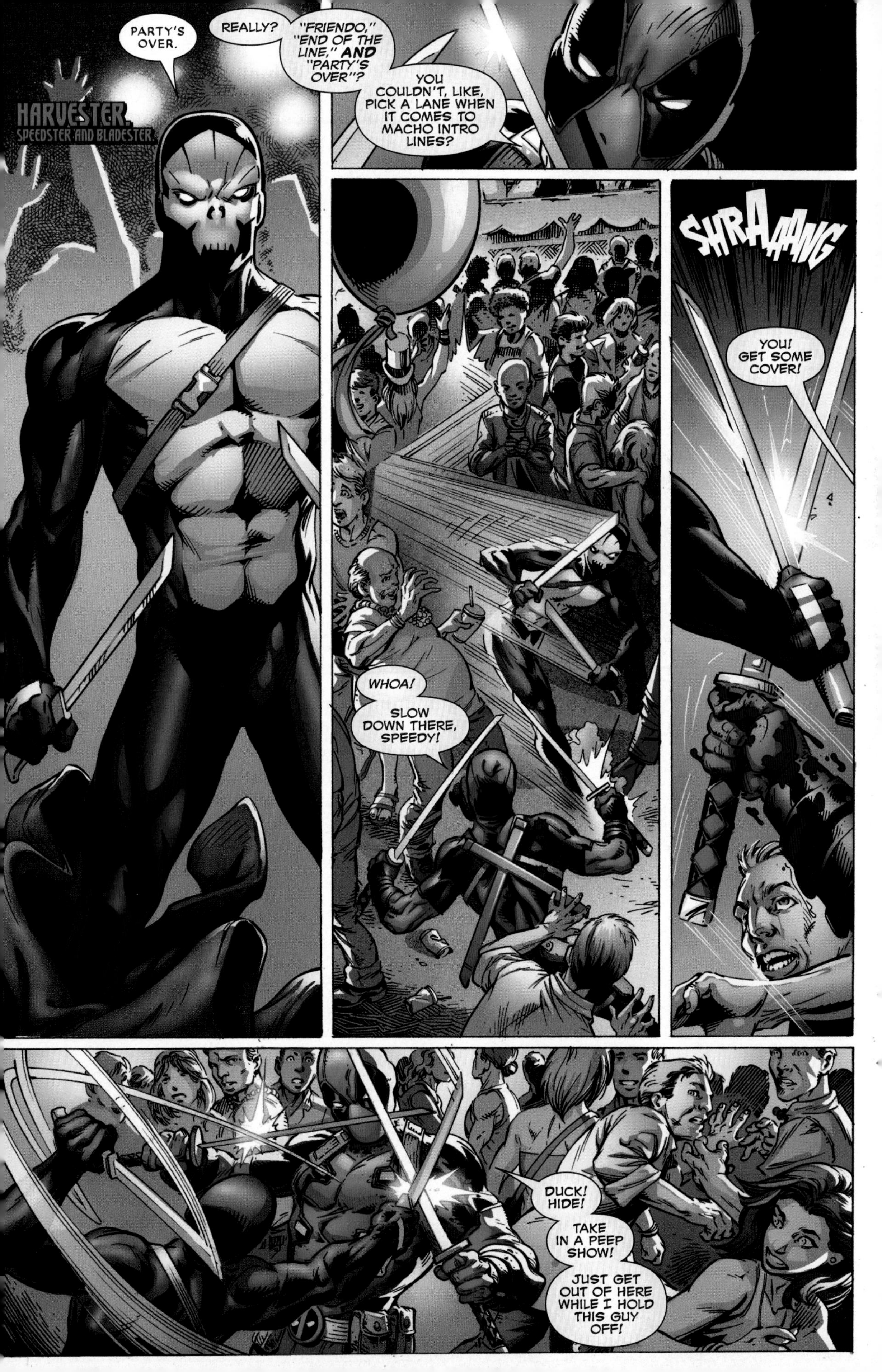
PARTY'S OVER.
HARVESTER.
SPEEDSTER AND BLADESTER.
REALLY?
"FRIENDO," "END OF THE LINE," AND "PARTY'S OVER"?
YOU COULDN'T, LIKE, PICK A LANE WHEN IT COMES TO MACHO INTRO LINES?
WHOA!
SLOW DOWN THERE, SPEEDY!
SHRAAAANG
YOU! GET SOME COVER!
DUCK! HIDE!
TAKE IN A PEEP SHOW!
JUST GET OUT OF HERE WHILE I HOLD THIS GUY OFF!

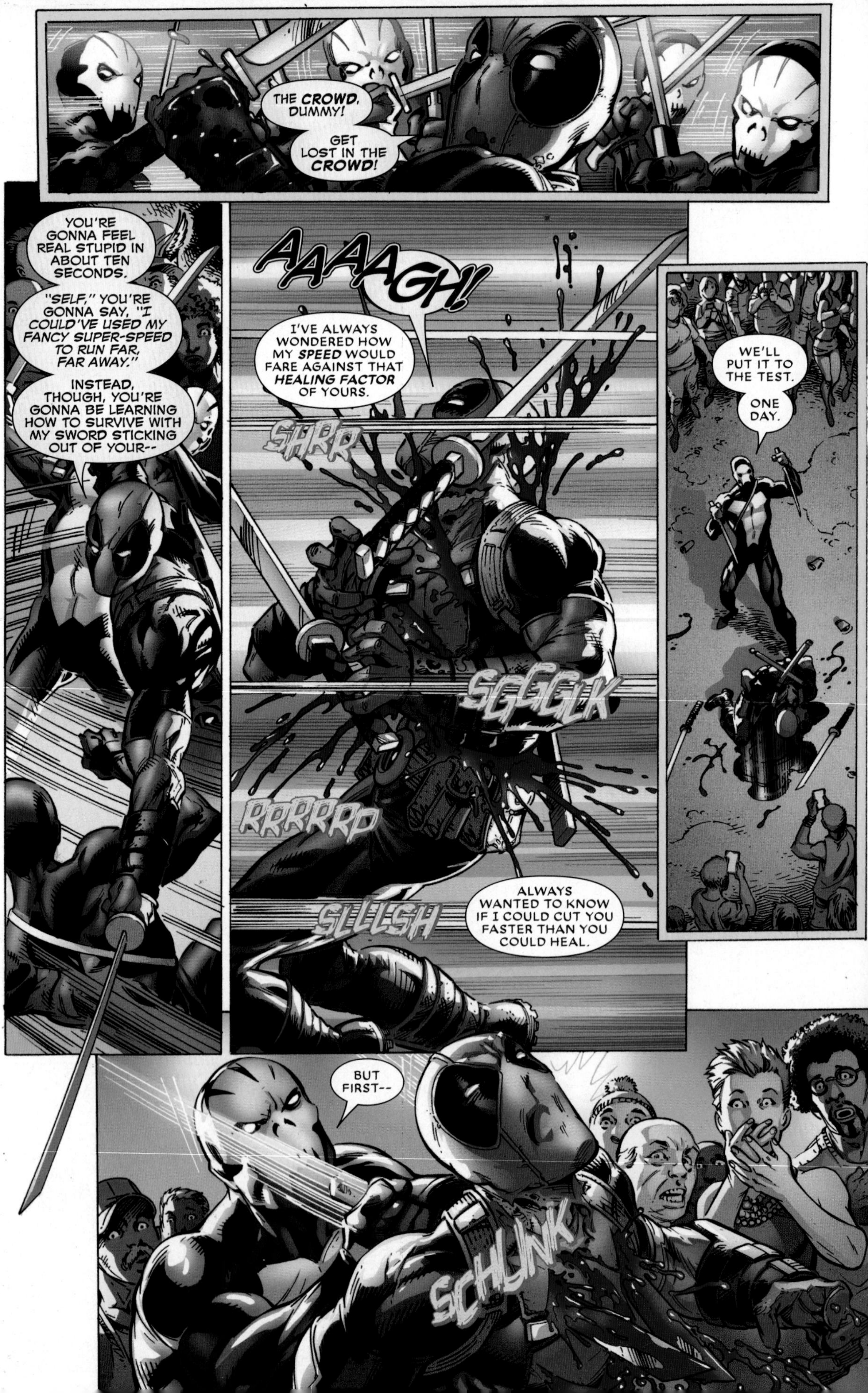

THE *CROWD*, DUMMY!
GET LOST IN THE *CROWD!*
YOU'RE GONNA FEEL REAL STUPID IN ABOUT TEN SECONDS.
"SELF," YOU'RE GONNA SAY, "I COULD'VE USED MY FANCY *SUPER-SPEED* TO RUN FAR, FAR AWAY."
INSTEAD, THOUGH, YOU'RE GONNA BE LEARNING HOW TO SURVIVE WITH MY SWORD STICKING OUT OF YOUR--
AAAAAGH!
I'VE ALWAYS WONDERED HOW MY *SPEED* WOULD FARE AGAINST THAT *HEALING FACTOR* OF YOURS.
SHRR
SGGGLK
RRRRRP
SLLLSH
ALWAYS WANTED TO KNOW IF I COULD CUT YOU FASTER THAN YOU COULD HEAL.
WE'LL PUT IT TO THE TEST.
ONE DAY.
BUT FIRST--
SCHUNK

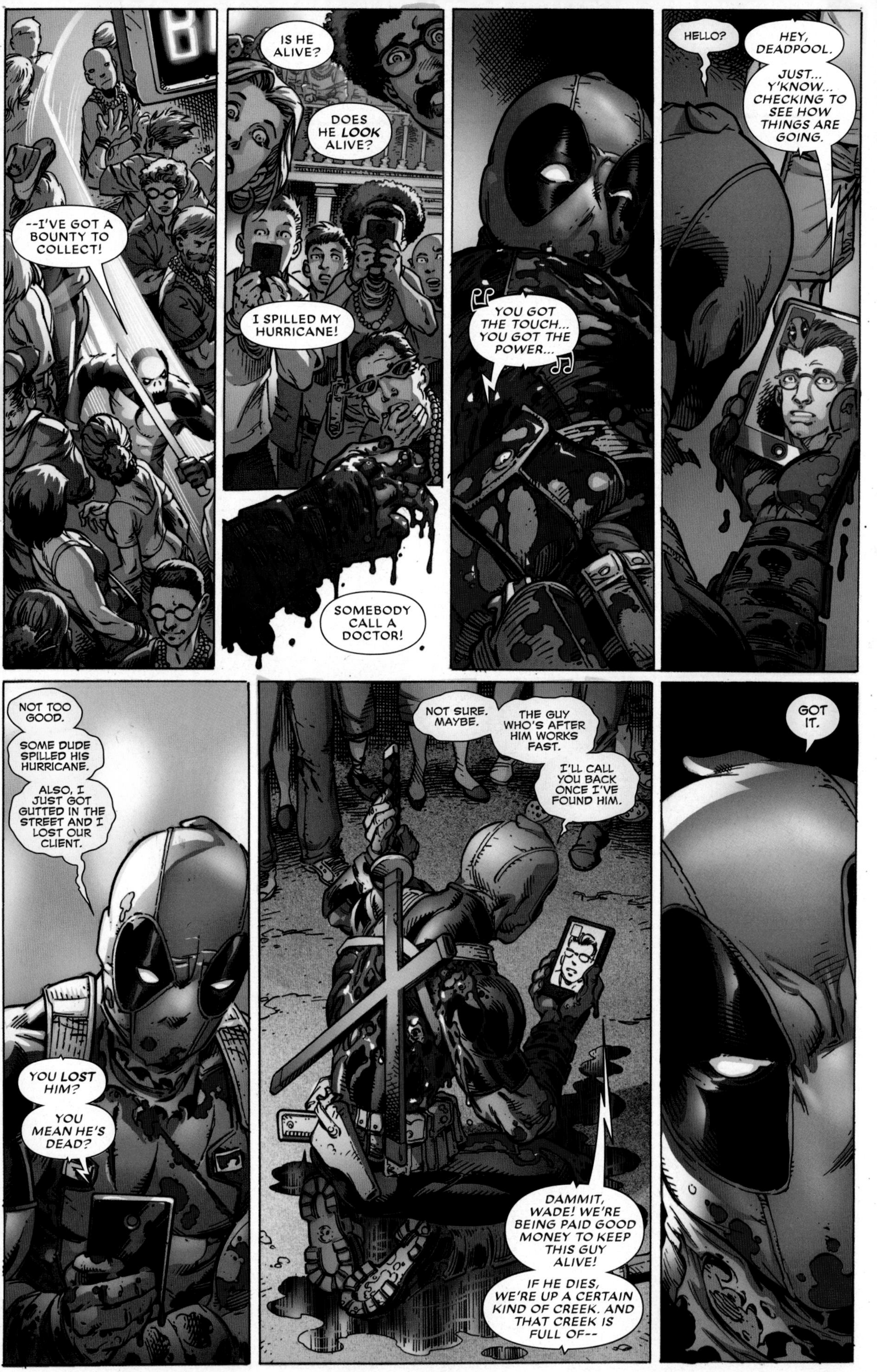
--I'VE GOT A BOUNTY TO COLLECT!
IS HE ALIVE?
DOES HE LOOK ALIVE?
I SPILLED MY HURRICANE!
SOMEBODY CALL A DOCTOR!
YOU GOT THE TOUCH... YOU GOT THE POWER...
HELLO?
HEY, DEADPOOL.
JUST... Y'KNOW... CHECKING TO SEE HOW THINGS ARE GOING.
NOT TOO GOOD.
SOME DUDE SPILLED HIS HURRICANE.
ALSO, I JUST GOT GUTTED IN THE STREET AND I LOST OUR CLIENT.
YOU LOST HIM?
YOU MEAN HE'S DEAD?
NOT SURE. MAYBE.
THE GUY WHO'S AFTER HIM WORKS FAST.
I'LL CALL YOU BACK ONCE I'VE FOUND HIM.
DAMMIT, WADE! WE'RE BEING PAID GOOD MONEY TO KEEP THIS GUY ALIVE!
IF HE DIES, WE'RE UP A CERTAIN KIND OF CREEK. AND THAT CREEK IS FULL OF--
GOT IT.

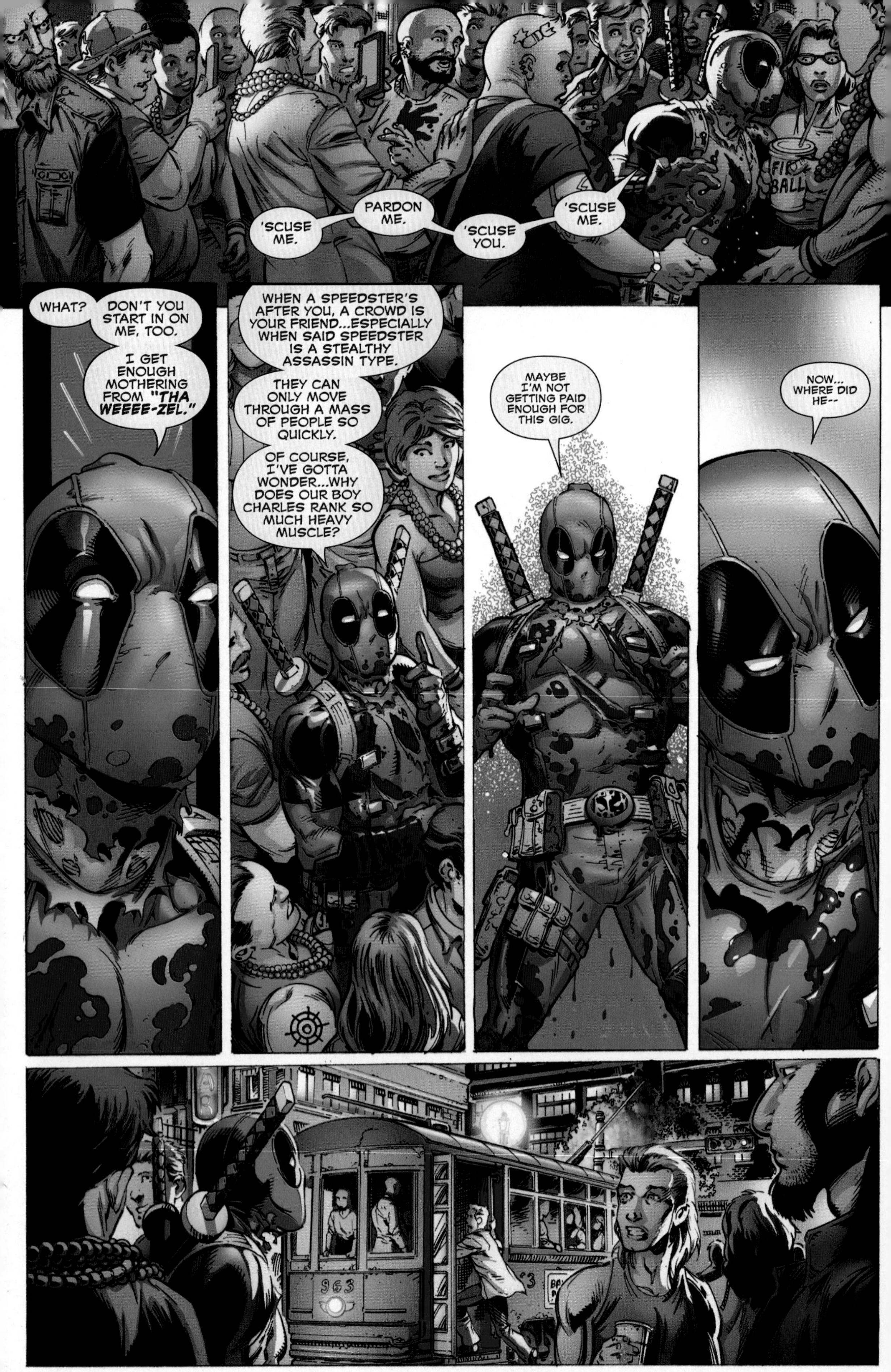
'SCUSE ME.
PARDON ME.
'SCUSE YOU.
'SCUSE ME.
WHAT?
DON'T YOU START IN ON ME, TOO.
I GET ENOUGH MOTHERING FROM "THA WEEEE-ZEL."
WHEN A SPEEDSTER'S AFTER YOU, A CROWD IS YOUR FRIEND...ESPECIALLY WHEN SAID SPEEDSTER IS A STEALTHY ASSASSIN TYPE.
THEY CAN ONLY MOVE THROUGH A MASS OF PEOPLE SO QUICKLY.
OF COURSE, I'VE GOTTA WONDER...WHY DOES OUR BOY CHARLES RANK SO MUCH HEAVY MUSCLE?
MAYBE I'M NOT GETTING PAID ENOUGH FOR THIS GIG.
NOW... WHERE DID HE--
963

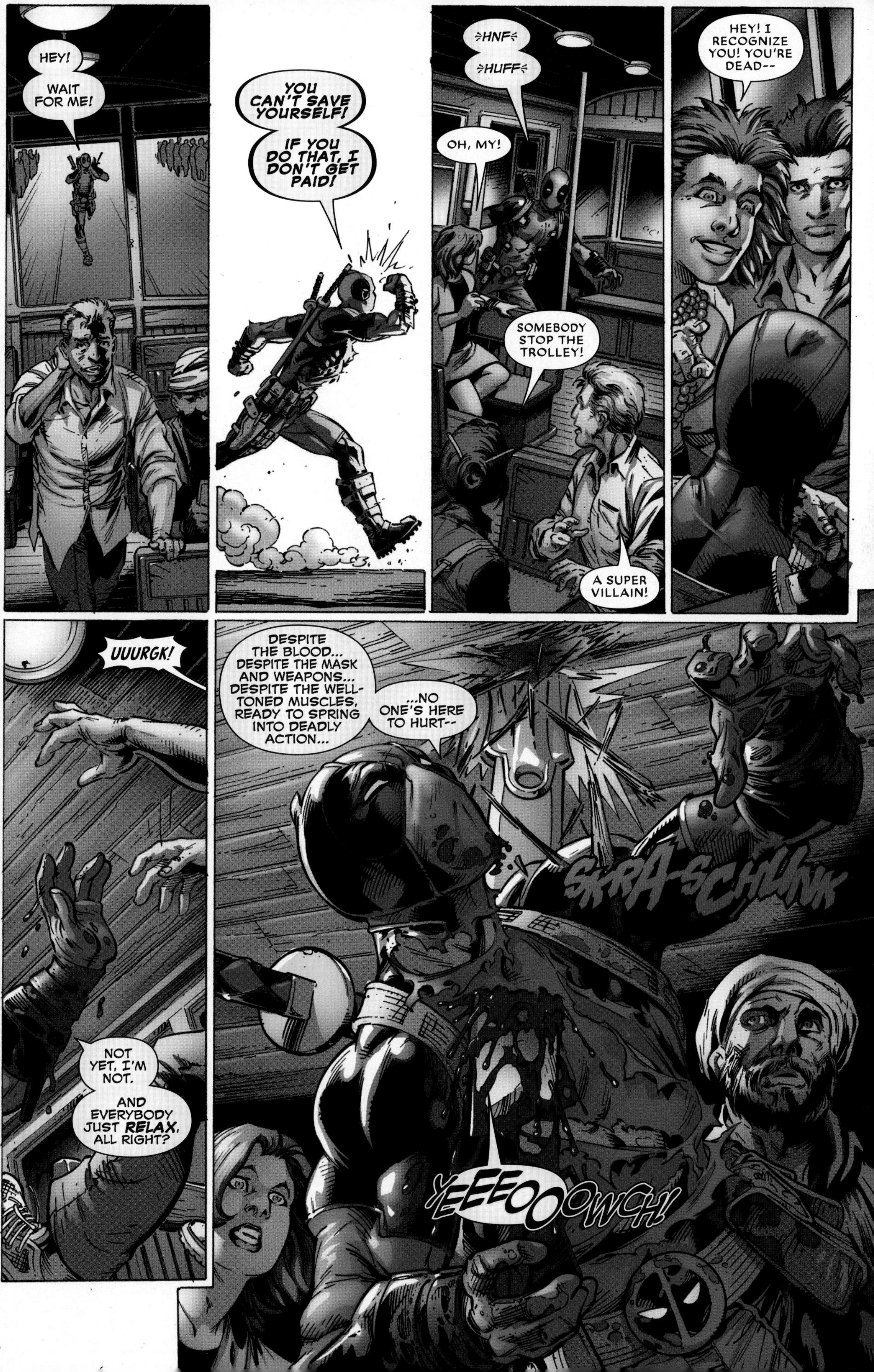
HEY!
WAIT FOR ME!
YOU CAN'T SAVE YOURSELF!
IF YOU DO THAT, I DON'T GET PAID!
HNF
HUFF
OH, MY!
SOMEBODY STOP THE TROLLEY!
A SUPER VILLAIN!
HEY! I RECOGNIZE YOU! YOU'RE DEAD--
UUURGK!
NOT YET, I'M NOT.
AND EVERYBODY JUST RELAX, ALL RIGHT?
DESPITE THE BLOOD... DESPITE THE MASK AND WEAPONS... DESPITE THE WELL-TONED MUSCLES, READY TO SPRING INTO DEADLY ACTION...
...NO ONE'S HERE TO HURT--
SKRA-SCHUNK
YEEEOOOWCH!

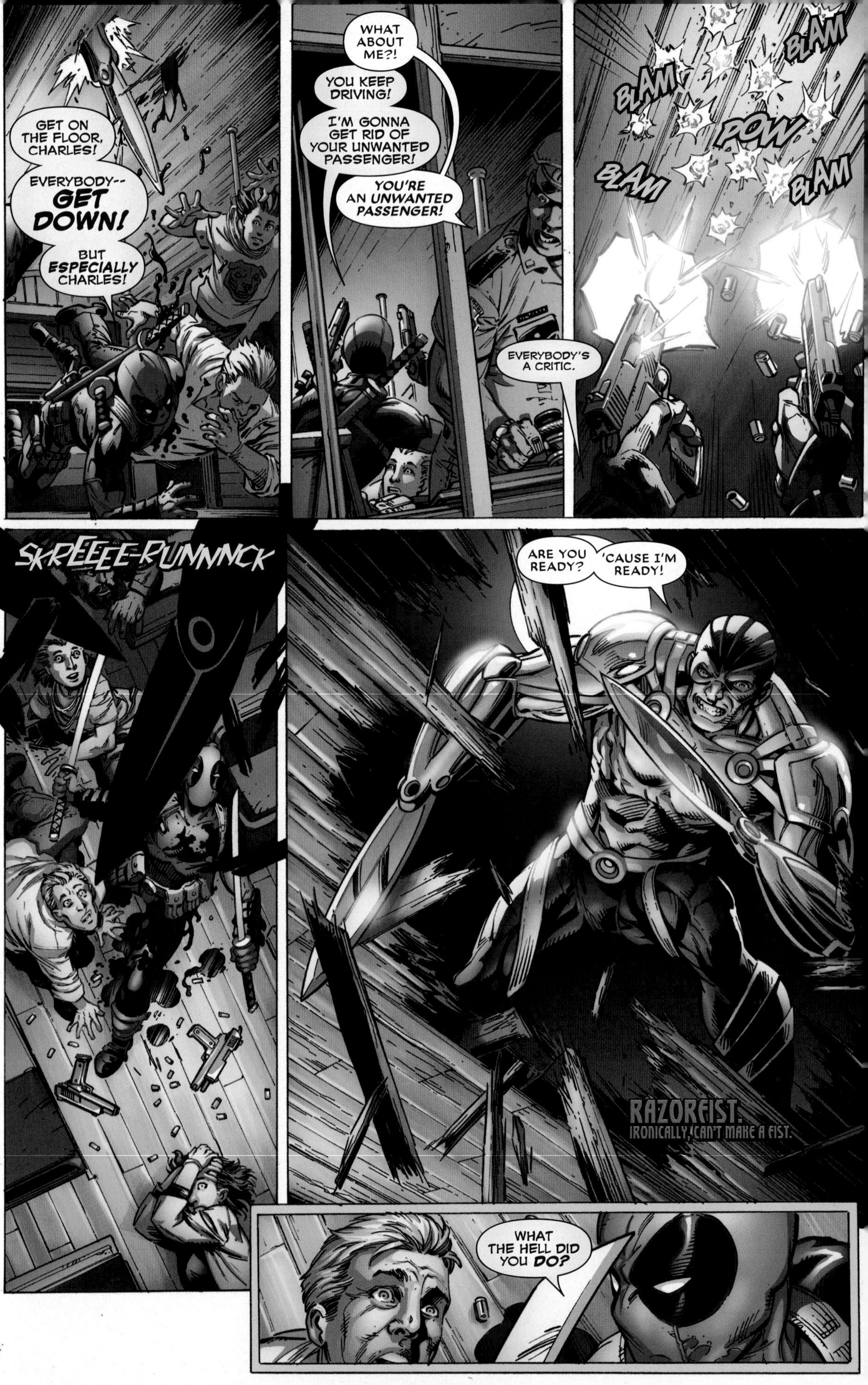
GET ON THE FLOOR, CHARLES!
EVERYBODY-- GET DOWN!
BUT ESPECIALLY CHARLES!
WHAT ABOUT ME?!
YOU KEEP DRIVING!
I'M GONNA GET RID OF YOUR UNWANTED PASSENGER!
YOU'RE AN UNWANTED PASSENGER!
EVERYBODY'S A CRITIC.
BLAM
BLAM
POW
BLAM
BLAM
SKREEEEE-RUNNNCK
ARE YOU READY?
'CAUSE I'M READY!
RAZORFIST.
IRONICALLY, CAN'T MAKE A FIST.
WHAT THE HELL DID YOU DO?

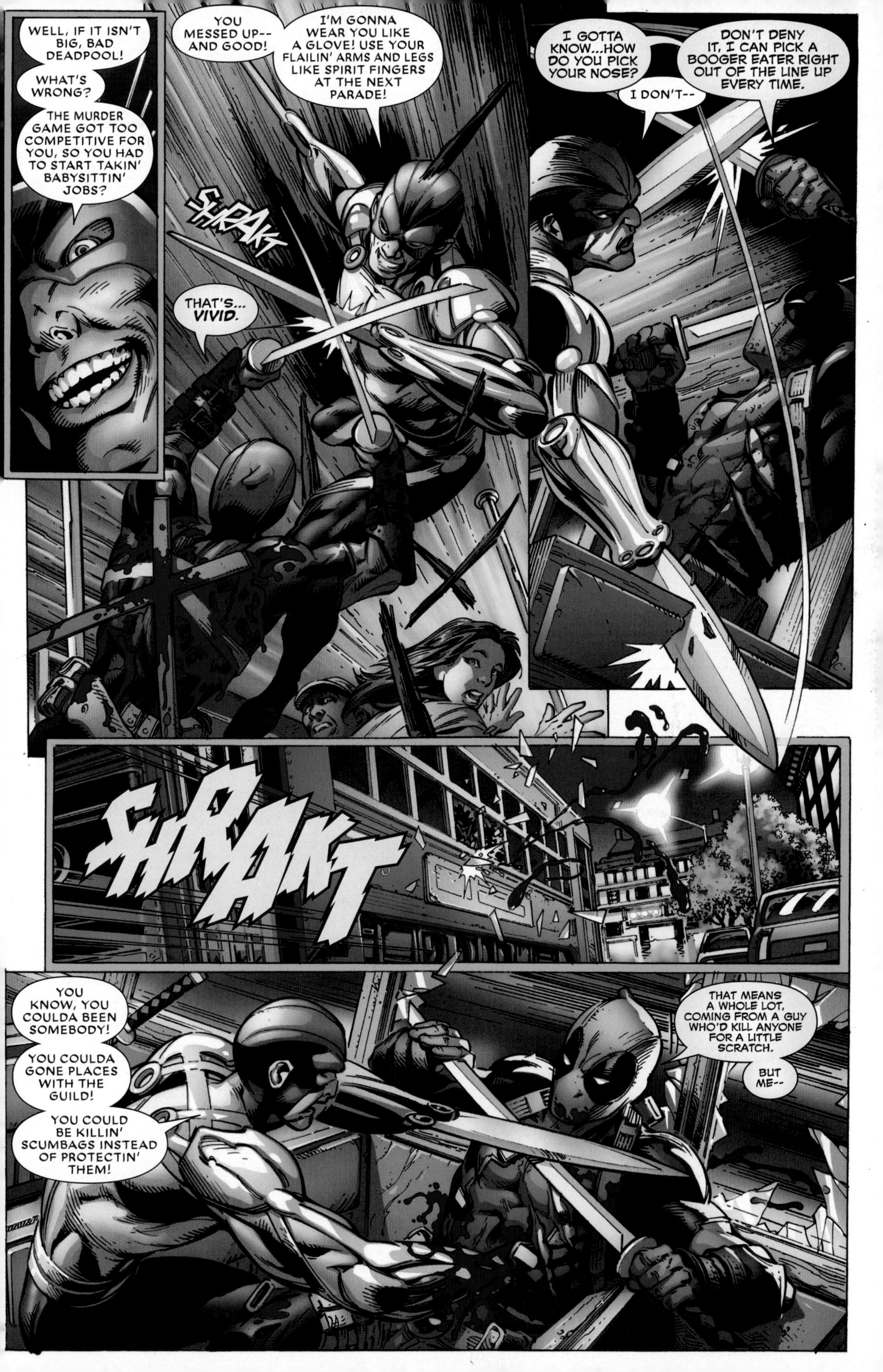
WELL, IF IT ISN'T BIG, BAD DEADPOOL!
WHAT'S WRONG?
THE MURDER GAME GOT TOO COMPETITIVE FOR YOU, SO YOU HAD TO START TAKIN' BABYSITTIN' JOBS?
YOU MESSED UP-- AND GOOD!
I'M GONNA WEAR YOU LIKE A GLOVE! USE YOUR FLAILIN' ARMS AND LEGS LIKE SPIRIT FINGERS AT THE NEXT PARADE!
SHRAKT
THAT'S... VIVID.
I GOTTA KNOW...HOW DO YOU PICK YOUR NOSE?
I DON'T--
DON'T DENY IT, I CAN PICK A BOOGER EATER RIGHT OUT OF THE LINE UP EVERY TIME.
SHRAKT
YOU KNOW, YOU COULDA BEEN SOMEBODY!
YOU COULDA GONE PLACES WITH THE GUILD!
YOU COULD BE KILLIN' SCUMBAGS INSTEAD OF PROTECTIN' THEM!
THAT MEANS A WHOLE LOT, COMING FROM A GUY WHO'D KILL ANYONE FOR A LITTLE SCRATCH.
BUT ME--

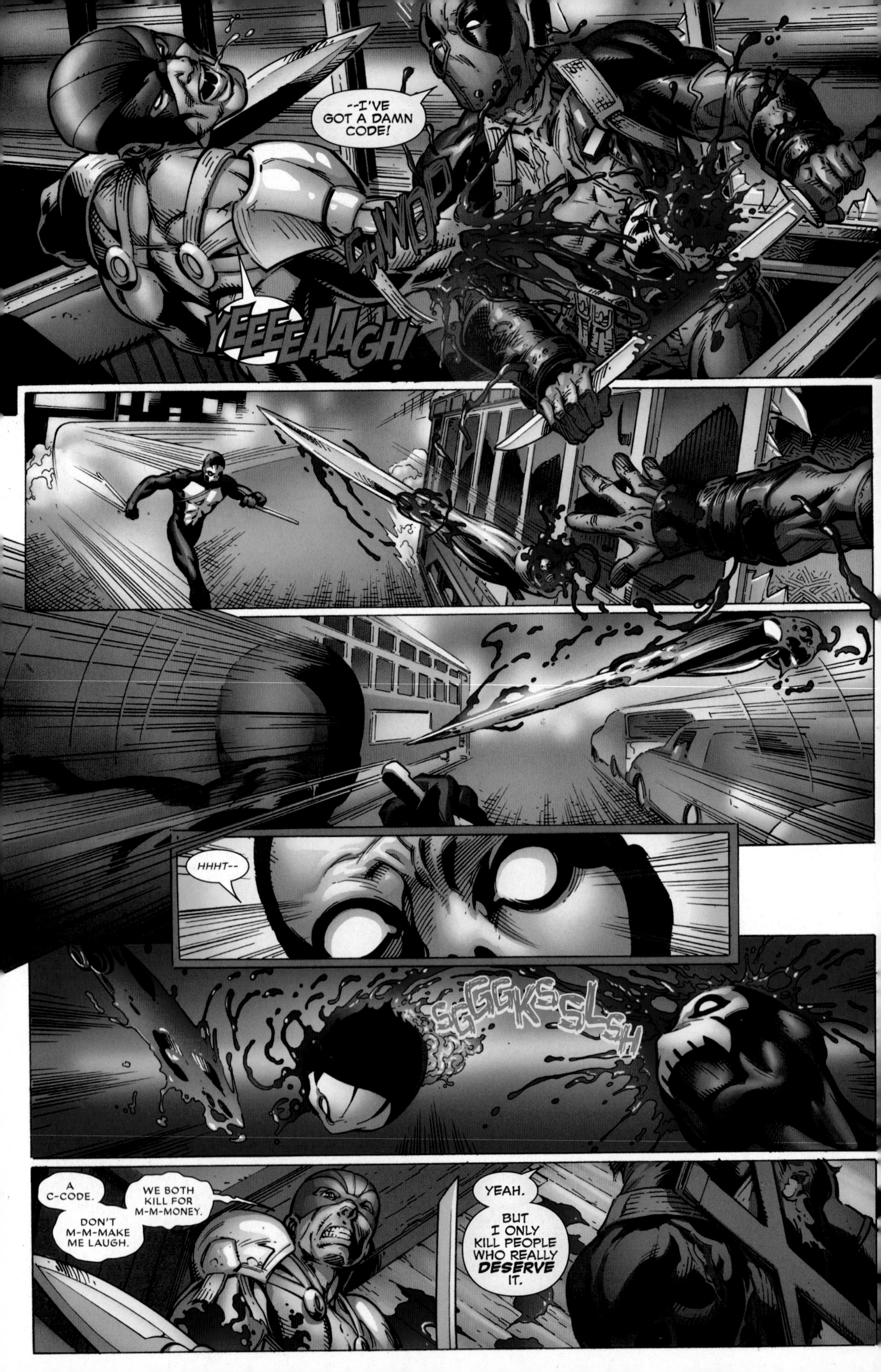

--I'VE GOT A DAMN CODE!
CHWOP
YEEEEAAGH!
HHHT--
SGGGKSSLSH
A C-CODE.
DON'T M-M-MAKE ME LAUGH.
WE BOTH KILL FOR M-M-MONEY.
YEAH.
BUT I ONLY KILL PEOPLE WHO REALLY **DESERVE** IT.

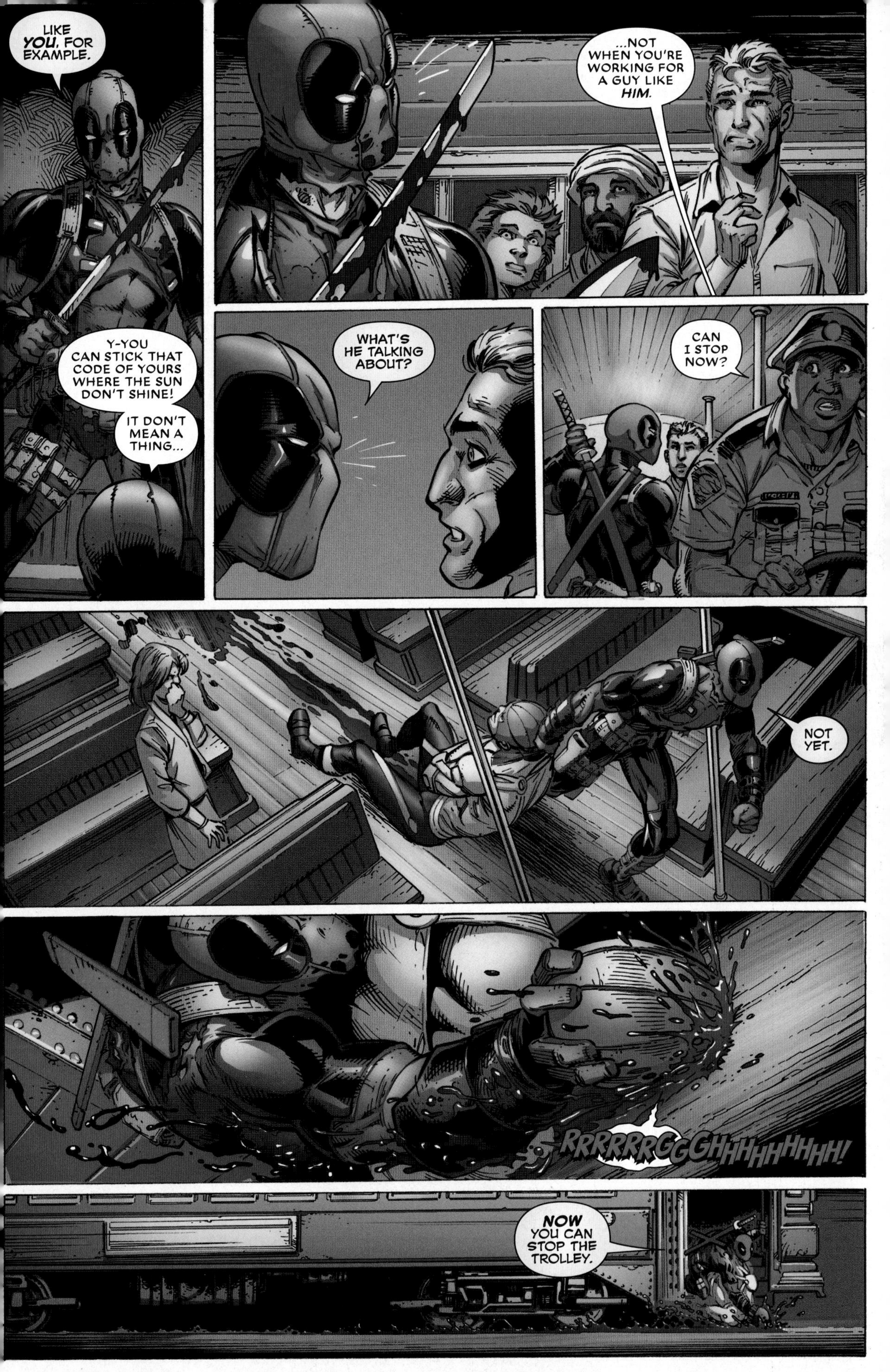
LIKE *YOU*, FOR EXAMPLE.
...NOT WHEN YOU'RE WORKING FOR A GUY LIKE *HIM*.
Y-YOU CAN STICK THAT CODE OF YOURS WHERE THE SUN DON'T SHINE!
IT DON'T MEAN A THING...
WHAT'S HE TALKING ABOUT?
CAN I STOP NOW?
NOT YET.
RRRRRRGGGHHHHHHHHH!
NOW YOU CAN STOP THE TROLLEY.

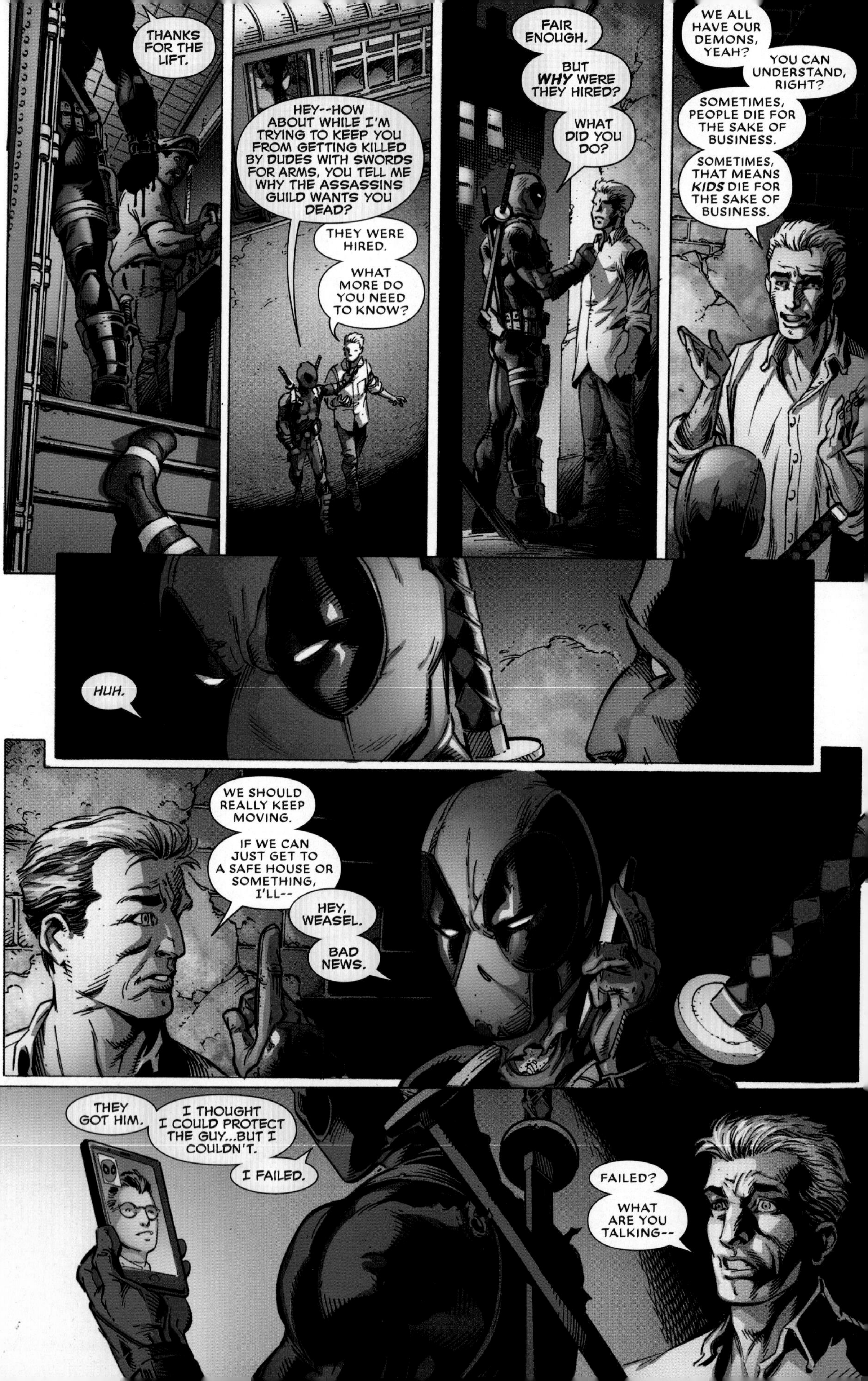
THANKS FOR THE LIFT.
HEY--HOW ABOUT WHILE I'M TRYING TO KEEP YOU FROM GETTING KILLED BY DUDES WITH SWORDS FOR ARMS, YOU TELL ME WHY THE ASSASSINS GUILD WANTS YOU DEAD?
THEY WERE HIRED.
WHAT MORE DO YOU NEED TO KNOW?
FAIR ENOUGH.
BUT WHY WERE THEY HIRED?
WHAT DID YOU DO?
WE ALL HAVE OUR DEMONS, YEAH?
YOU CAN UNDERSTAND, RIGHT?
SOMETIMES, PEOPLE DIE FOR THE SAKE OF BUSINESS.
SOMETIMES, THAT MEANS KIDS DIE FOR THE SAKE OF BUSINESS.
HUH.
WE SHOULD REALLY KEEP MOVING.
IF WE CAN JUST GET TO A SAFE HOUSE OR SOMETHING, I'LL--
HEY, WEASEL.
BAD NEWS.
THEY GOT HIM.
I THOUGHT I COULD PROTECT THE GUY...BUT I COULDN'T.
I FAILED.
FAILED?
WHAT ARE YOU TALKING--

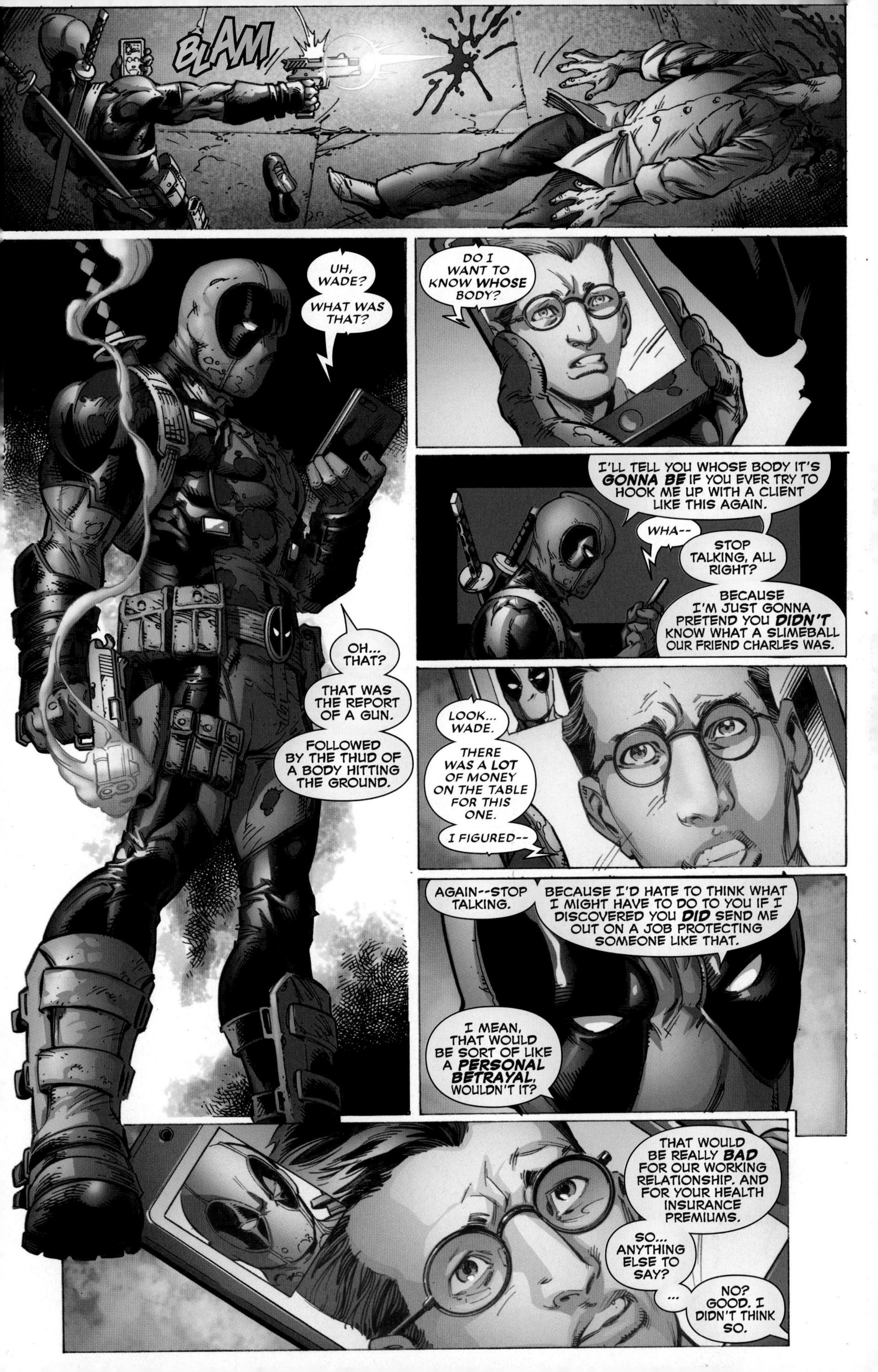
BLAM
UH, WADE?
WHAT WAS THAT?
DO I WANT TO KNOW WHOSE BODY?
OH... THAT?
THAT WAS THE REPORT OF A GUN.
FOLLOWED BY THE THUD OF A BODY HITTING THE GROUND.
I'LL TELL YOU WHOSE BODY IT'S GONNA BE IF YOU EVER TRY TO HOOK ME UP WITH A CLIENT LIKE THIS AGAIN.
WHA--
STOP TALKING, ALL RIGHT?
BECAUSE I'M JUST GONNA PRETEND YOU DIDN'T KNOW WHAT A SLIMEBALL OUR FRIEND CHARLES WAS.
LOOK... WADE.
THERE WAS A LOT OF MONEY ON THE TABLE FOR THIS ONE.
I FIGURED--
AGAIN--STOP TALKING.
BECAUSE I'D HATE TO THINK WHAT I MIGHT HAVE TO DO TO YOU IF I DISCOVERED YOU DID SEND ME OUT ON A JOB PROTECTING SOMEONE LIKE THAT.
I MEAN, THAT WOULD BE SORT OF LIKE A PERSONAL BETRAYAL, WOULDN'T IT?
THAT WOULD BE REALLY BAD FOR OUR WORKING RELATIONSHIP. AND FOR YOUR HEALTH INSURANCE PREMIUMS.
SO... ANYTHING ELSE TO SAY?
...
NO? GOOD. I DIDN'T THINK SO.

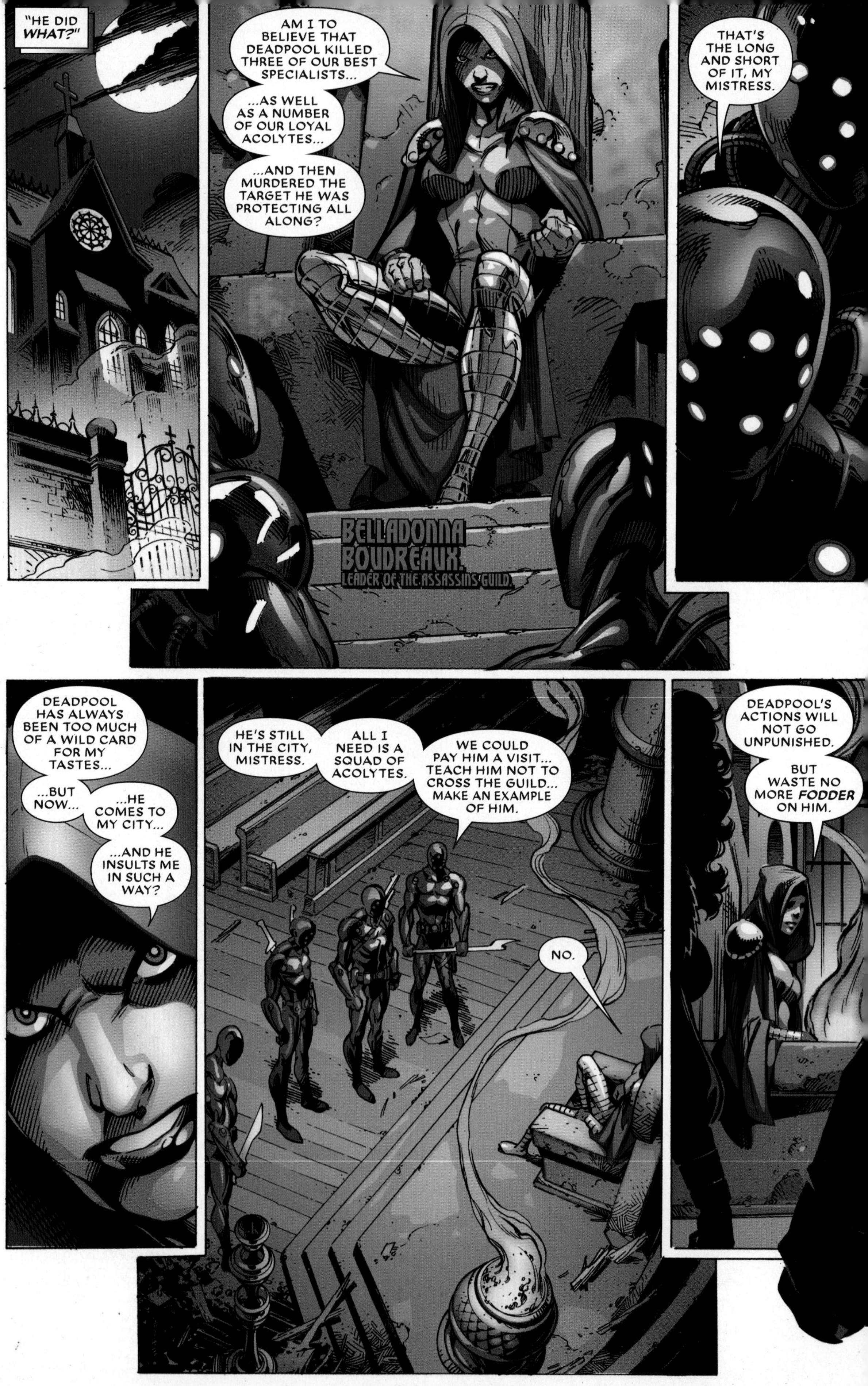
"HE DID WHAT?"
AM I TO BELIEVE THAT DEADPOOL KILLED THREE OF OUR BEST SPECIALISTS...
...AS WELL AS A NUMBER OF OUR LOYAL ACOLYTES...
...AND THEN MURDERED THE TARGET HE WAS PROTECTING ALL ALONG?
BELLADONNA BOUDREAUX. LEADER OF THE ASSASSINS GUILD.
THAT'S THE LONG AND SHORT OF IT, MY MISTRESS.
DEADPOOL HAS ALWAYS BEEN TOO MUCH OF A WILD CARD FOR MY TASTES...
...BUT NOW...
...HE COMES TO MY CITY...
...AND HE INSULTS ME IN SUCH A WAY?
HE'S STILL IN THE CITY, MISTRESS.
ALL I NEED IS A SQUAD OF ACOLYTES.
WE COULD PAY HIM A VISIT... TEACH HIM NOT TO CROSS THE GUILD... MAKE AN EXAMPLE OF HIM.
NO.
DEADPOOL'S ACTIONS WILL NOT GO UNPUNISHED.
BUT WASTE NO MORE FODDER ON HIM.

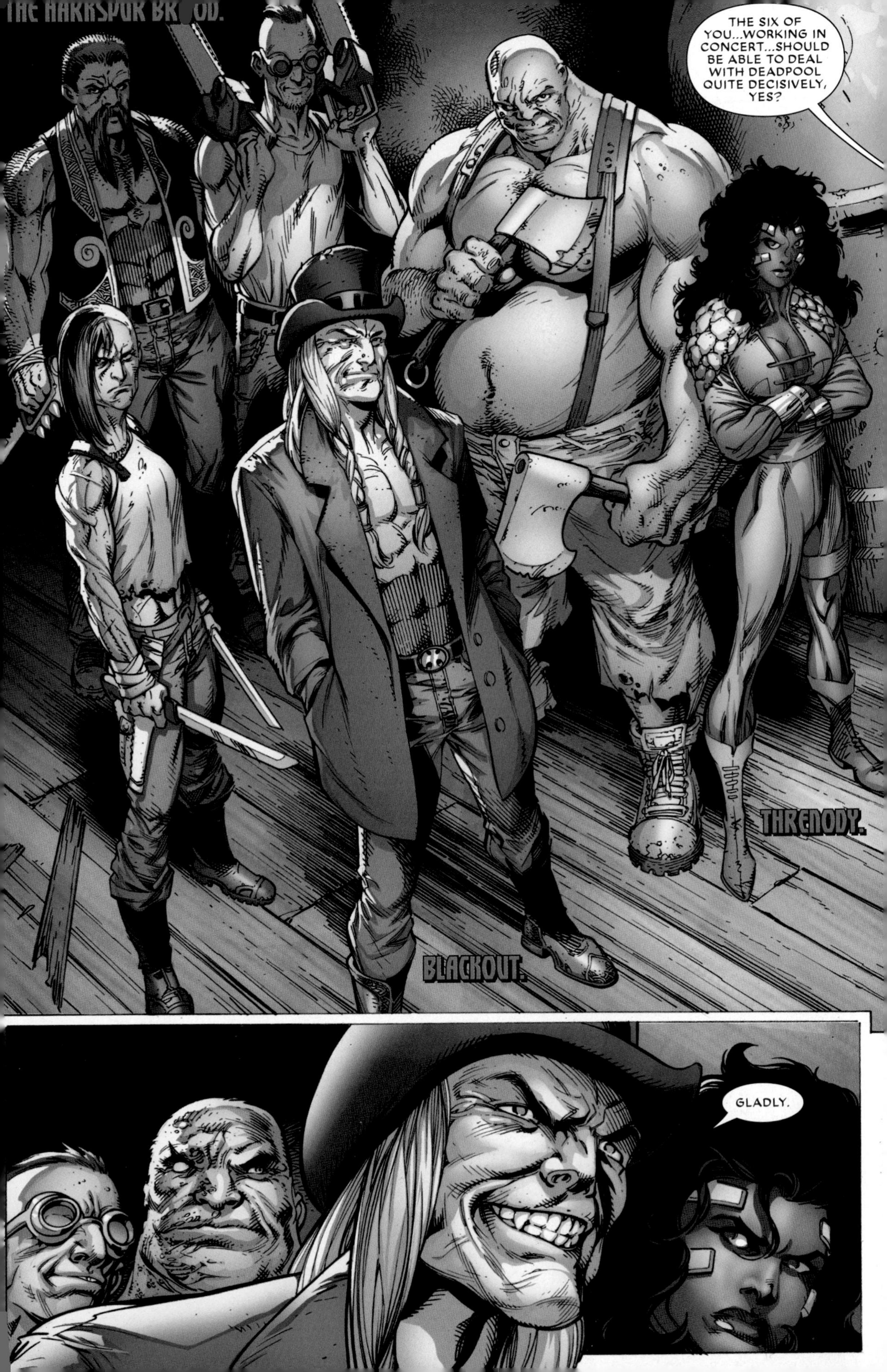
THE HARKSPUR BR OD.
THE SIX OF YOU...WORKING IN CONCERT...SHOULD BE ABLE TO DEAL WITH DEADPOOL QUITE DECISIVELY, YES?
THRENODY.
BLACKOUT.
GLADLY.

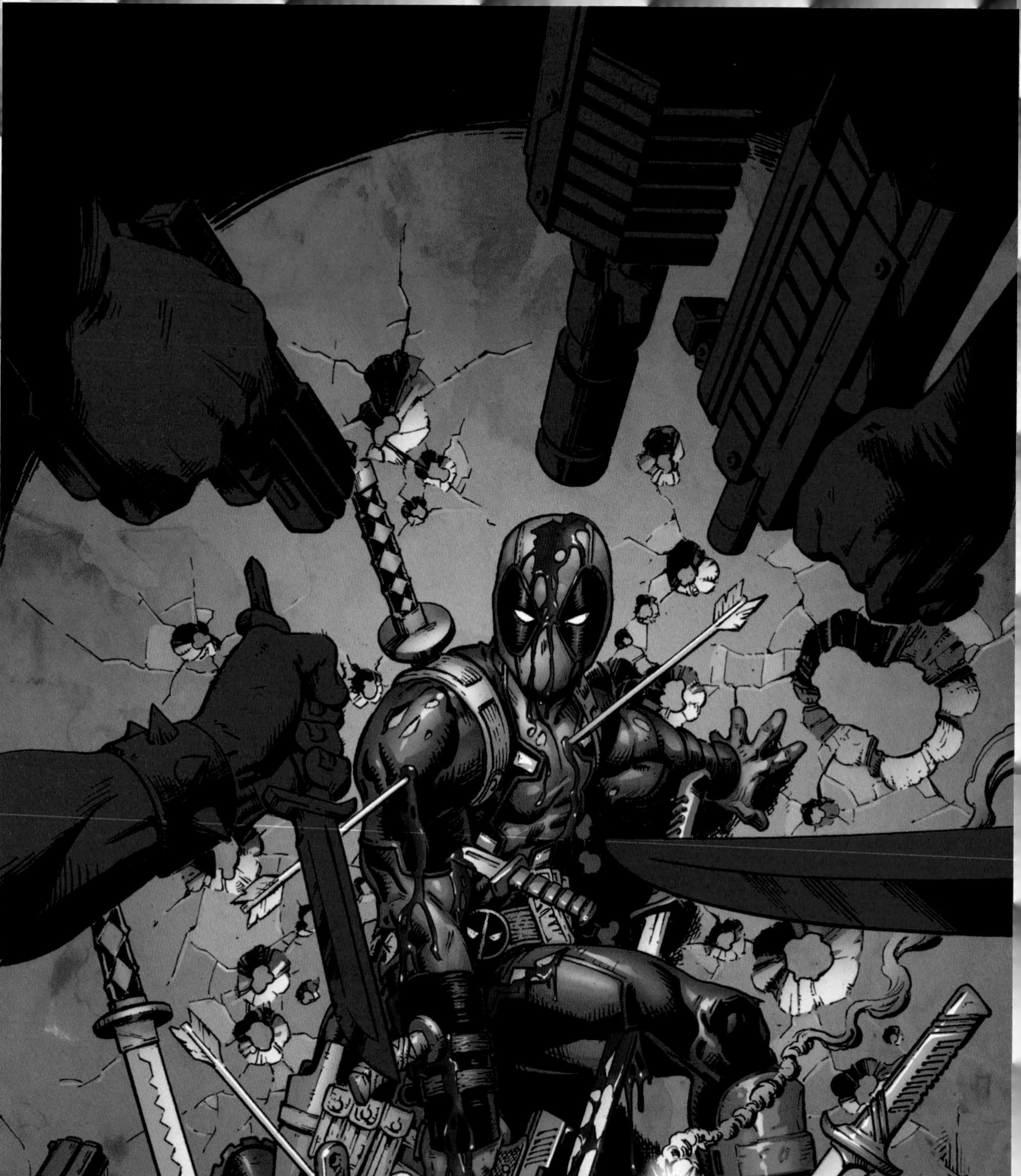

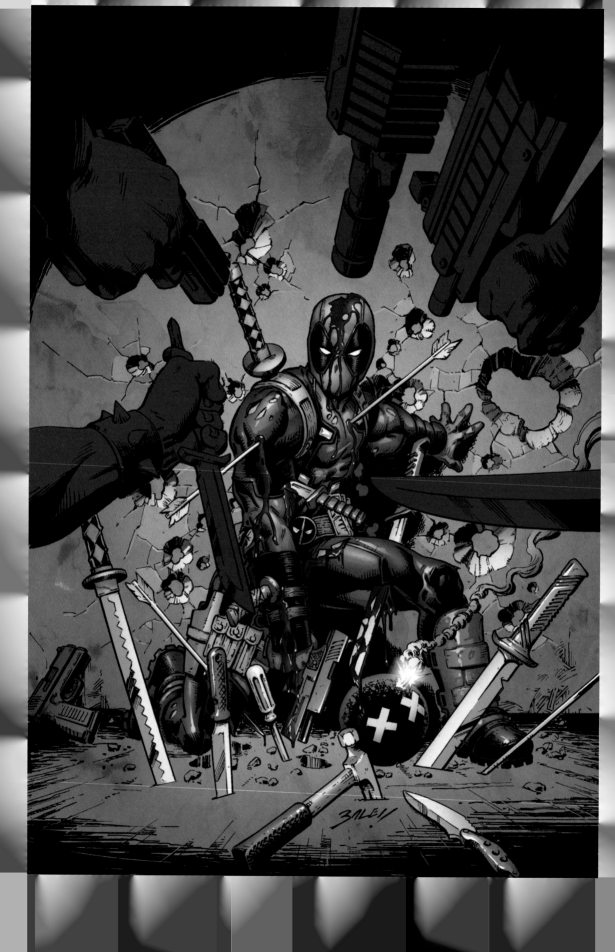

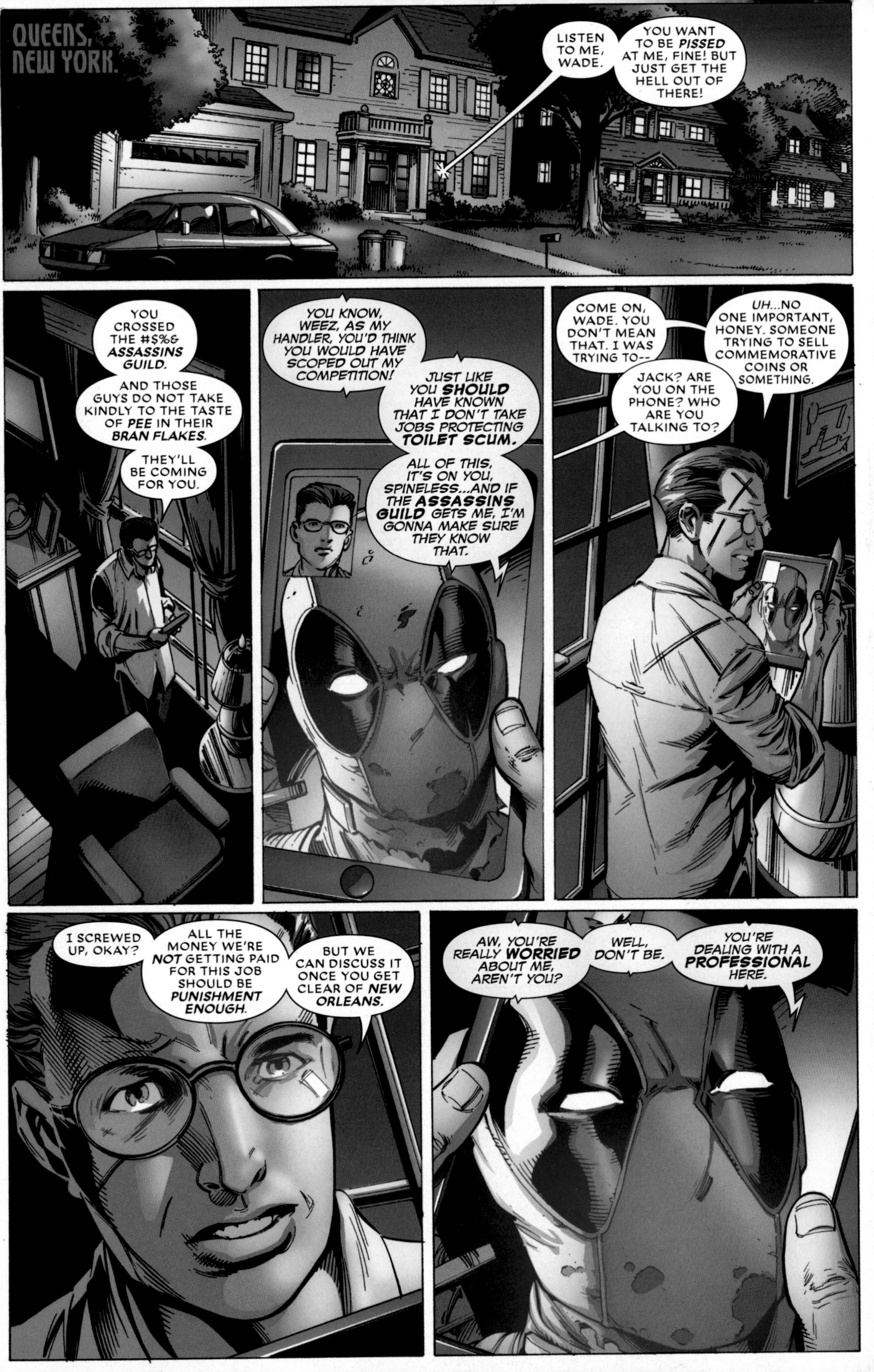
QUEENS, NEW YORK.
LISTEN TO ME, WADE.
YOU WANT TO BE PISSED AT ME, FINE! BUT JUST GET THE HELL OUT OF THERE!
YOU CROSSED THE #$%& ASSASSINS GUILD.
AND THOSE GUYS DO NOT TAKE KINDLY TO THE TASTE OF PEE IN THEIR BRAN FLAKES.
THEY'LL BE COMING FOR YOU.
YOU KNOW, WEEZ, AS MY HANDLER, YOU'D THINK YOU WOULD HAVE SCOPED OUT MY COMPETITION!
JUST LIKE YOU SHOULD HAVE KNOWN THAT I DON'T TAKE JOBS PROTECTING TOILET SCUM.
ALL OF THIS, IT'S ON YOU, SPINELESS...AND IF THE ASSASSINS GUILD GETS ME, I'M GONNA MAKE SURE THEY KNOW THAT.
COME ON, WADE. YOU DON'T MEAN THAT. I WAS TRYING TO--
JACK? ARE YOU ON THE PHONE? WHO ARE YOU TALKING TO?
UH...NO ONE IMPORTANT, HONEY. SOMEONE TRYING TO SELL COMMEMORATIVE COINS OR SOMETHING.
I SCREWED UP, OKAY?
ALL THE MONEY WE'RE NOT GETTING PAID FOR THIS JOB SHOULD BE PUNISHMENT ENOUGH.
BUT WE CAN DISCUSS IT ONCE YOU GET CLEAR OF NEW ORLEANS.
AW, YOU'RE REALLY WORRIED ABOUT ME, AREN'T YOU?
WELL, DON'T BE.
YOU'RE DEALING WITH A PROFESSIONAL HERE.

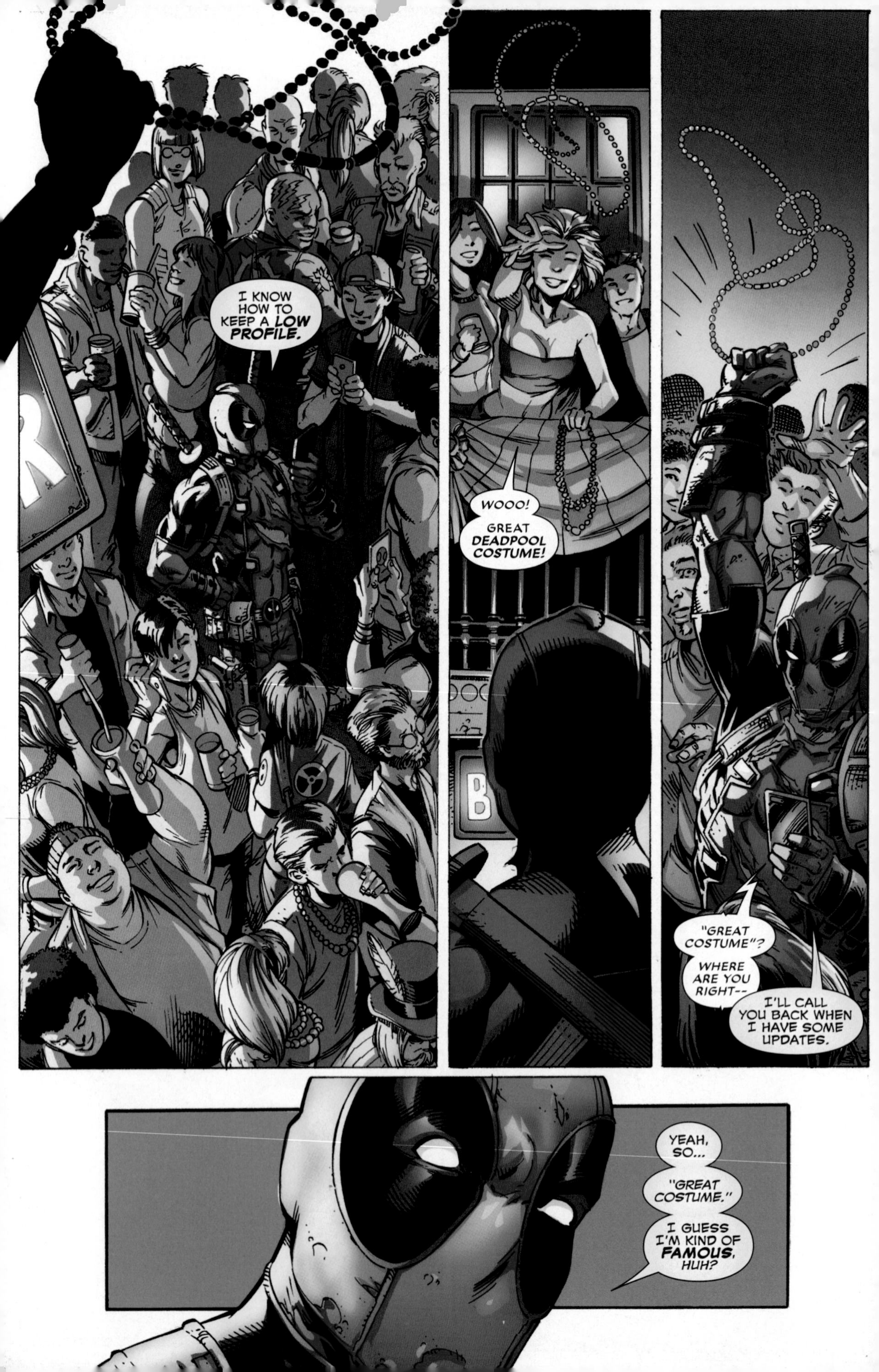

I KNOW HOW TO KEEP A LOW PROFILE.
WOOO! GREAT DEADPOOL COSTUME!
"GREAT COSTUME"?
WHERE ARE YOU RIGHT--
I'LL CALL YOU BACK WHEN I HAVE SOME UPDATES.
YEAH, SO...
"GREAT COSTUME."
I GUESS I'M KIND OF FAMOUS, HUH?

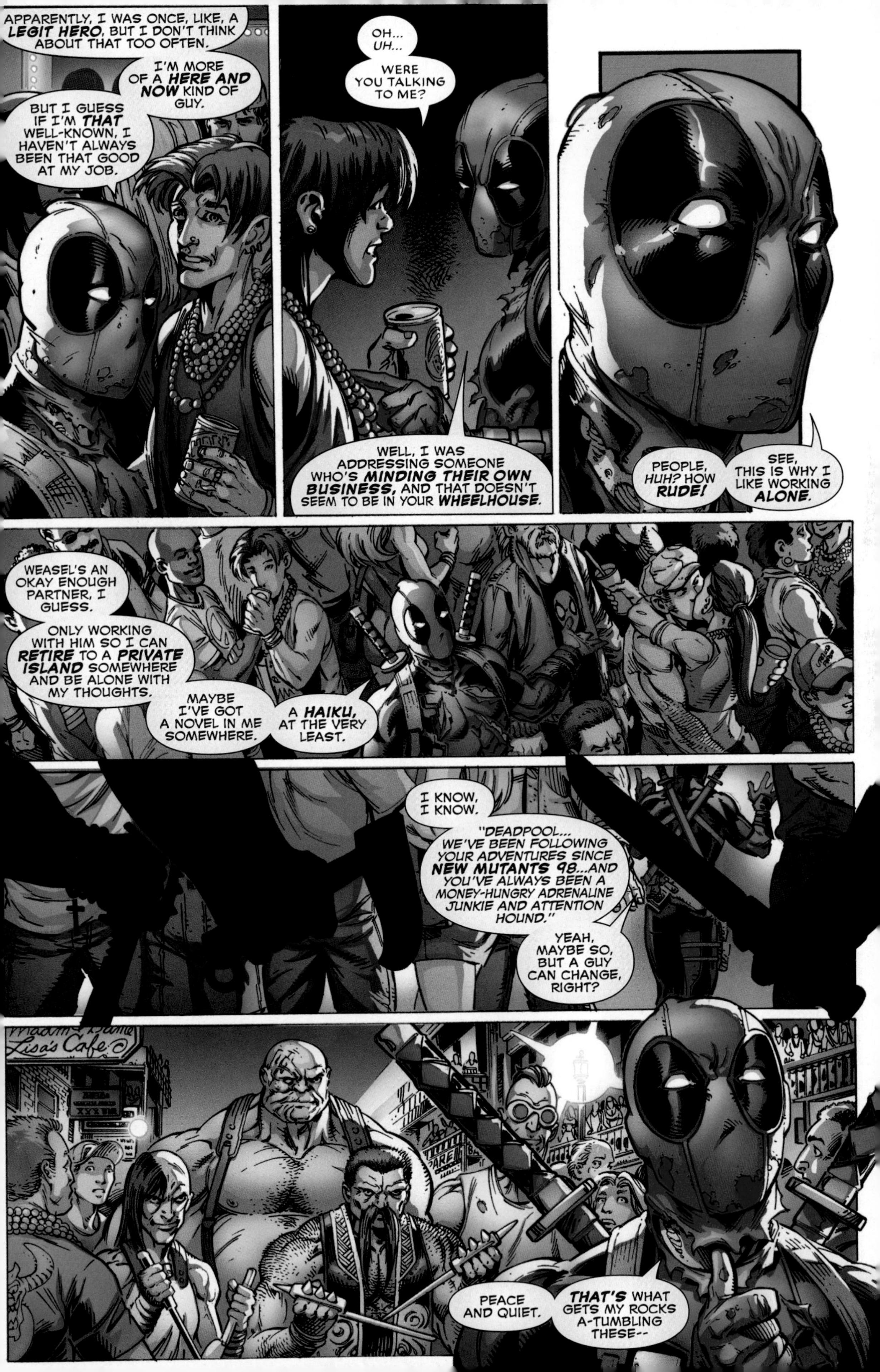

APPARENTLY, I WAS ONCE, LIKE, A LEGIT HERO, BUT I DON'T THINK ABOUT THAT TOO OFTEN.
I'M MORE OF A HERE AND NOW KIND OF GUY.
BUT I GUESS IF I'M THAT WELL-KNOWN, I HAVEN'T ALWAYS BEEN THAT GOOD AT MY JOB.
OH... UH...
WERE YOU TALKING TO ME?
WELL, I WAS ADDRESSING SOMEONE WHO'S MINDING THEIR OWN BUSINESS, AND THAT DOESN'T SEEM TO BE IN YOUR WHEELHOUSE.
PEOPLE, HUH? HOW RUDE!
SEE, THIS IS WHY I LIKE WORKING ALONE.
WEASEL'S AN OKAY ENOUGH PARTNER, I GUESS.
ONLY WORKING WITH HIM SO I CAN RETIRE TO A PRIVATE ISLAND SOMEWHERE AND BE ALONE WITH MY THOUGHTS.
MAYBE I'VE GOT A NOVEL IN ME SOMEWHERE.
A HAIKU, AT THE VERY LEAST.
I KNOW, I KNOW.
"DEADPOOL... WE'VE BEEN FOLLOWING YOUR ADVENTURES SINCE NEW MUTANTS 98...AND YOU'VE ALWAYS BEEN A MONEY-HUNGRY ADRENALINE JUNKIE AND ATTENTION HOUND."
YEAH, MAYBE SO, BUT A GUY CAN CHANGE, RIGHT?
Lisa's Cafe
PEACE AND QUIET.
THAT'S WHAT GETS MY ROCKS A-TUMBLING THESE--

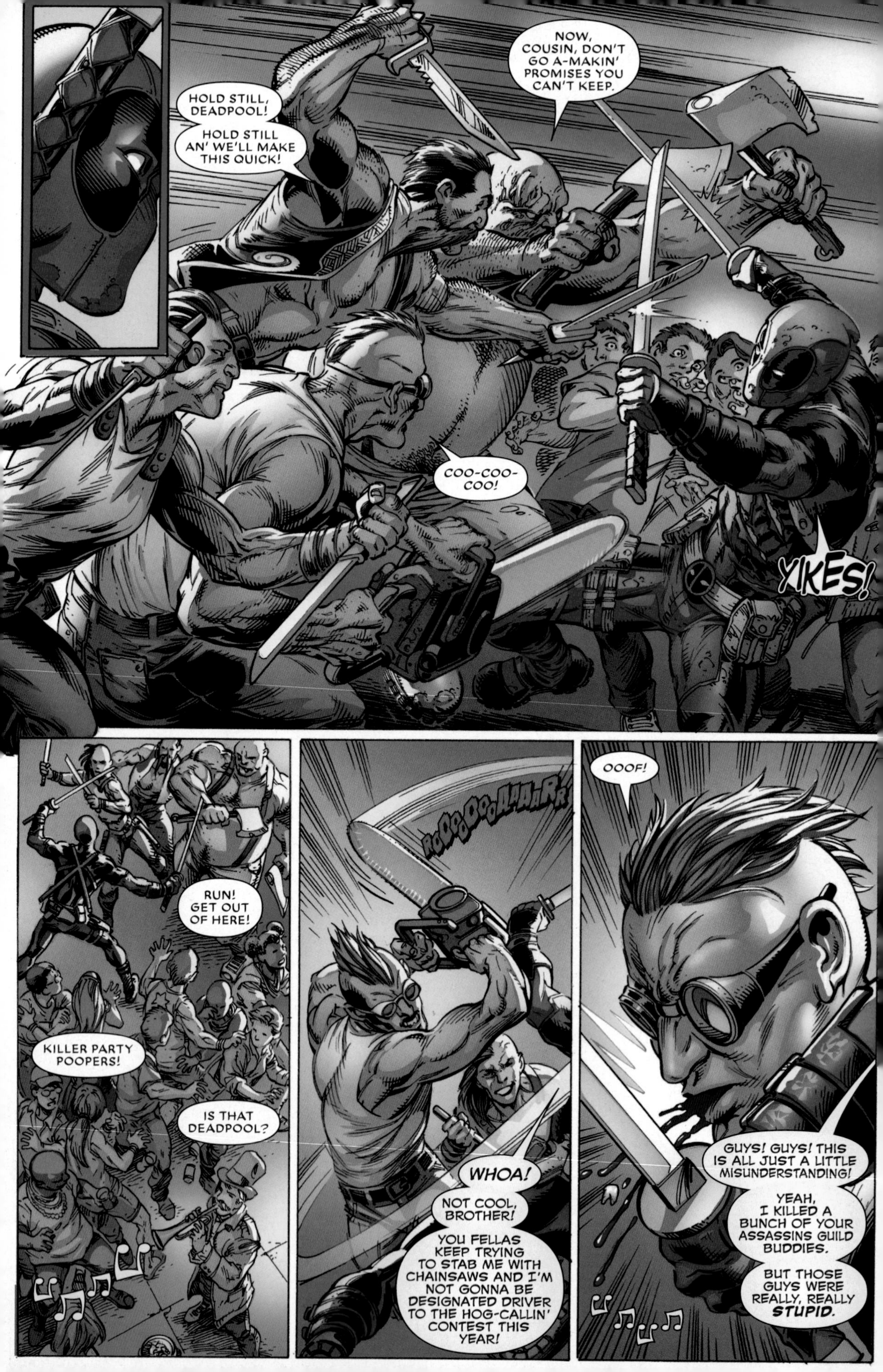
HOLD STILL, DEADPOOL!
HOLD STILL AN' WE'LL MAKE THIS QUICK!
NOW, COUSIN, DON'T GO A-MAKIN' PROMISES YOU CAN'T KEEP.
COO-COO-COO!
YIKES!
RUN! GET OUT OF HERE!
KILLER PARTY POOPERS!
IS THAT DEADPOOL?
RoOoOoOoAAARR
WHOA!
NOT COOL, BROTHER!
YOU FELLAS KEEP TRYING TO STAB ME WITH CHAINSAWS AND I'M NOT GONNA BE DESIGNATED DRIVER TO THE HOG-CALLIN' CONTEST THIS YEAR!
OOOF!
GUYS! GUYS! THIS IS ALL JUST A LITTLE MISUNDERSTANDING!
YEAH, I KILLED A BUNCH OF YOUR ASSASSINS GUILD BUDDIES.
BUT THOSE GUYS WERE REALLY, REALLY STUPID.

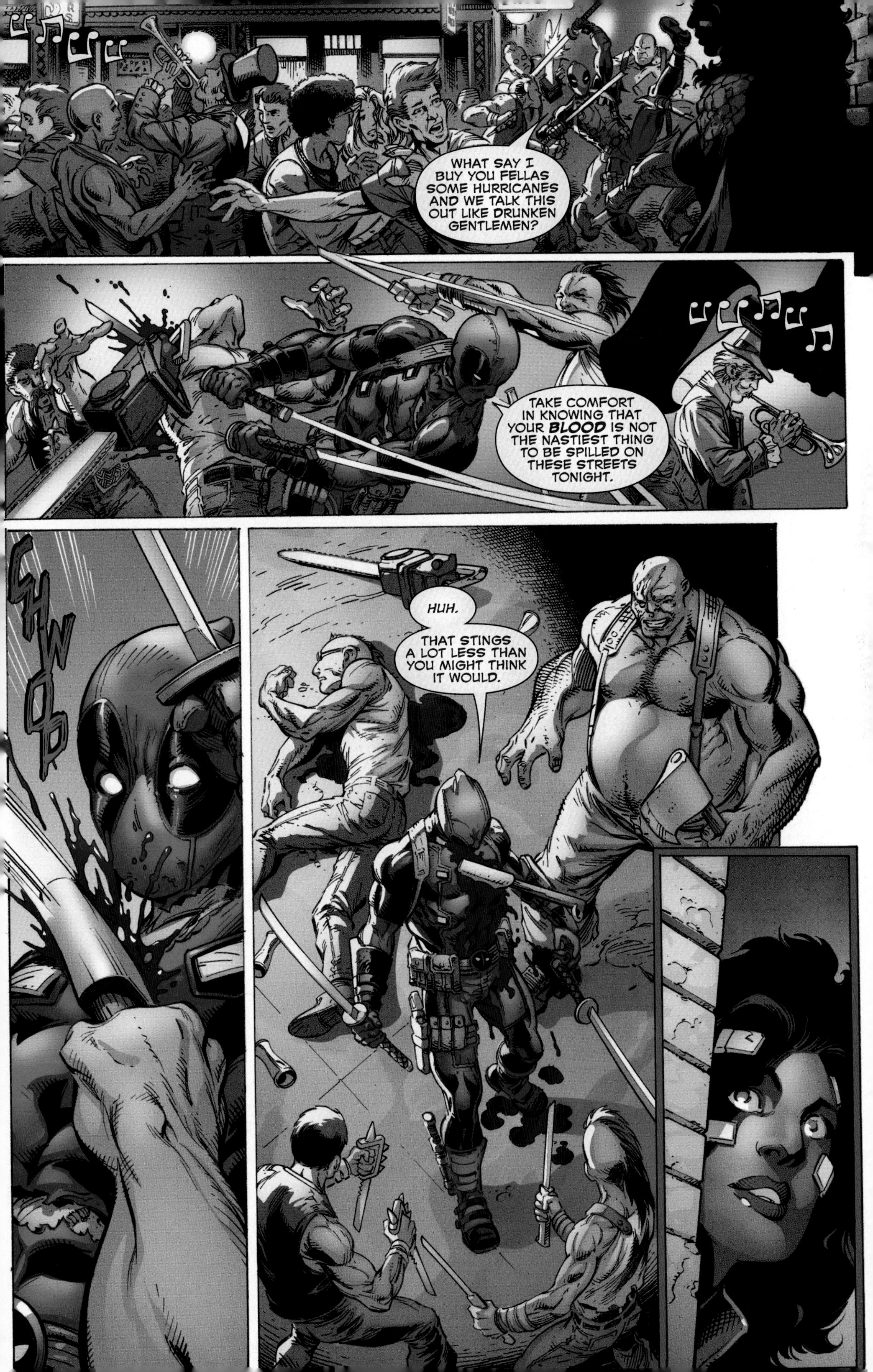
WHAT SAY I BUY YOU FELLAS SOME HURRICANES AND WE TALK THIS OUT LIKE DRUNKEN GENTLEMEN?
TAKE COMFORT IN KNOWING THAT YOUR **BLOOD** IS NOT THE NASTIEST THING TO BE SPILLED ON THESE STREETS TONIGHT.
CHWOD
HUH.
THAT STINGS A LOT LESS THAN YOU MIGHT THINK IT WOULD.

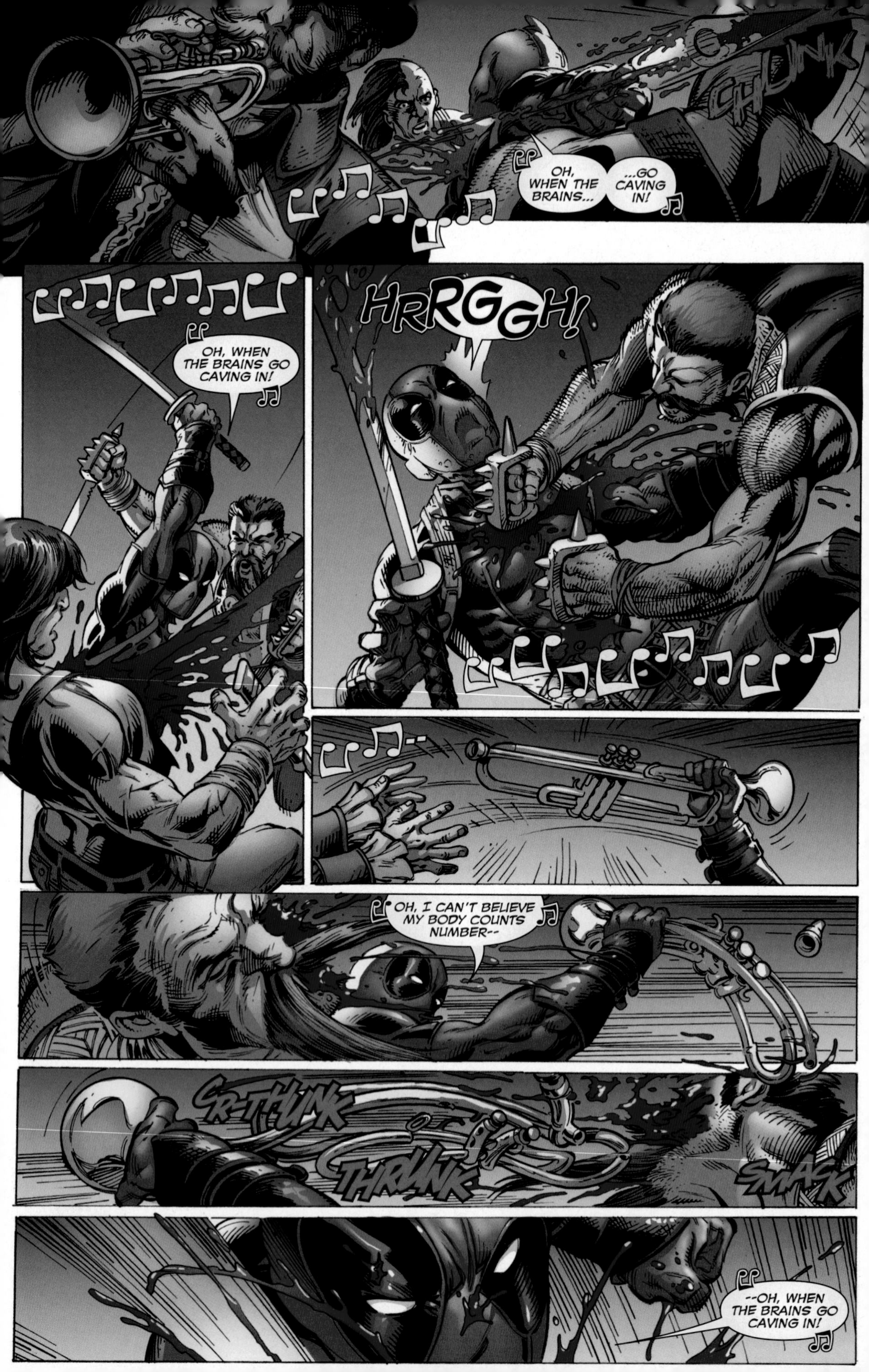
CHUNK
OH, WHEN THE BRAINS...
...GO CAVING IN!
OH, WHEN THE BRAINS GO CAVING IN!
HRRGGH!
OH, I CAN'T BELIEVE MY BODY COUNTS NUMBER--
CR-THUNK
THRUNK
SMACK
--OH, WHEN THE BRAINS GO CAVING IN!

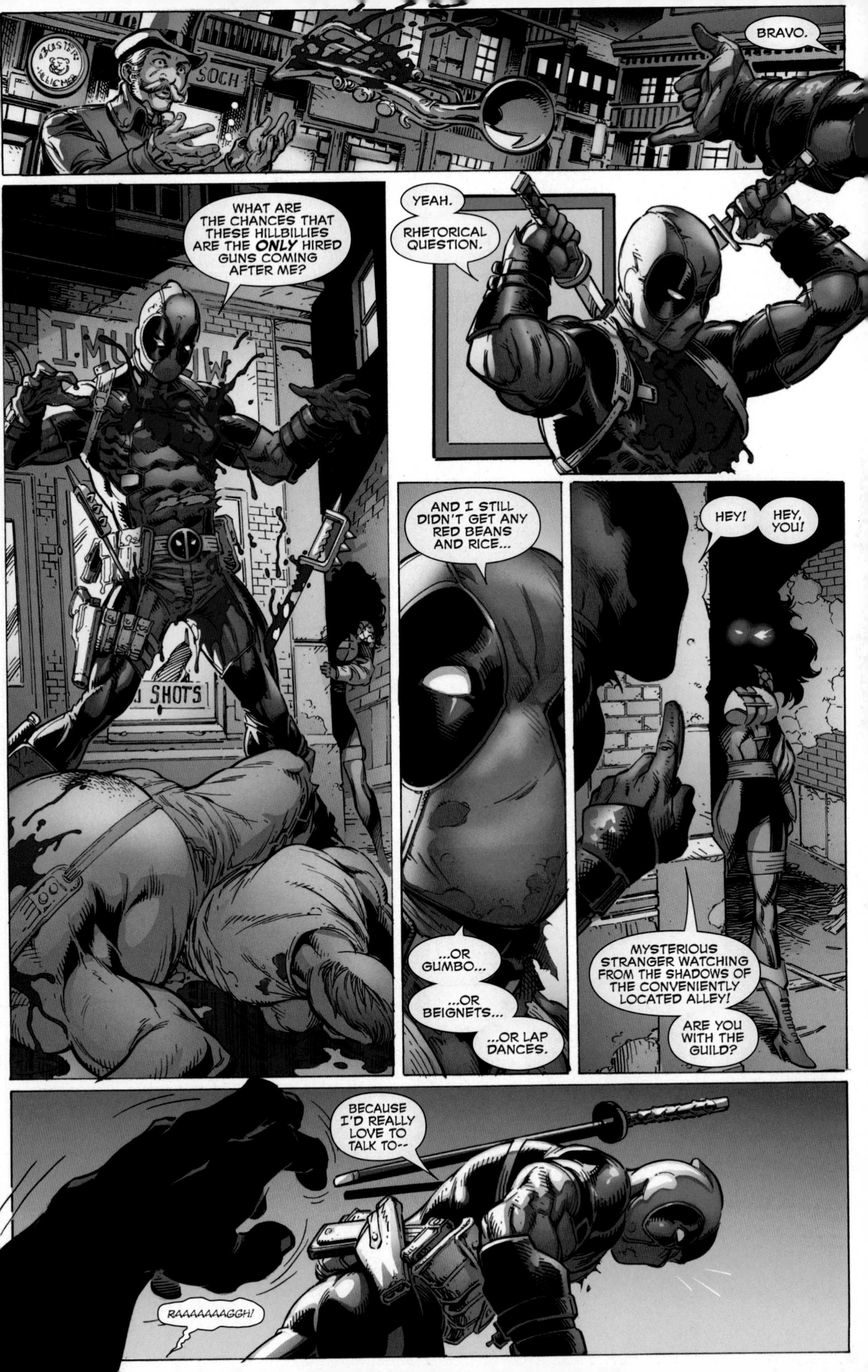

BRAVO.
WHAT ARE THE CHANCES THAT THESE HILLBILLIES ARE THE ONLY HIRED GUNS COMING AFTER ME?
YEAH.
RHETORICAL QUESTION.
AND I STILL DIDN'T GET ANY RED BEANS AND RICE...
...OR GUMBO...
...OR BEIGNETS...
...OR LAP DANCES.
HEY!
HEY, YOU!
MYSTERIOUS STRANGER WATCHING FROM THE SHADOWS OF THE CONVENIENTLY LOCATED ALLEY!
ARE YOU WITH THE GUILD?
BECAUSE I'D REALLY LOVE TO TALK TO--
RAAAAAAAAGGH!

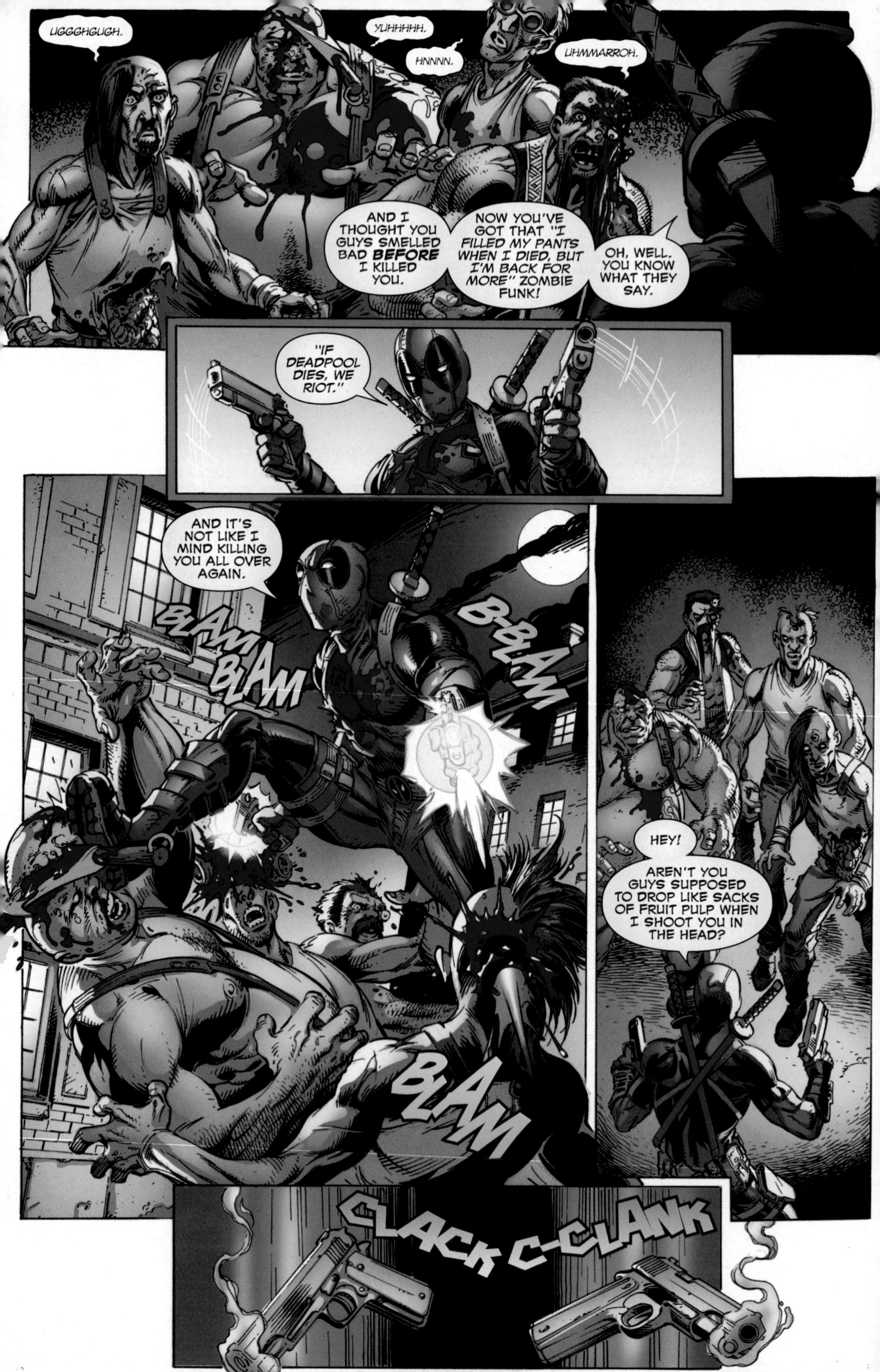
UGGGHGUGH.
YUHHHHH.
HNNNN.
UHMMARROH.
AND I THOUGHT YOU GUYS SMELLED BAD BEFORE I KILLED YOU.
NOW YOU'VE GOT THAT "I FILLED MY PANTS WHEN I DIED, BUT I'M BACK FOR MORE" ZOMBIE FUNK!
OH, WELL. YOU KNOW WHAT THEY SAY.
"IF DEADPOOL DIES, WE RIOT."
AND IT'S NOT LIKE I MIND KILLING YOU ALL OVER AGAIN.
BLAM BLAM BLAM
B-BLAM
BLAM
HEY!
AREN'T YOU GUYS SUPPOSED TO DROP LIKE SACKS OF FRUIT PULP WHEN I SHOOT YOU IN THE HEAD?
CLACK C-CLANK

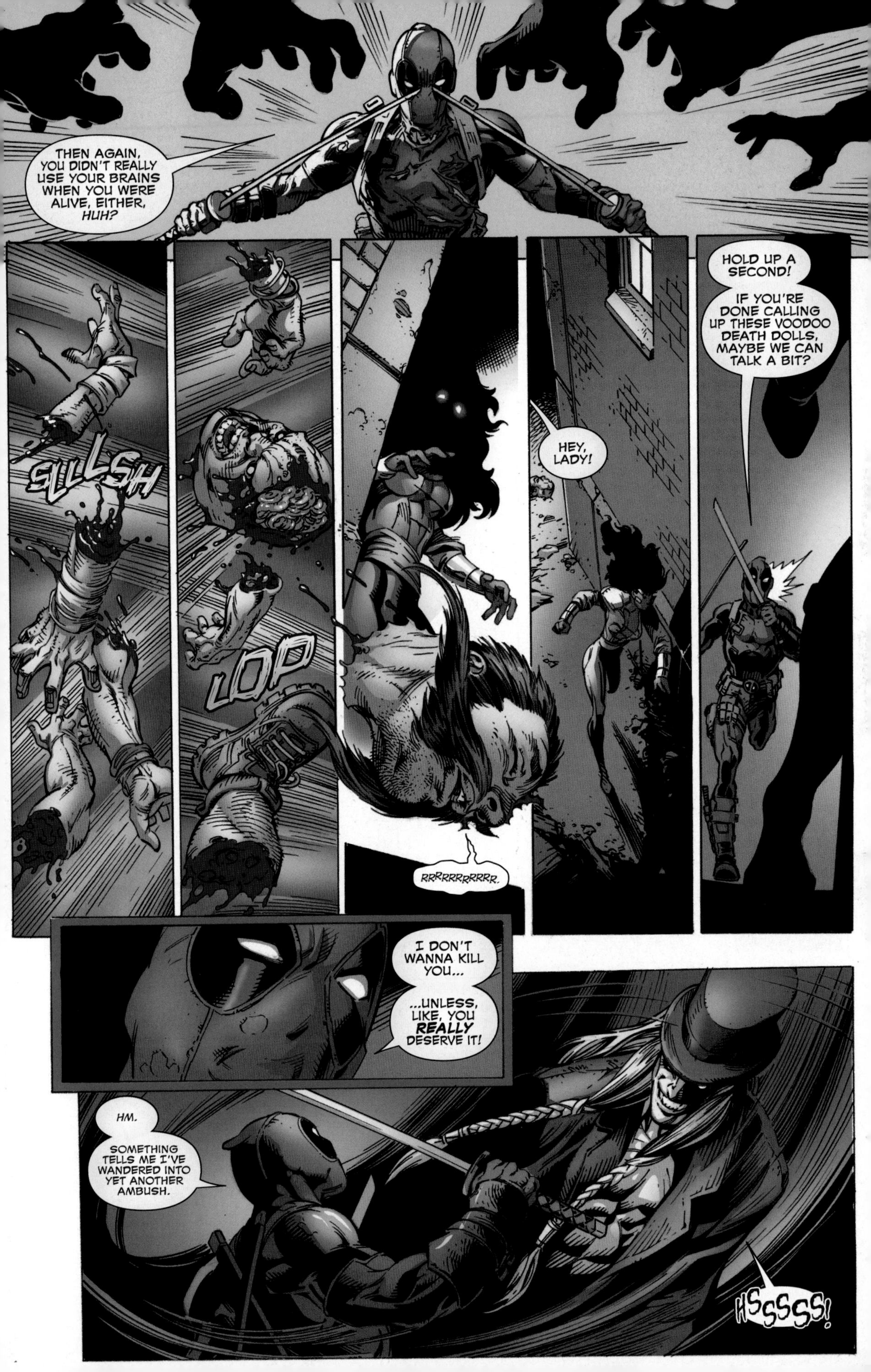
THEN AGAIN, YOU DIDN'T REALLY USE YOUR BRAINS WHEN YOU WERE ALIVE, EITHER, HUH?
SHLLSH
LOP
RRRRRRRRRRR.
HEY, LADY!
HOLD UP A SECOND!
IF YOU'RE DONE CALLING UP THESE VOODOO DEATH DOLLS, MAYBE WE CAN TALK A BIT?
I DON'T WANNA KILL YOU...
...UNLESS, LIKE, YOU REALLY DESERVE IT!
HM.
SOMETHING TELLS ME I'VE WANDERED INTO YET ANOTHER AMBUSH.
HSSSSS!

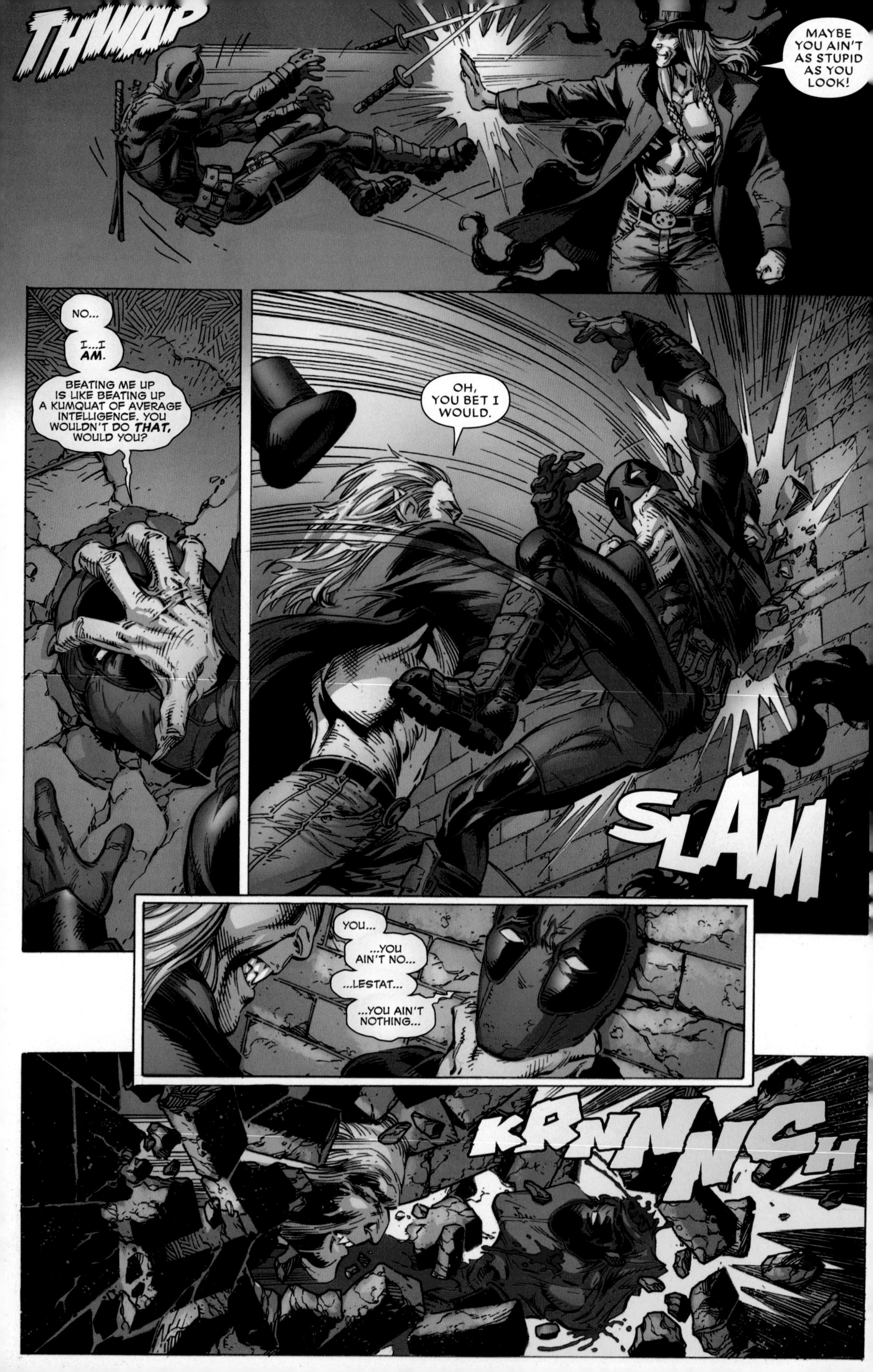
THWAP
MAYBE YOU AIN'T AS STUPID AS YOU LOOK!
NO...
I...I AM.
BEATING ME UP IS LIKE BEATING UP A KUMQUAT OF AVERAGE INTELLIGENCE. YOU WOULDN'T DO THAT, WOULD YOU?
OH, YOU BET I WOULD.
SLAM
YOU...
...YOU AIN'T NO...
...LESTAT...
...YOU AIN'T NOTHING...
KRNNNCH

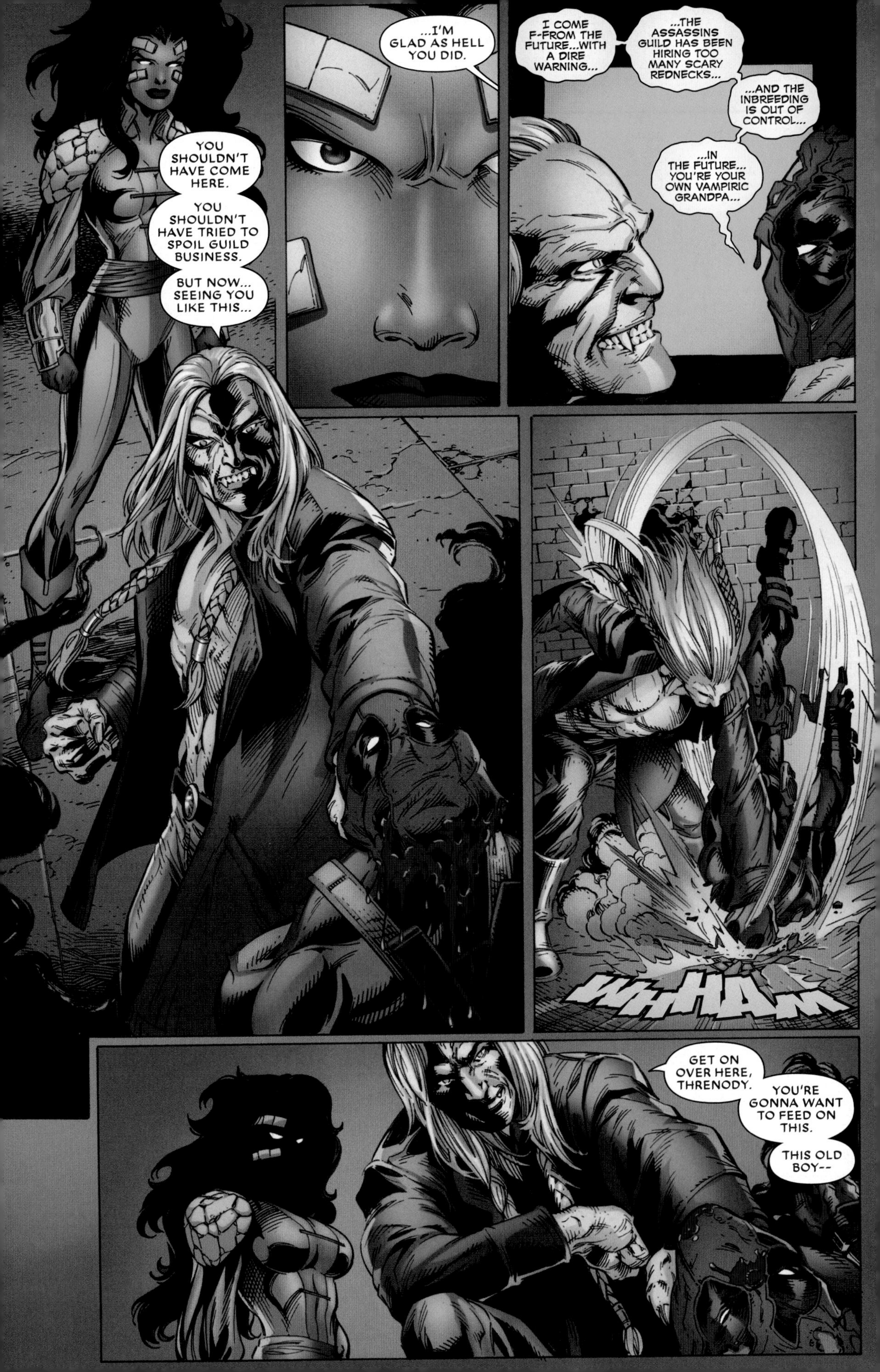
YOU SHOULDN'T HAVE COME HERE.
YOU SHOULDN'T HAVE TRIED TO SPOIL GUILD BUSINESS.
BUT NOW... SEEING YOU LIKE THIS...
...I'M GLAD AS HELL YOU DID.
I COME F-FROM THE FUTURE...WITH A DIRE WARNING...
...THE ASSASSINS GUILD HAS BEEN HIRING TOO MANY SCARY REDNECKS...
...AND THE INBREEDING IS OUT OF CONTROL...
...IN THE FUTURE... YOU'RE YOUR OWN VAMPIRIC GRANDPA...
WHHAM
GET ON OVER HERE, THRENODY.
YOU'RE GONNA WANT TO FEED ON THIS.
THIS OLD BOY--

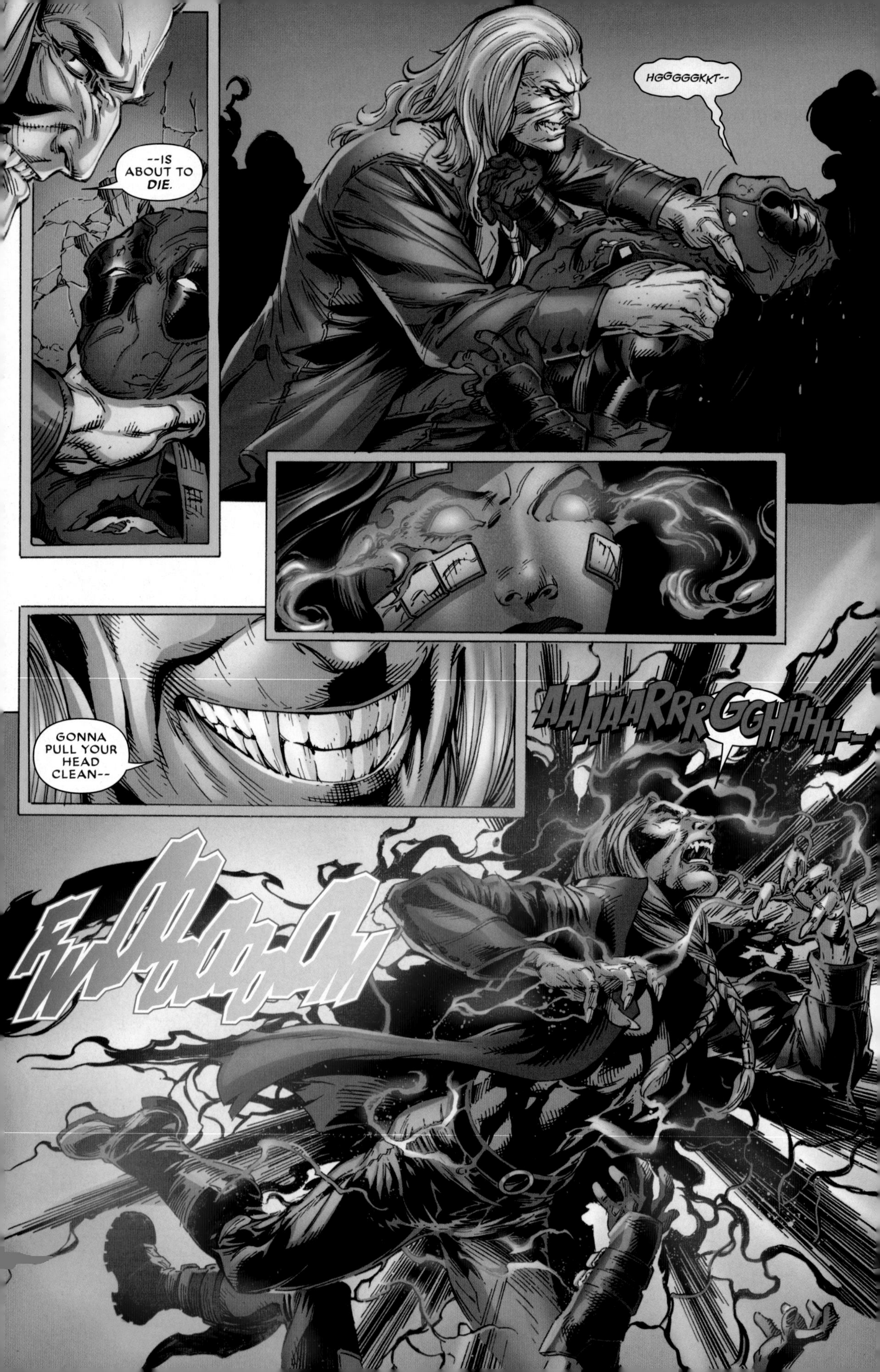
--IS ABOUT TO DIE.
HGGGGGKKT--
GONNA PULL YOUR HEAD CLEAN--
AAAAARRRGGHHHH--
FWOOOOM

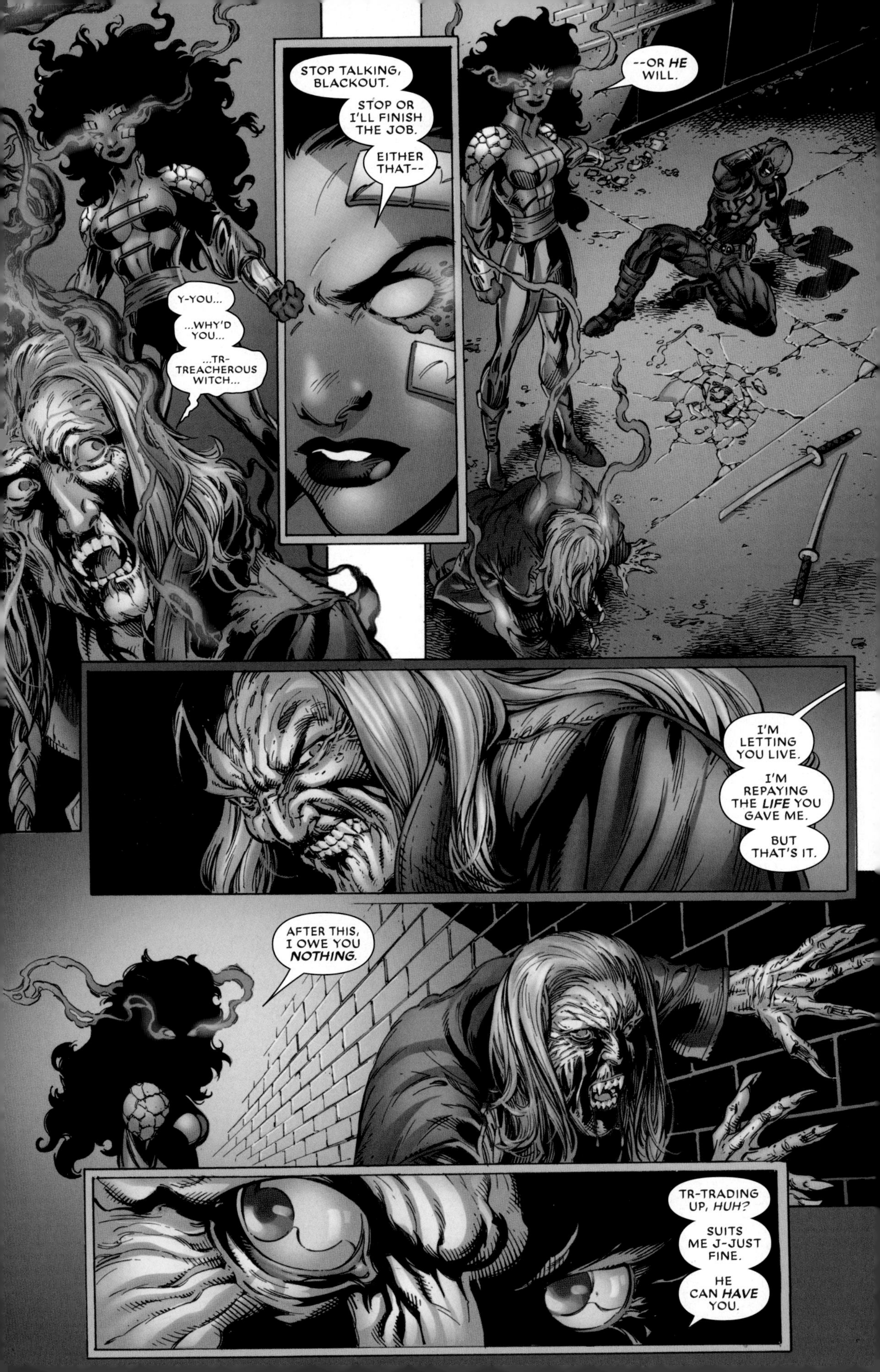
STOP TALKING, BLACKOUT.
STOP OR I'LL FINISH THE JOB.
EITHER THAT--
--OR HE WILL.
Y-YOU...
...WHY'D YOU...
...TR-TREACHEROUS WITCH...
I'M LETTING YOU LIVE.
I'M REPAYING THE LIFE YOU GAVE ME.
BUT THAT'S IT.
AFTER THIS, I OWE YOU NOTHING.
TR-TRADING UP, HUH?
SUITS ME J-JUST FINE.
HE CAN HAVE YOU.

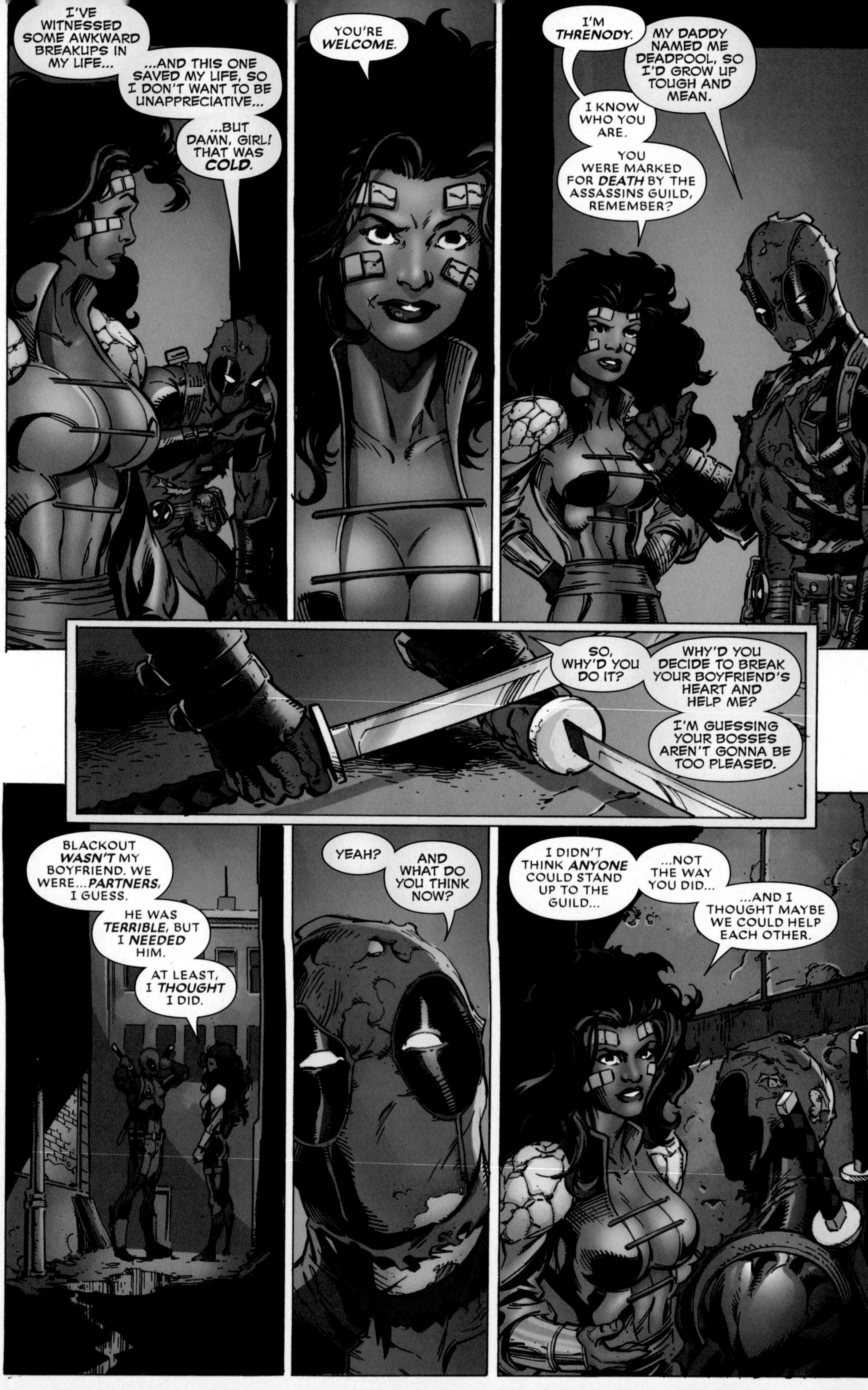
I'VE WITNESSED SOME AWKWARD BREAKUPS IN MY LIFE...
...AND THIS ONE SAVED MY LIFE, SO I DON'T WANT TO BE UNAPPRECIATIVE...
...BUT DAMN, GIRL! THAT WAS *COLD*.
YOU'RE *WELCOME*.
I'M *THRENODY*.
MY DADDY NAMED ME DEADPOOL, SO I'D GROW UP TOUGH AND MEAN.
I KNOW WHO YOU ARE.
YOU WERE MARKED FOR *DEATH* BY THE ASSASSINS GUILD, REMEMBER?
SO, WHY'D YOU DO IT?
WHY'D YOU DECIDE TO BREAK YOUR BOYFRIEND'S HEART AND HELP ME?
I'M GUESSING YOUR BOSSES AREN'T GONNA BE TOO PLEASED.
BLACKOUT *WASN'T* MY BOYFRIEND. WE WERE...*PARTNERS*, I GUESS.
HE WAS *TERRIBLE*, BUT I *NEEDED* HIM.
AT LEAST, I *THOUGHT* I DID.
YEAH?
AND WHAT DO YOU THINK NOW?
I DIDN'T THINK *ANYONE* COULD STAND UP TO THE GUILD...
...NOT THE WAY YOU DID...
...AND I THOUGHT MAYBE WE COULD HELP EACH OTHER.

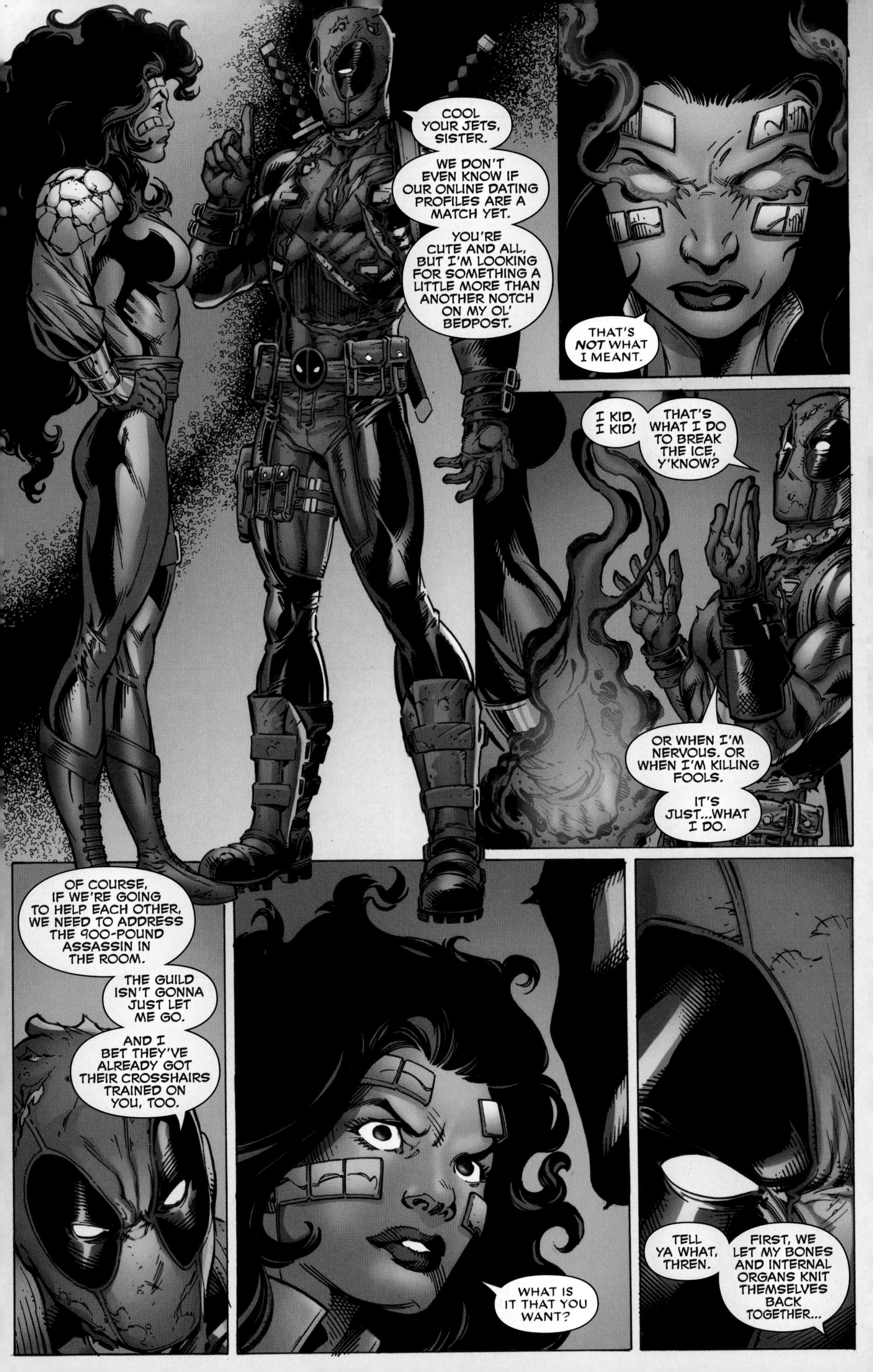

COOL YOUR JETS, SISTER.
WE DON'T EVEN KNOW IF OUR ONLINE DATING PROFILES ARE A MATCH YET.
YOU'RE CUTE AND ALL, BUT I'M LOOKING FOR SOMETHING A LITTLE MORE THAN ANOTHER NOTCH ON MY OL' BEDPOST.
THAT'S *NOT* WHAT I MEANT.
I KID, I KID!
THAT'S WHAT I DO TO BREAK THE ICE, Y'KNOW?
OR WHEN I'M NERVOUS. OR WHEN I'M KILLING FOOLS.
IT'S JUST...WHAT I DO.
OF COURSE, IF WE'RE GOING TO HELP EACH OTHER, WE NEED TO ADDRESS THE 900-POUND ASSASSIN IN THE ROOM.
THE GUILD ISN'T GONNA JUST LET ME GO.
AND I BET THEY'VE ALREADY GOT THEIR CROSSHAIRS TRAINED ON YOU, TOO.
WHAT IS IT THAT YOU WANT?
TELL YA WHAT, THREN.
FIRST, WE LET MY BONES AND INTERNAL ORGANS KNIT THEMSELVES BACK TOGETHER...

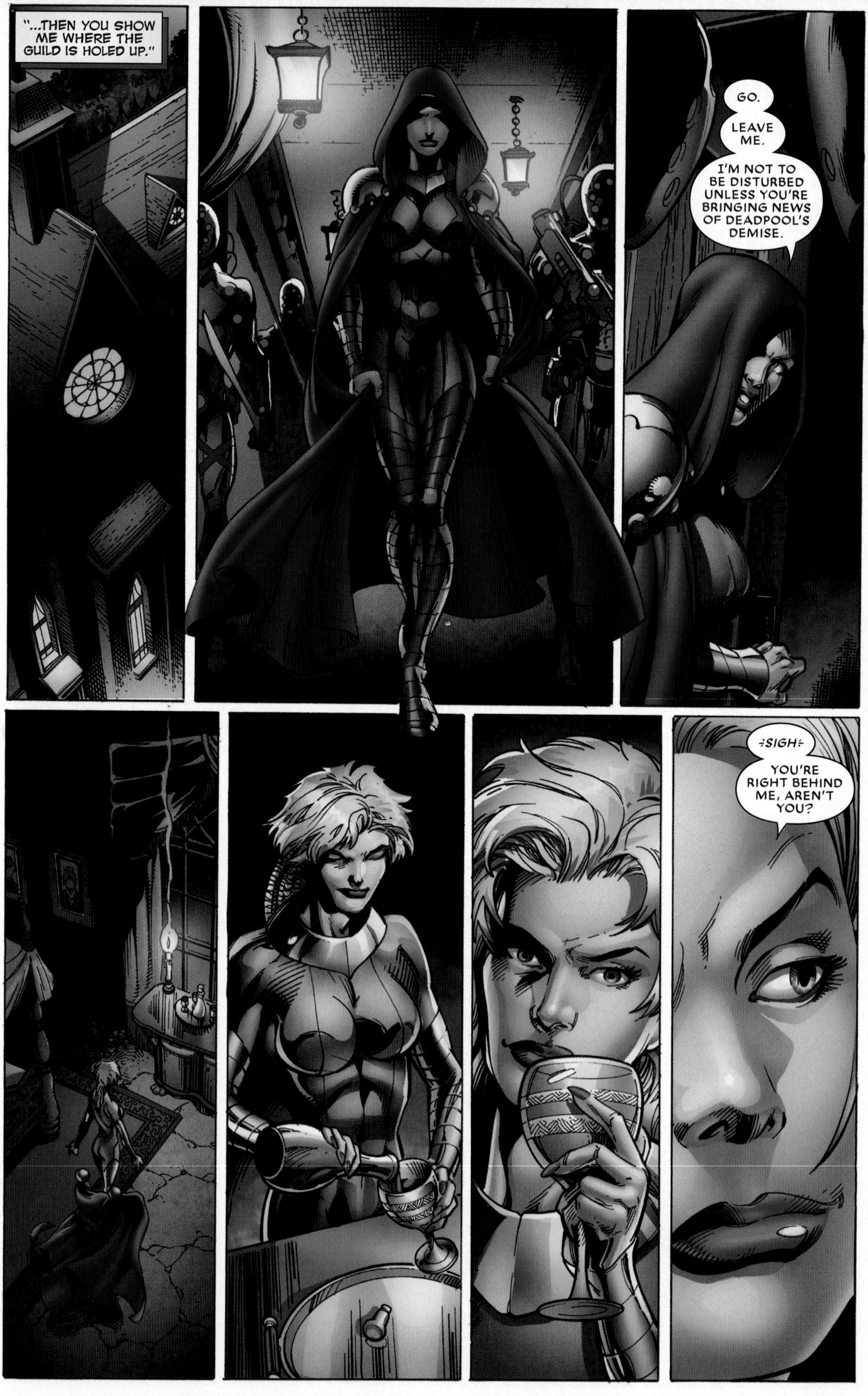
"...THEN YOU SHOW ME WHERE THE GUILD IS HOLED UP."
GO.
LEAVE ME.
I'M NOT TO BE DISTURBED UNLESS YOU'RE BRINGING NEWS OF DEADPOOL'S DEMISE.
=SIGH=
YOU'RE RIGHT BEHIND ME, AREN'T YOU?

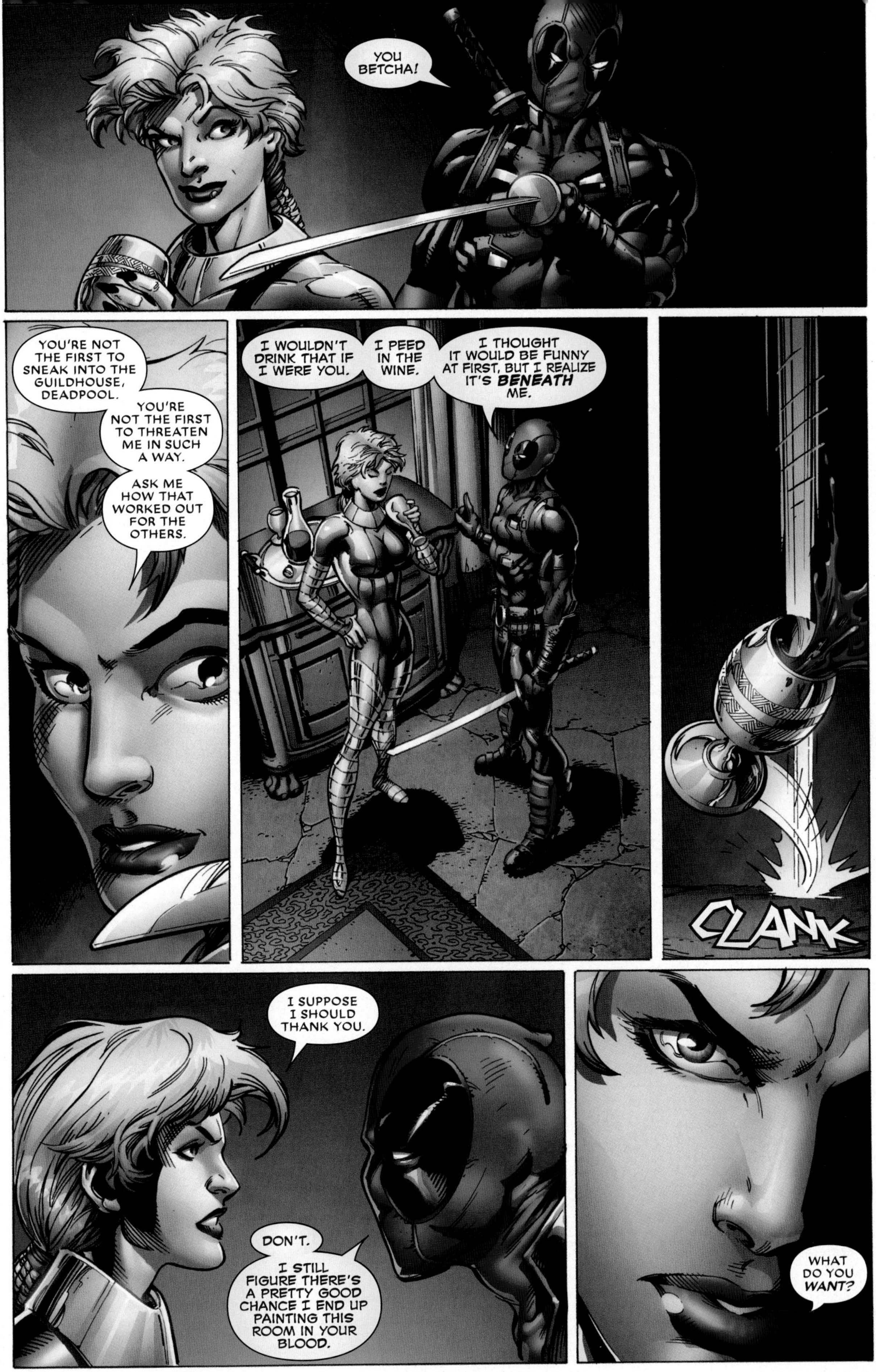
YOU BETCHA!
YOU'RE NOT THE FIRST TO SNEAK INTO THE GUILDHOUSE, DEADPOOL.
YOU'RE NOT THE FIRST TO THREATEN ME IN SUCH A WAY.
ASK ME HOW THAT WORKED OUT FOR THE OTHERS.
I WOULDN'T DRINK THAT IF I WERE YOU.
I PEED IN THE WINE.
I THOUGHT IT WOULD BE FUNNY AT FIRST, BUT I REALIZE IT'S BENEATH ME.
CLANK
I SUPPOSE I SHOULD THANK YOU.
DON'T.
I STILL FIGURE THERE'S A PRETTY GOOD CHANCE I END UP PAINTING THIS ROOM IN YOUR BLOOD.
WHAT DO YOU WANT?

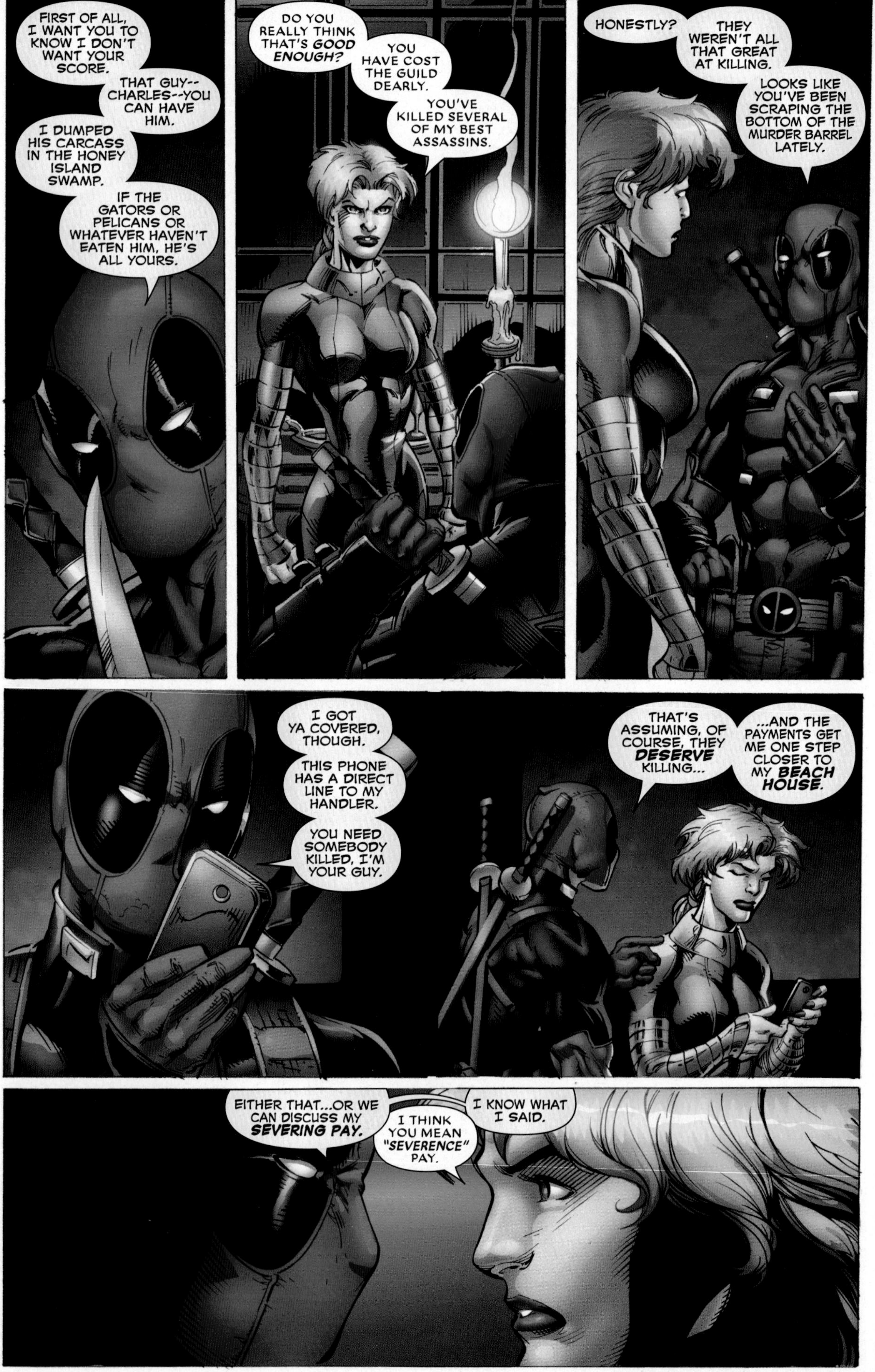
FIRST OF ALL, I WANT YOU TO KNOW I DON'T WANT YOUR SCORE.
THAT GUY-- CHARLES--YOU CAN HAVE HIM.
I DUMPED HIS CARCASS IN THE HONEY ISLAND SWAMP.
IF THE GATORS OR PELICANS OR WHATEVER HAVEN'T EATEN HIM, HE'S ALL YOURS.
DO YOU REALLY THINK THAT'S *GOOD ENOUGH?*
YOU HAVE COST THE GUILD DEARLY.
YOU'VE KILLED SEVERAL OF MY BEST ASSASSINS.
HONESTLY?
THEY WEREN'T ALL THAT GREAT AT KILLING.
LOOKS LIKE YOU'VE BEEN SCRAPING THE BOTTOM OF THE MURDER BARREL LATELY.
I GOT YA COVERED, THOUGH.
THIS PHONE HAS A DIRECT LINE TO MY HANDLER.
YOU NEED SOMEBODY KILLED, I'M YOUR GUY.
THAT'S ASSUMING, OF COURSE, THEY *DESERVE* KILLING...
...AND THE PAYMENTS GET ME ONE STEP CLOSER TO MY *BEACH HOUSE.*
EITHER THAT...OR WE CAN DISCUSS MY *SEVERING PAY.*
I THINK YOU MEAN *"SEVERENCE"* PAY.
I KNOW WHAT I SAID.

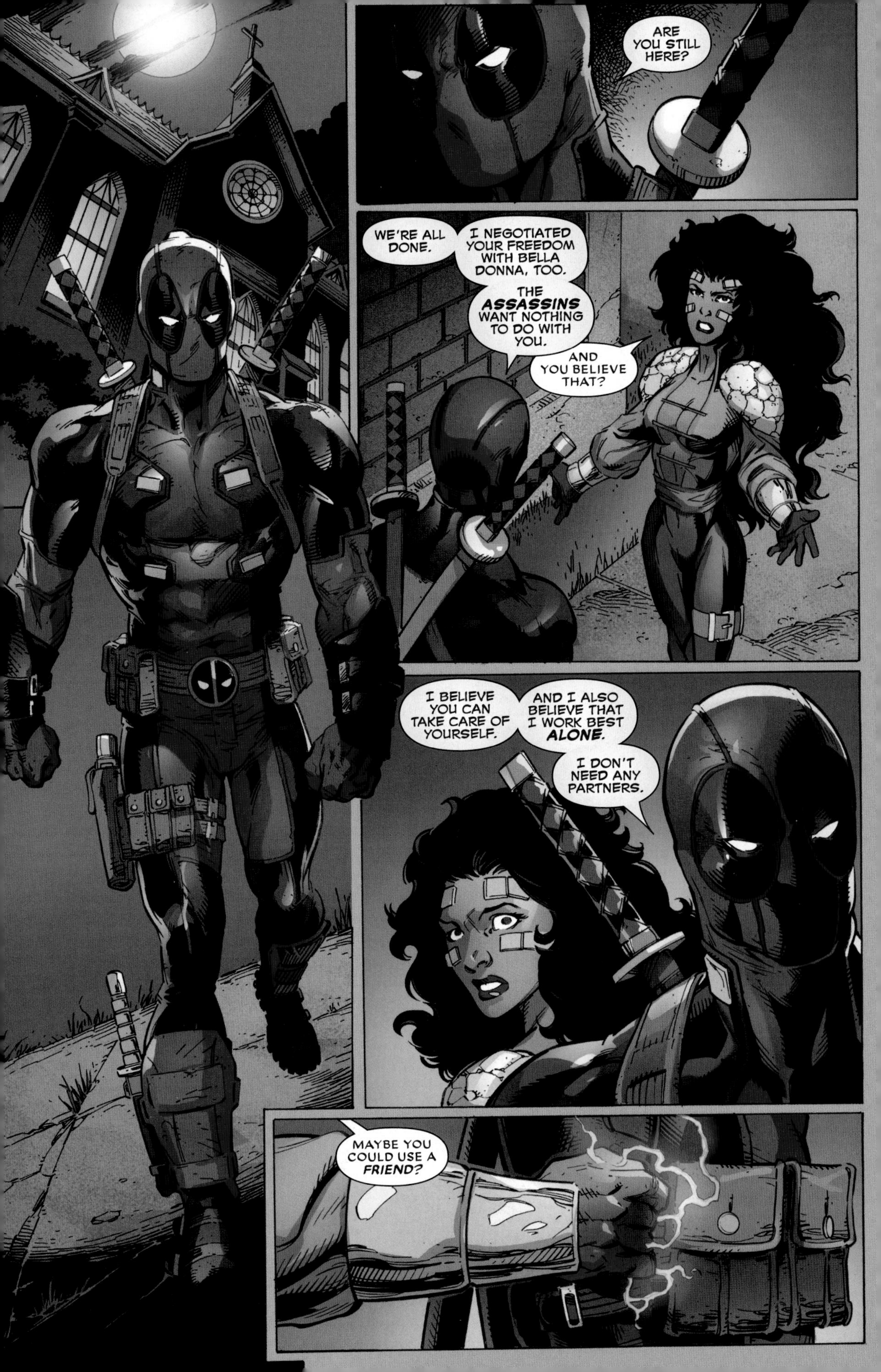
ARE YOU STILL HERE?
WE'RE ALL DONE.
I NEGOTIATED YOUR FREEDOM WITH BELLA DONNA, TOO.
THE ASSASSINS WANT NOTHING TO DO WITH YOU.
AND YOU BELIEVE THAT?
I BELIEVE YOU CAN TAKE CARE OF YOURSELF.
AND I ALSO BELIEVE THAT I WORK BEST ALONE.
I DON'T NEED ANY PARTNERS.
MAYBE YOU COULD USE A FRIEND?

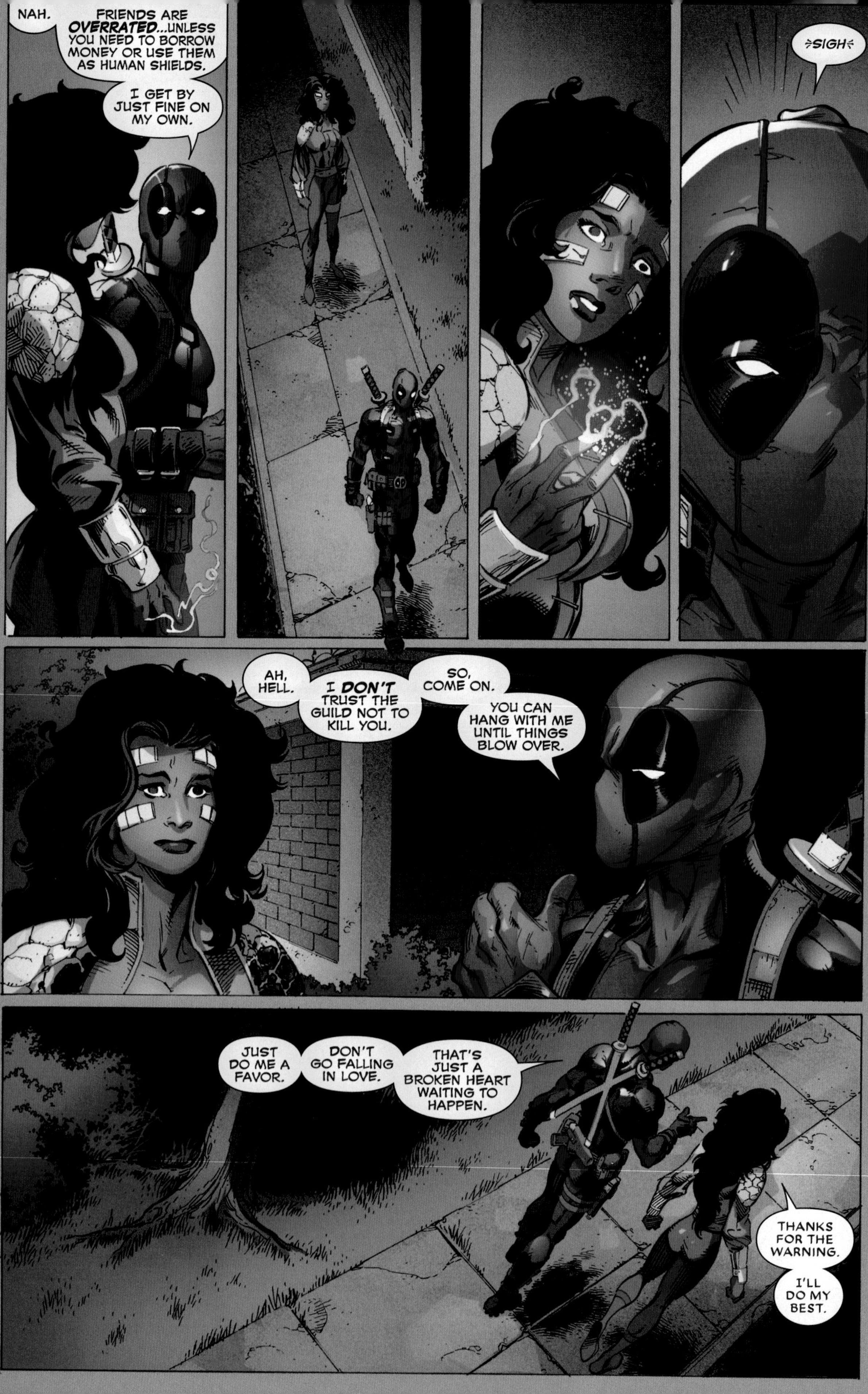

NAH.
FRIENDS ARE **OVERRATED**...UNLESS YOU NEED TO BORROW MONEY OR USE THEM AS HUMAN SHIELDS.
I GET BY JUST FINE ON MY OWN.
SIGH
AH, HELL.
I **DON'T** TRUST THE GUILD NOT TO KILL YOU.
SO, COME ON.
YOU CAN HANG WITH ME UNTIL THINGS BLOW OVER.
JUST DO ME A FAVOR.
DON'T GO FALLING IN LOVE.
THAT'S JUST A BROKEN HEART WAITING TO HAPPEN.
THANKS FOR THE WARNING.
I'LL DO MY BEST.

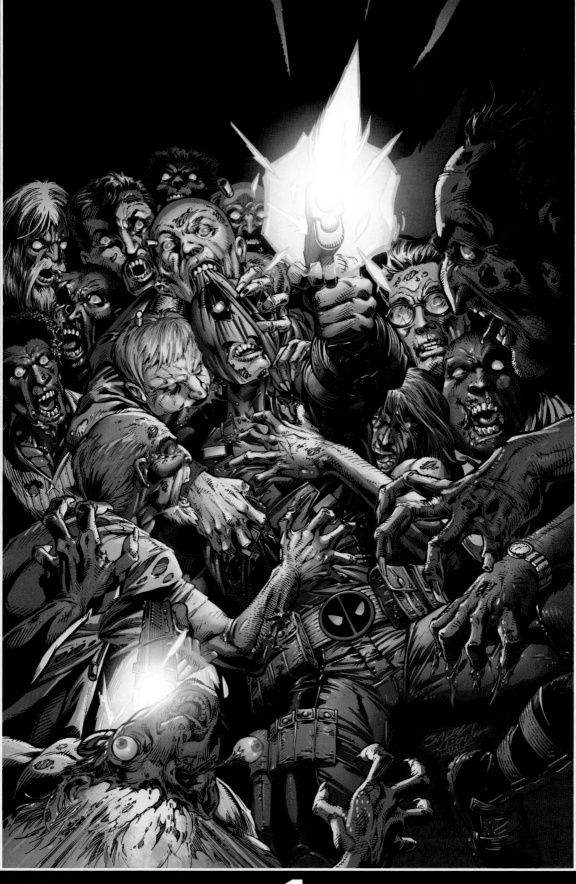

4

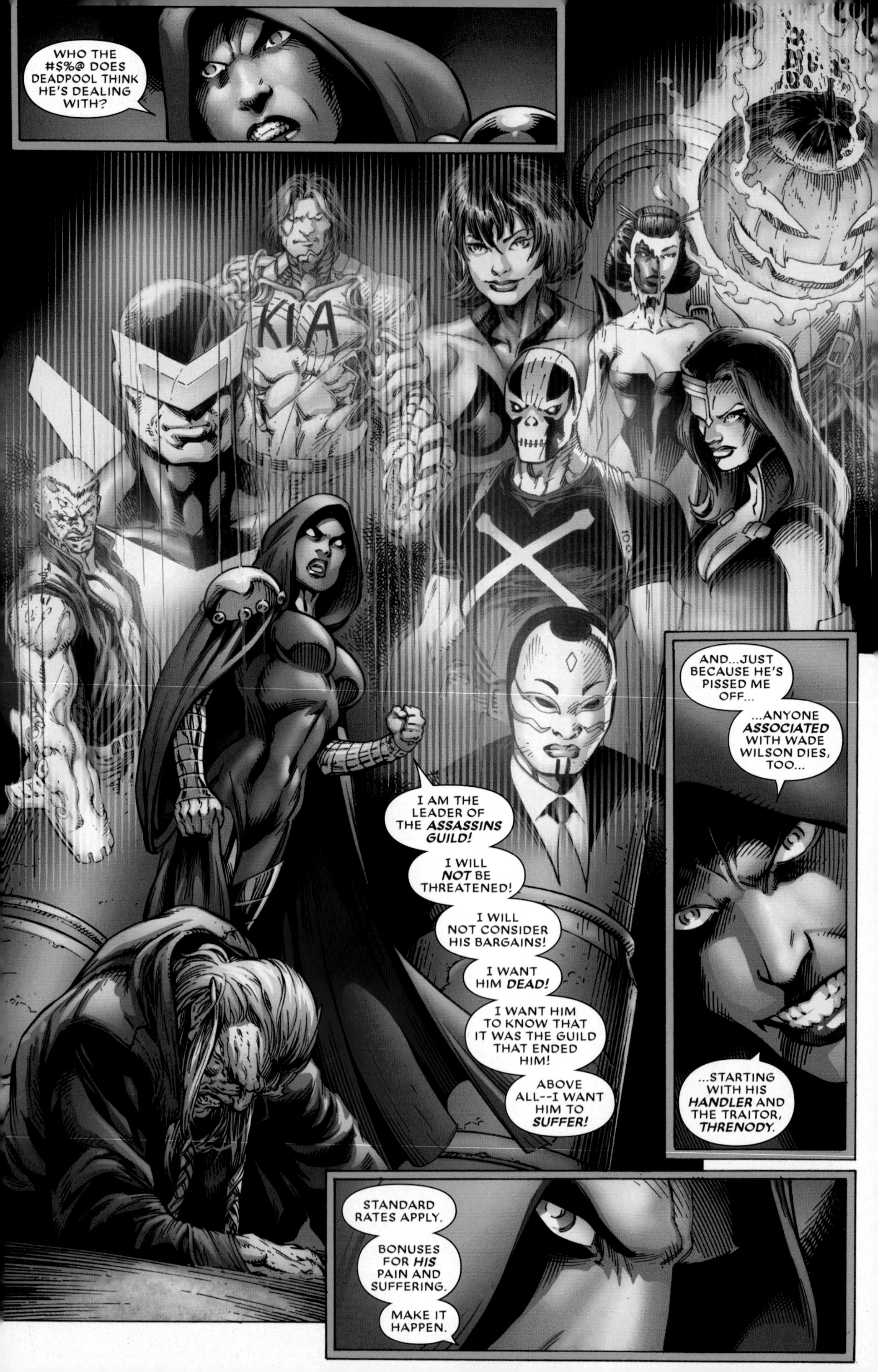

WHO THE #$%@ DOES DEADPOOL THINK HE'S DEALING WITH?
KIA
I AM THE LEADER OF THE ASSASSINS GUILD!
I WILL NOT BE THREATENED!
I WILL NOT CONSIDER HIS BARGAINS!
I WANT HIM DEAD!
I WANT HIM TO KNOW THAT IT WAS THE GUILD THAT ENDED HIM!
ABOVE ALL--I WANT HIM TO SUFFER!
AND...JUST BECAUSE HE'S PISSED ME OFF...
...ANYONE ASSOCIATED WITH WADE WILSON DIES, TOO...
...STARTING WITH HIS HANDLER AND THE TRAITOR, THRENODY.
STANDARD RATES APPLY.
BONUSES FOR HIS PAIN AND SUFFERING.
MAKE IT HAPPEN.

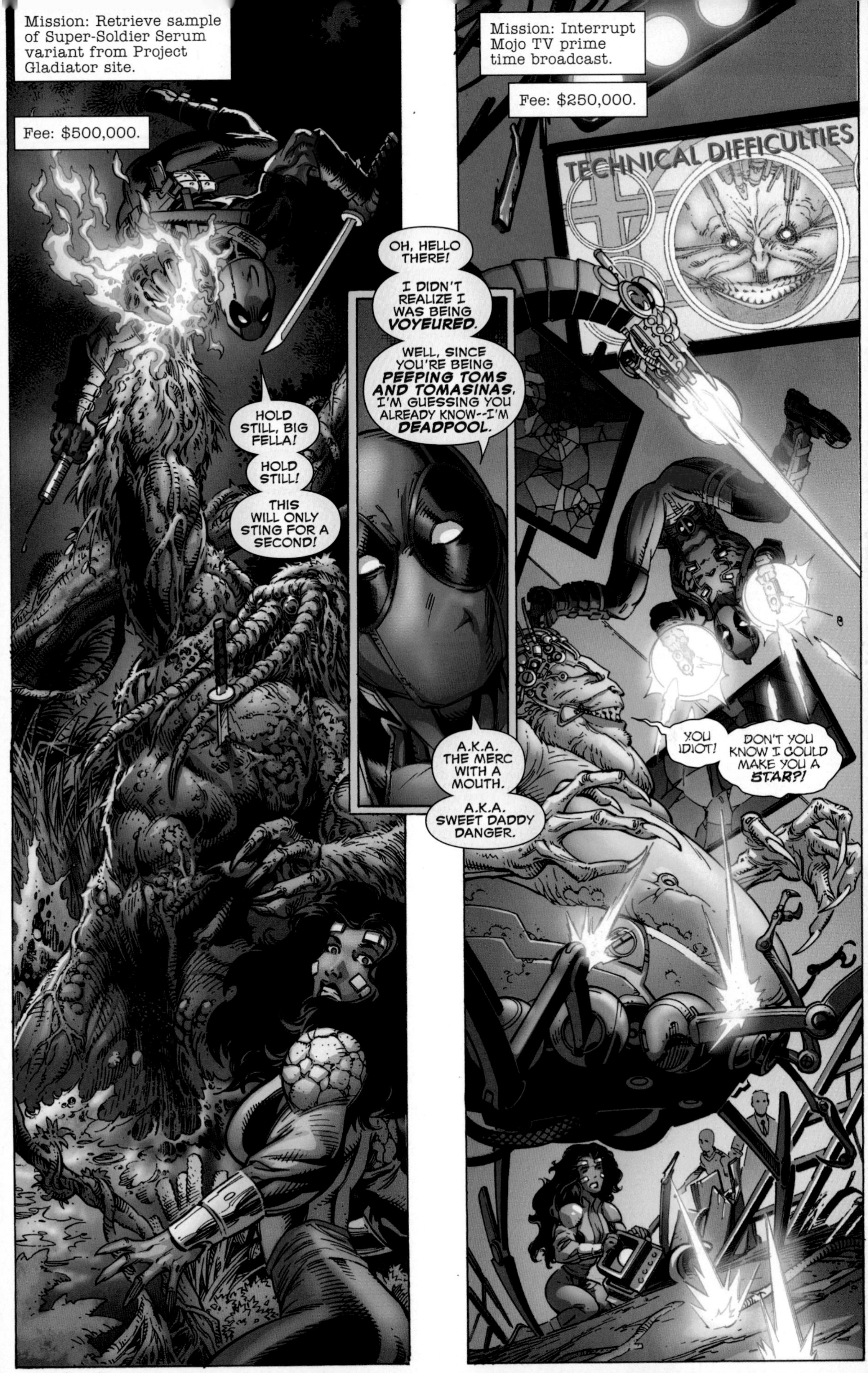
Mission: Retrieve sample of Super-Soldier Serum variant from Project Gladiator site.
Fee: $500,000.
HOLD STILL, BIG FELLA!
HOLD STILL!
THIS WILL ONLY STING FOR A SECOND!
OH, HELLO THERE!
I DIDN'T REALIZE I WAS BEING VOYEURED.
WELL, SINCE YOU'RE BEING PEEPING TOMS AND TOMASINAS, I'M GUESSING YOU ALREADY KNOW--I'M DEADPOOL.
A.K.A. THE MERC WITH A MOUTH.
A.K.A. SWEET DADDY DANGER.
Mission: Interrupt Mojo TV prime time broadcast.
Fee: $250,000.
TECHNICAL DIFFICULTIES
YOU IDIOT!
DON'T YOU KNOW I COULD MAKE YOU A STAR?!

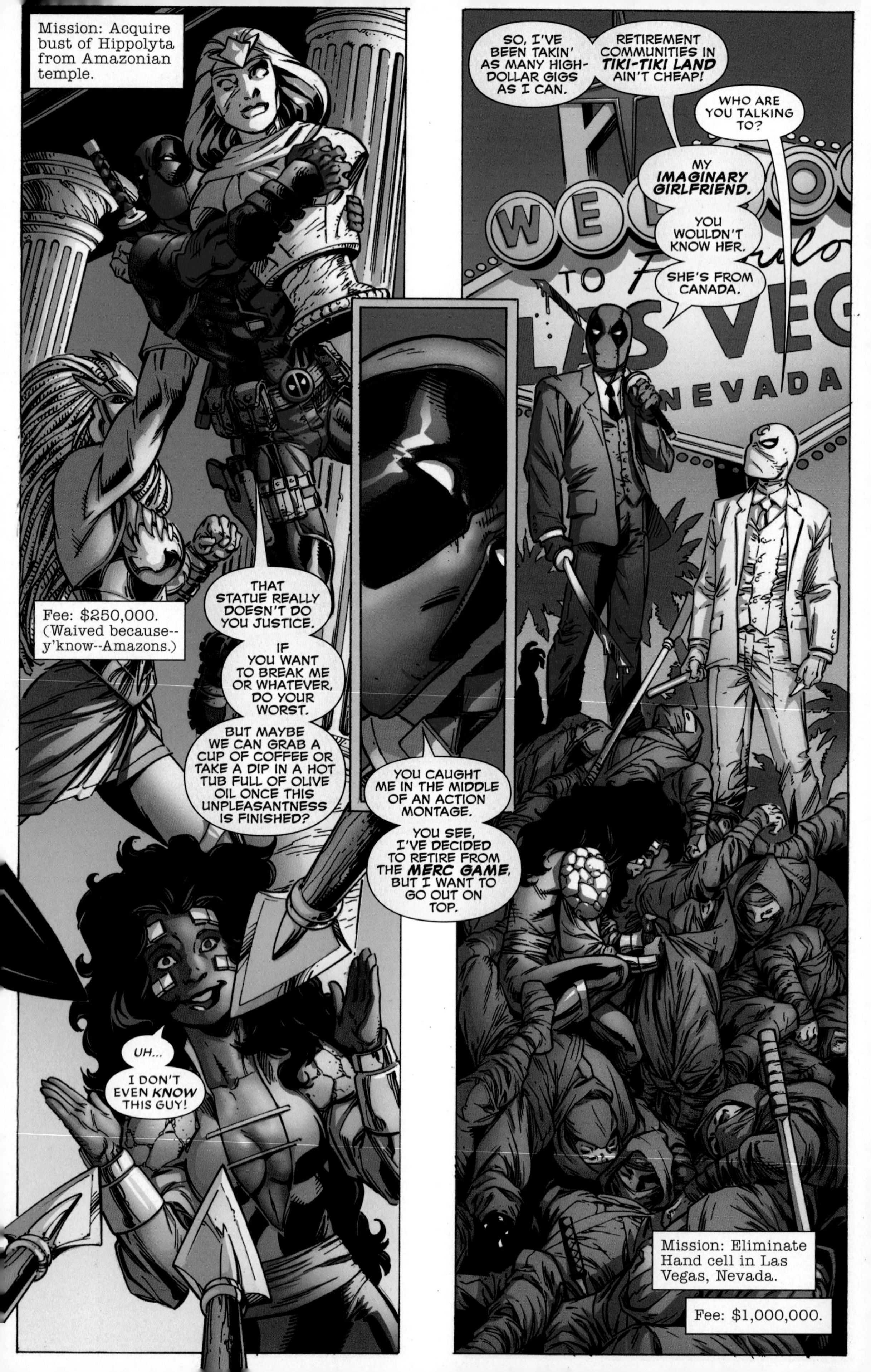

Mission: Acquire bust of Hippolyta from Amazonian temple.
THAT STATUE REALLY DOESN'T DO YOU JUSTICE.
IF YOU WANT TO BREAK ME OR WHATEVER, DO YOUR WORST.
BUT MAYBE WE CAN GRAB A CUP OF COFFEE OR TAKE A DIP IN A HOT TUB FULL OF OLIVE OIL ONCE THIS UNPLEASANTNESS IS FINISHED?
Fee: $250,000. (Waived because--y'know--Amazons.)
YOU CAUGHT ME IN THE MIDDLE OF AN ACTION MONTAGE.
YOU SEE, I'VE DECIDED TO RETIRE FROM THE *MERC GAME*, BUT I WANT TO GO OUT ON TOP.
UH...
I DON'T EVEN *KNOW* THIS GUY!
SO, I'VE BEEN TAKIN' AS MANY HIGH-DOLLAR GIGS AS I CAN.
RETIREMENT COMMUNITIES IN *TIKI-TIKI LAND* AIN'T CHEAP!
WHO ARE YOU TALKING TO?
MY *IMAGINARY GIRLFRIEND.*
YOU WOULDN'T KNOW HER.
SHE'S FROM CANADA.
NEVADA
Mission: Eliminate Hand cell in Las Vegas, Nevada.
Fee: $1,000,000.

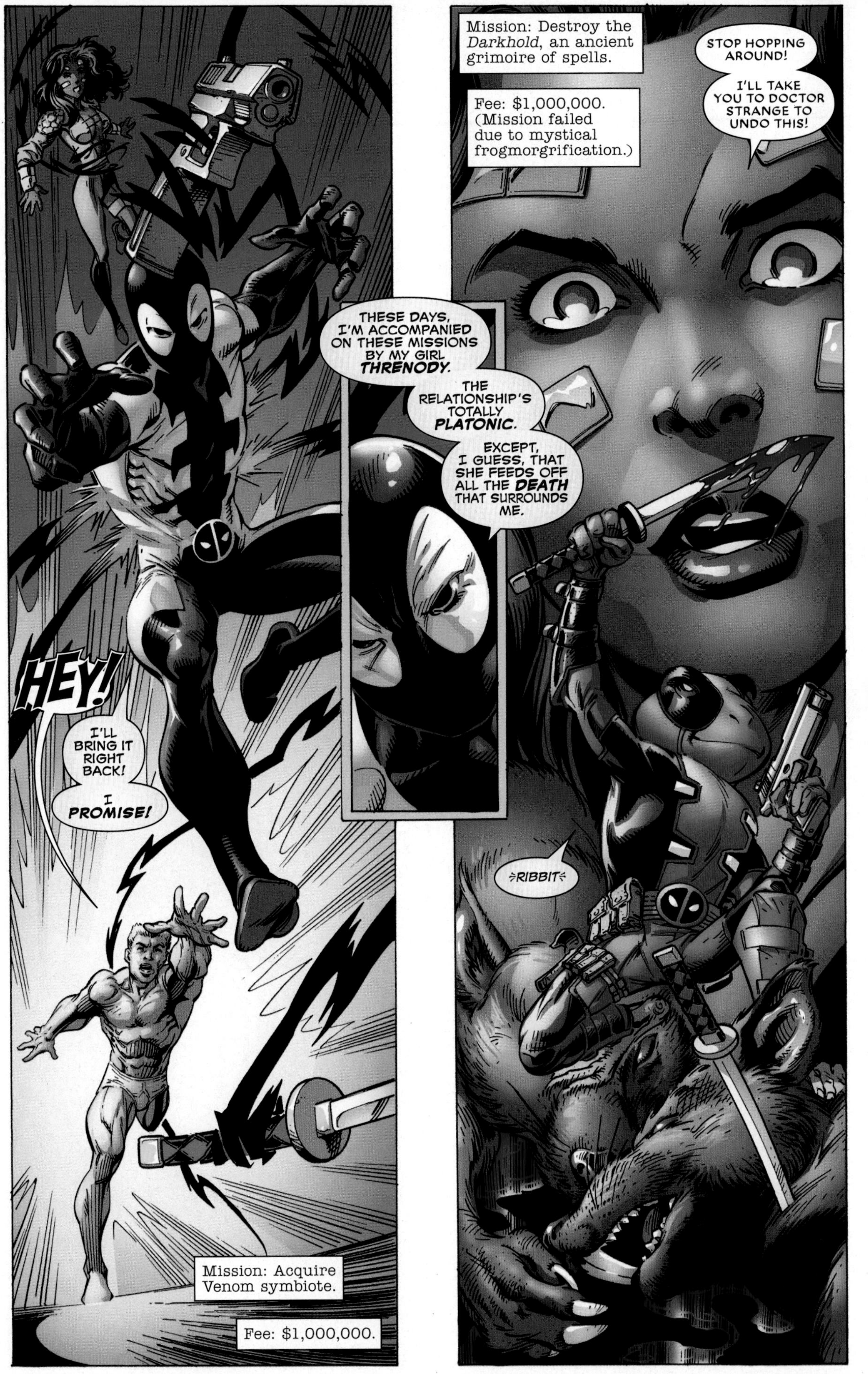
HEY!
I'LL BRING IT RIGHT BACK!
I PROMISE!
Mission: Acquire Venom symbiote.
Fee: $1,000,000.
THESE DAYS, I'M ACCOMPANIED ON THESE MISSIONS BY MY GIRL THRENODY.
THE RELATIONSHIP'S TOTALLY PLATONIC.
EXCEPT, I GUESS, THAT SHE FEEDS OFF ALL THE DEATH THAT SURROUNDS ME.
Mission: Destroy the Darkhold, an ancient grimoire of spells.
Fee: $1,000,000. (Mission failed due to mystical frogmorgrification.)
STOP HOPPING AROUND!
I'LL TAKE YOU TO DOCTOR STRANGE TO UNDO THIS!
RIBBIT

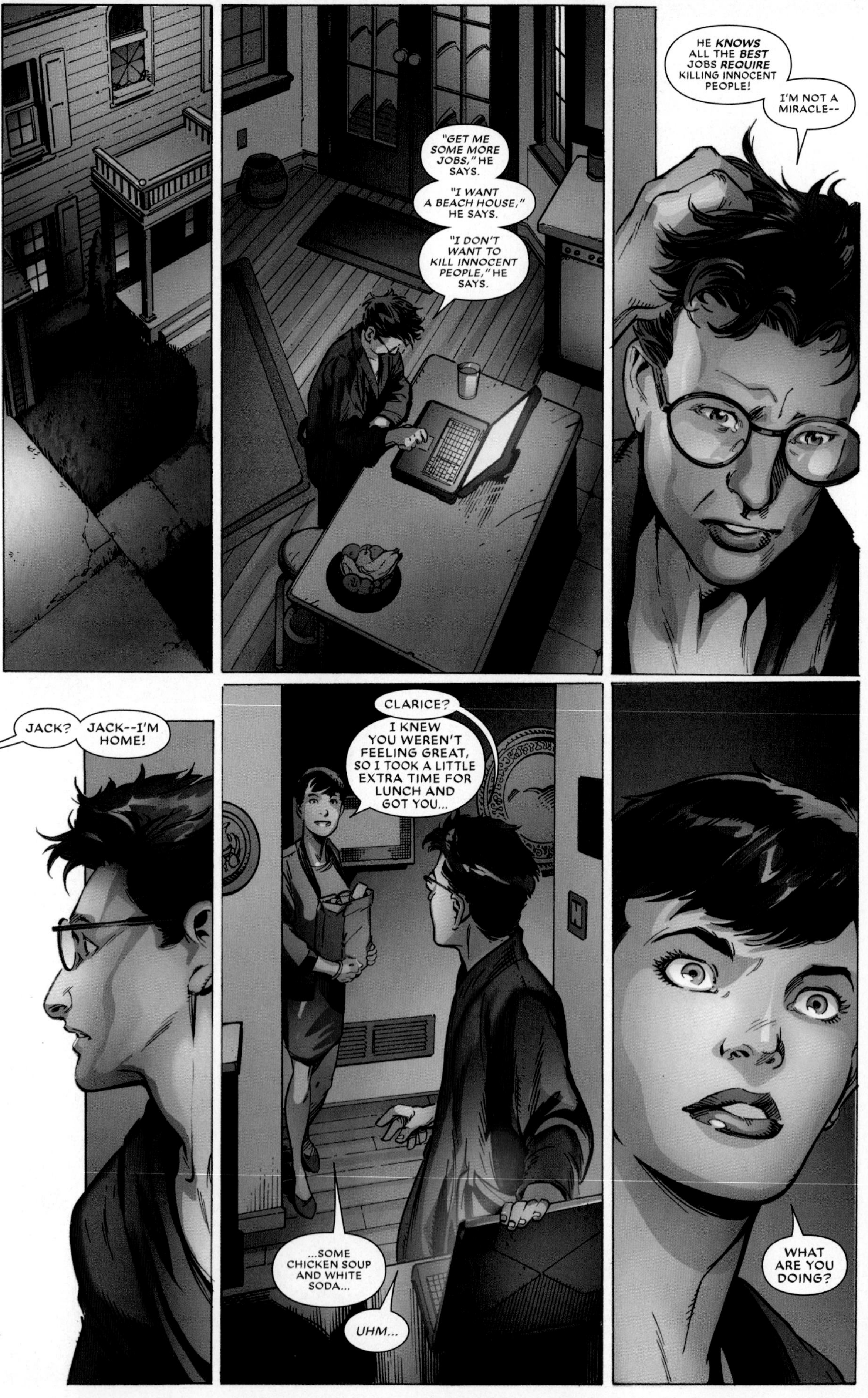

"GET ME SOME MORE JOBS," HE SAYS.
"I WANT A BEACH HOUSE," HE SAYS.
"I DON'T WANT TO KILL INNOCENT PEOPLE," HE SAYS.
HE *KNOWS* ALL THE *BEST* JOBS *REQUIRE* KILLING INNOCENT PEOPLE!
I'M NOT A MIRACLE--
JACK?
JACK--I'M HOME!
CLARICE?
I KNEW YOU WEREN'T FEELING GREAT, SO I TOOK A LITTLE EXTRA TIME FOR LUNCH AND GOT YOU...
...SOME CHICKEN SOUP AND WHITE SODA...
UHM...
WHAT ARE YOU DOING?

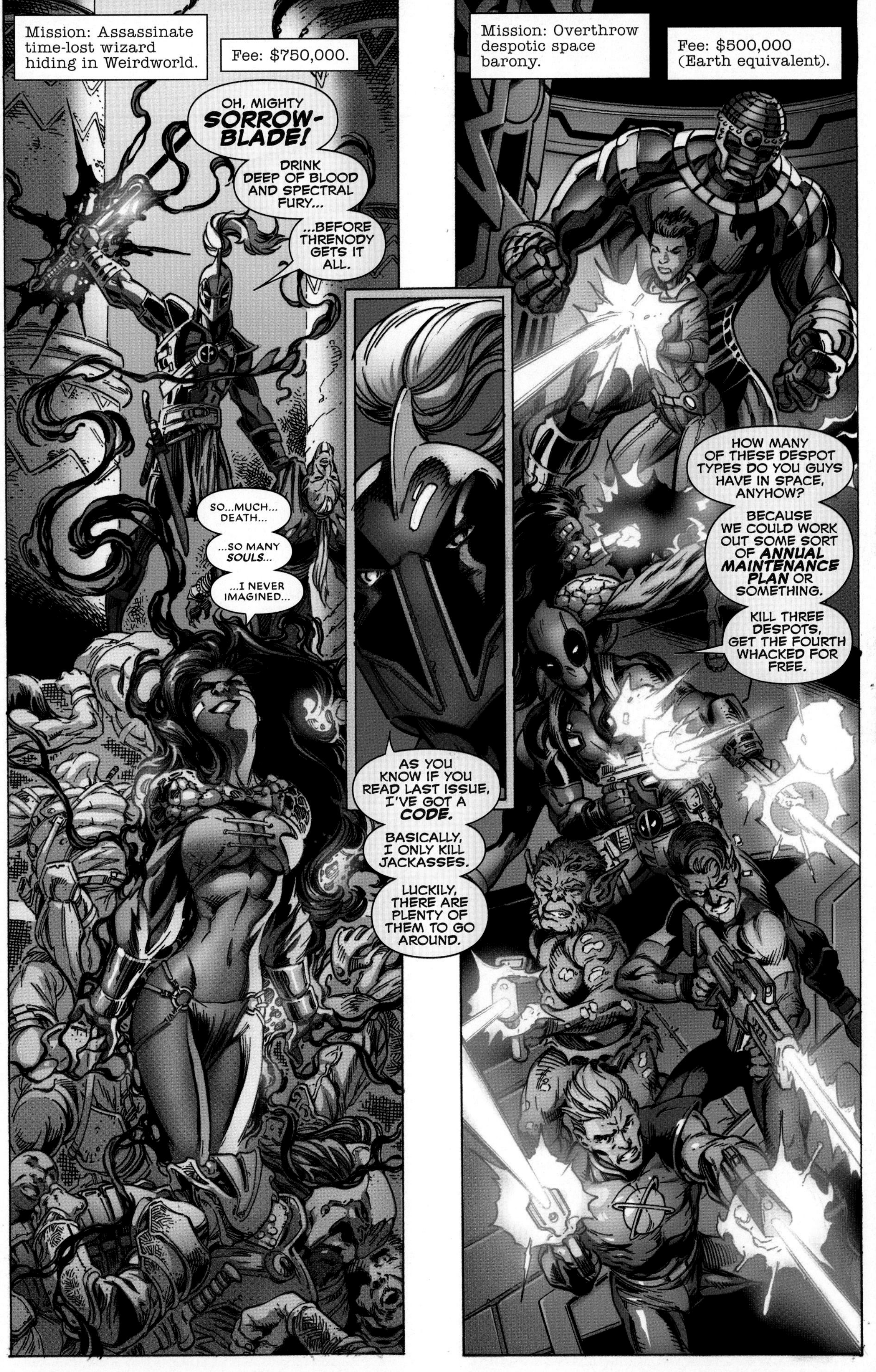
Mission: Assassinate time-lost wizard hiding in Weirdworld.
Fee: $750,000.
OH, MIGHTY SORROW-BLADE!
DRINK DEEP OF BLOOD AND SPECTRAL FURY...
...BEFORE THRENODY GETS IT ALL.
SO...MUCH... DEATH...
...SO MANY SOULS...
...I NEVER IMAGINED...
AS YOU KNOW IF YOU READ LAST ISSUE, I'VE GOT A CODE.
BASICALLY, I ONLY KILL JACKASSES.
LUCKILY, THERE ARE PLENTY OF THEM TO GO AROUND.
Mission: Overthrow despotic space barony.
Fee: $500,000 (Earth equivalent).
HOW MANY OF THESE DESPOT TYPES DO YOU GUYS HAVE IN SPACE, ANYHOW?
BECAUSE WE COULD WORK OUT SOME SORT OF ANNUAL MAINTENANCE PLAN OR SOMETHING.
KILL THREE DESPOTS, GET THE FOURTH WHACKED FOR FREE.

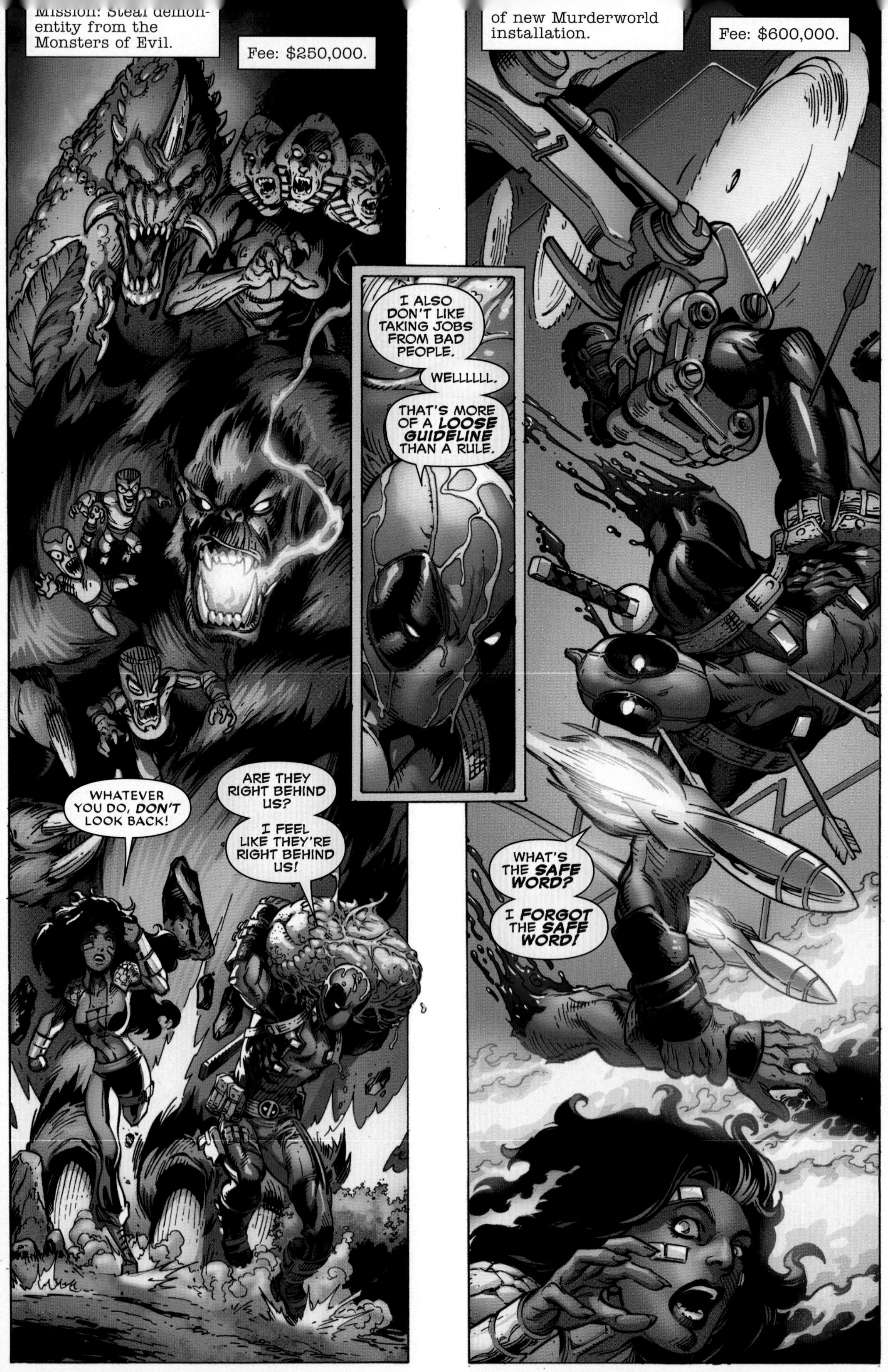

Mission: Steal demon-entity from the Monsters of Evil.
Fee: $250,000.
of new Murderworld installation.
Fee: $600,000.
I ALSO DON'T LIKE TAKING JOBS FROM BAD PEOPLE.
WELLLLLLL.
THAT'S MORE OF A LOOSE GUIDELINE THAN A RULE.
WHATEVER YOU DO, DON'T LOOK BACK!
ARE THEY RIGHT BEHIND US?
I FEEL LIKE THEY'RE RIGHT BEHIND US!
WHAT'S THE SAFE WORD?
I FORGOT THE SAFE WORD!

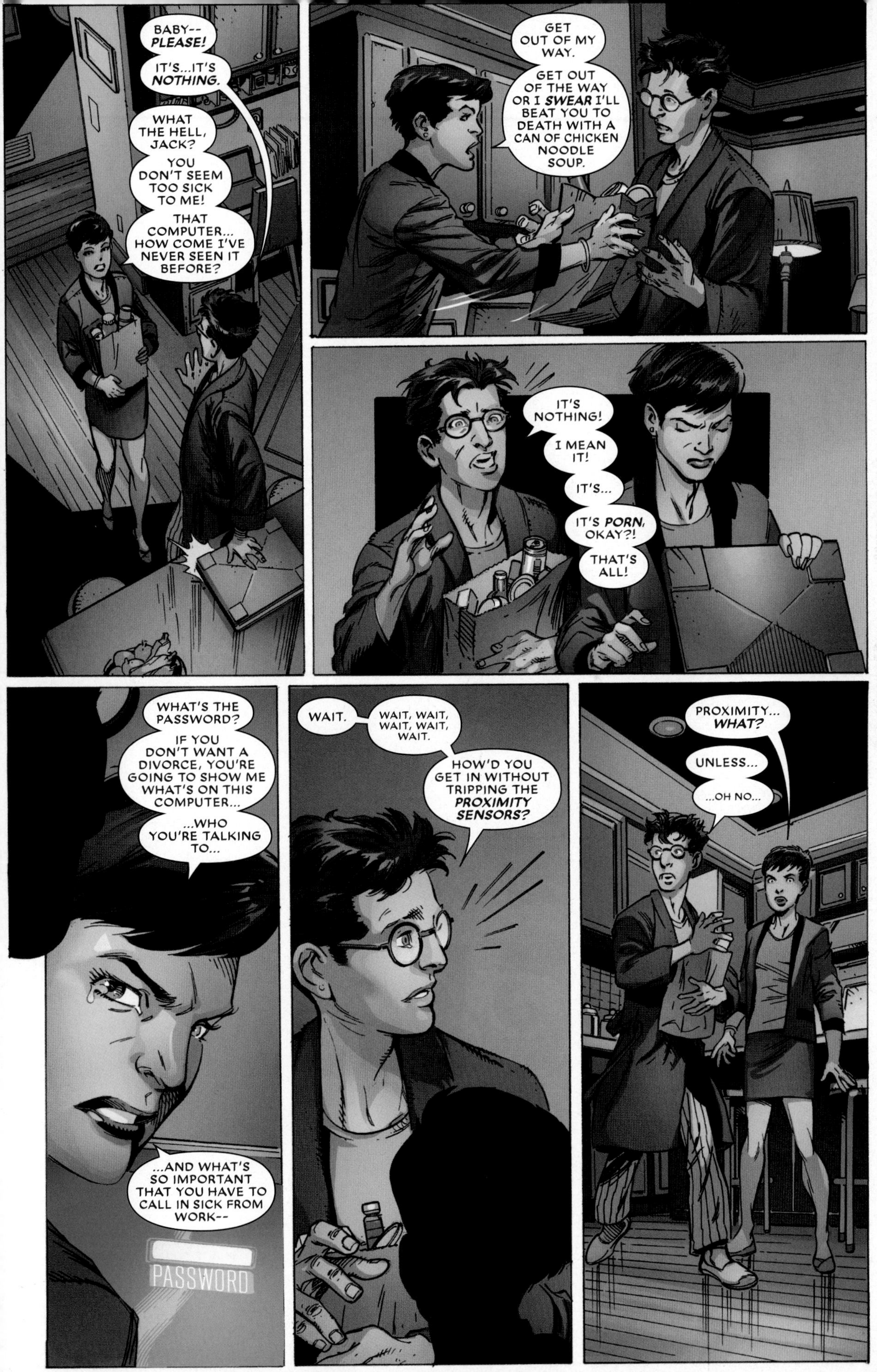
BABY-- PLEASE!
IT'S...IT'S NOTHING.
WHAT THE HELL, JACK?
YOU DON'T SEEM TOO SICK TO ME!
THAT COMPUTER... HOW COME I'VE NEVER SEEN IT BEFORE?
GET OUT OF MY WAY.
GET OUT OF THE WAY OR I SWEAR I'LL BEAT YOU TO DEATH WITH A CAN OF CHICKEN NOODLE SOUP.
IT'S NOTHING!
I MEAN IT!
IT'S...
IT'S PORN, OKAY?!
THAT'S ALL!
WHAT'S THE PASSWORD?
IF YOU DON'T WANT A DIVORCE, YOU'RE GOING TO SHOW ME WHAT'S ON THIS COMPUTER...
...WHO YOU'RE TALKING TO...
...AND WHAT'S SO IMPORTANT THAT YOU HAVE TO CALL IN SICK FROM WORK--
PASSWORD
WAIT.
WAIT, WAIT, WAIT, WAIT, WAIT.
HOW'D YOU GET IN WITHOUT TRIPPING THE PROXIMITY SENSORS?
PROXIMITY... WHAT?
UNLESS...
...OH NO...

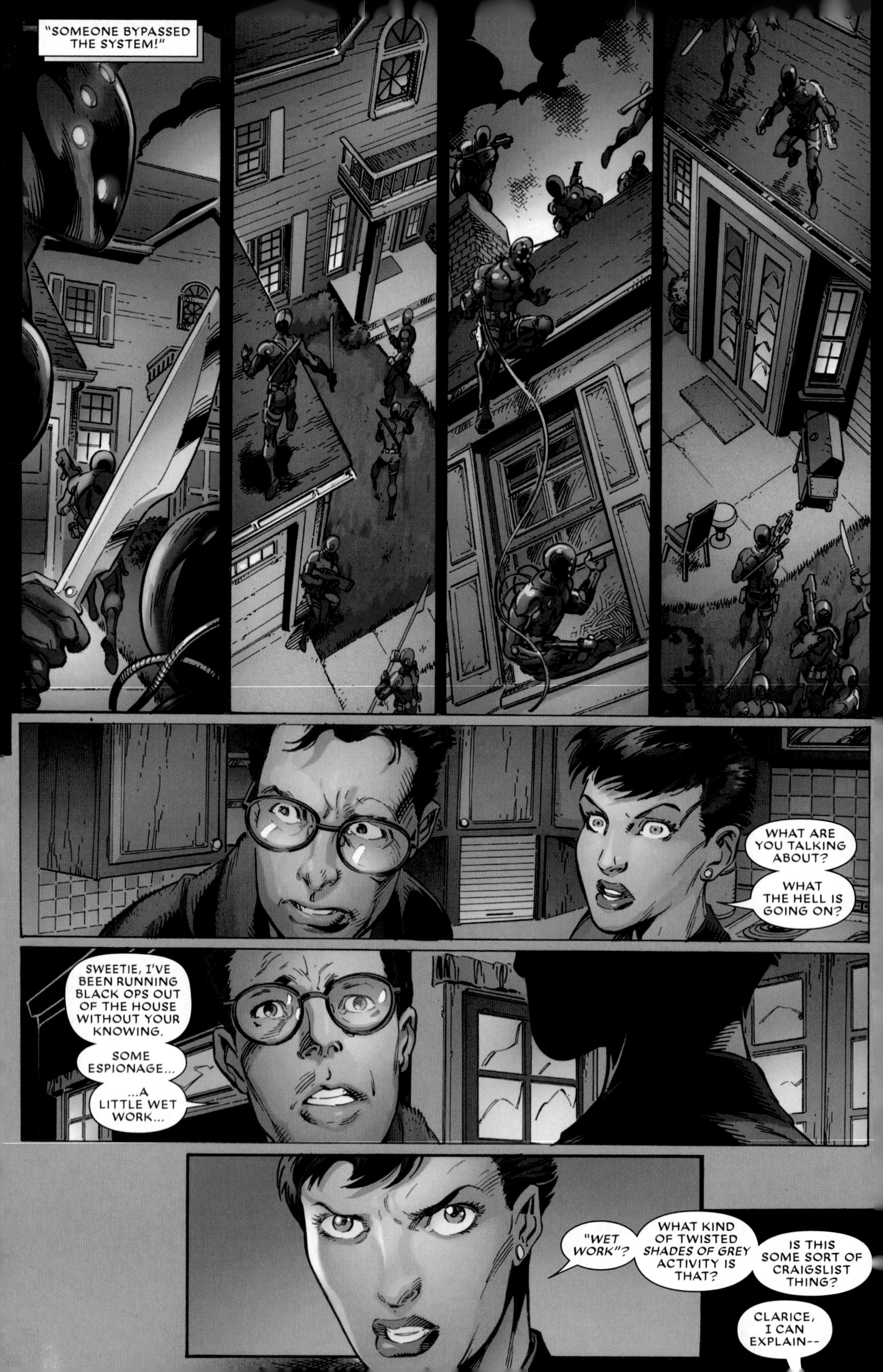
"SOMEONE BYPASSED THE SYSTEM!"
WHAT ARE YOU TALKING ABOUT?
WHAT THE HELL IS GOING ON?
SWEETIE, I'VE BEEN RUNNING BLACK OPS OUT OF THE HOUSE WITHOUT YOUR KNOWING.
SOME ESPIONAGE...
...A LITTLE WET WORK...
"WET WORK"?
WHAT KIND OF TWISTED SHADES OF GREY ACTIVITY IS THAT?
IS THIS SOME SORT OF CRAIGSLIST THING?
CLARICE, I CAN EXPLAIN--

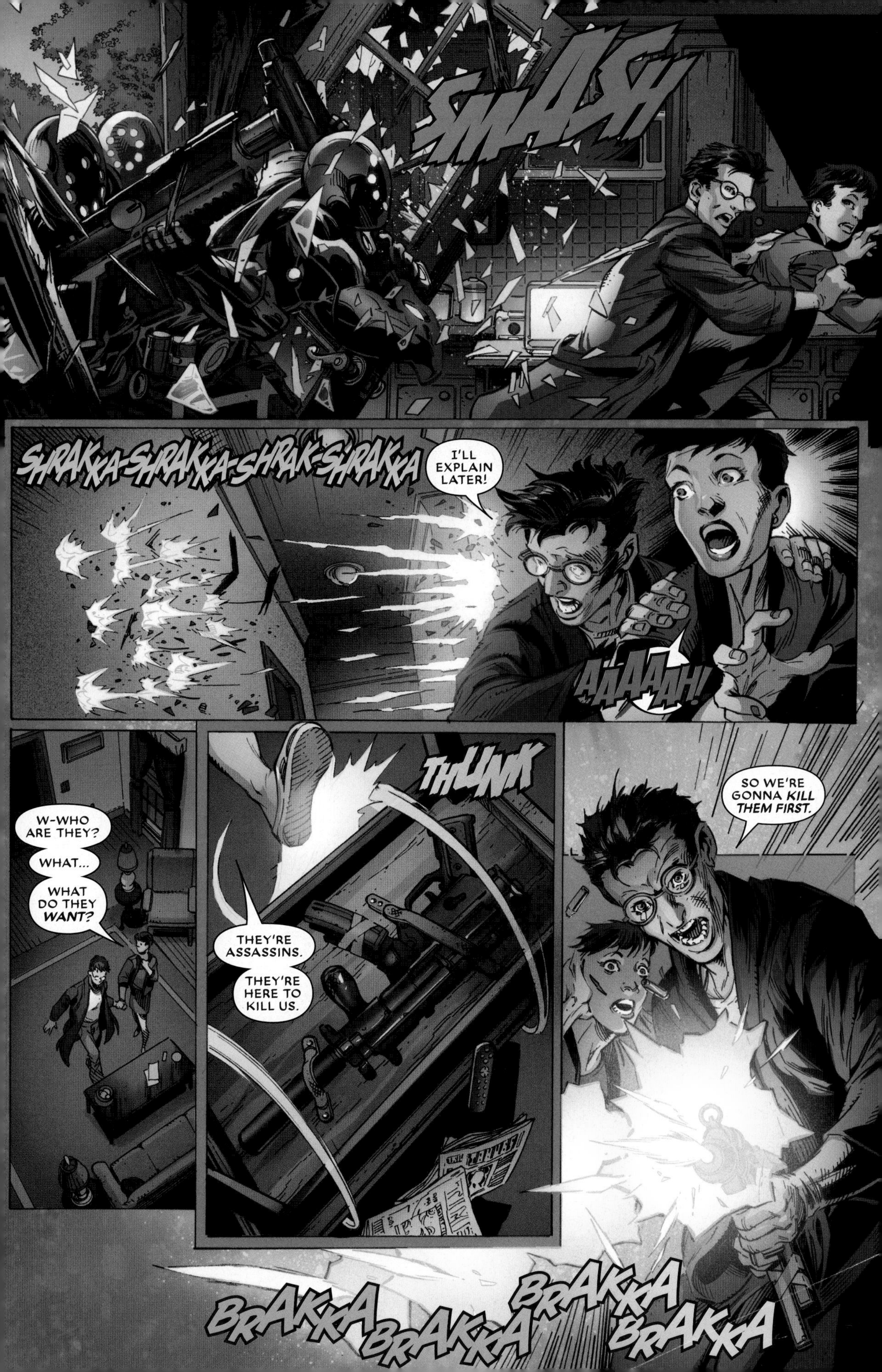
SMASH
SHRAKKA-SHRAKKA-SHRAK-SHRAKKA
I'LL EXPLAIN LATER!
AAAAAH!
W-WHO ARE THEY?
WHAT...
WHAT DO THEY WANT?
THUNK
THEY'RE ASSASSINS.
THEY'RE HERE TO KILL US.
SO WE'RE GONNA KILL THEM FIRST.
BRAKKA BRAKKA BRAKKA BRAKKA

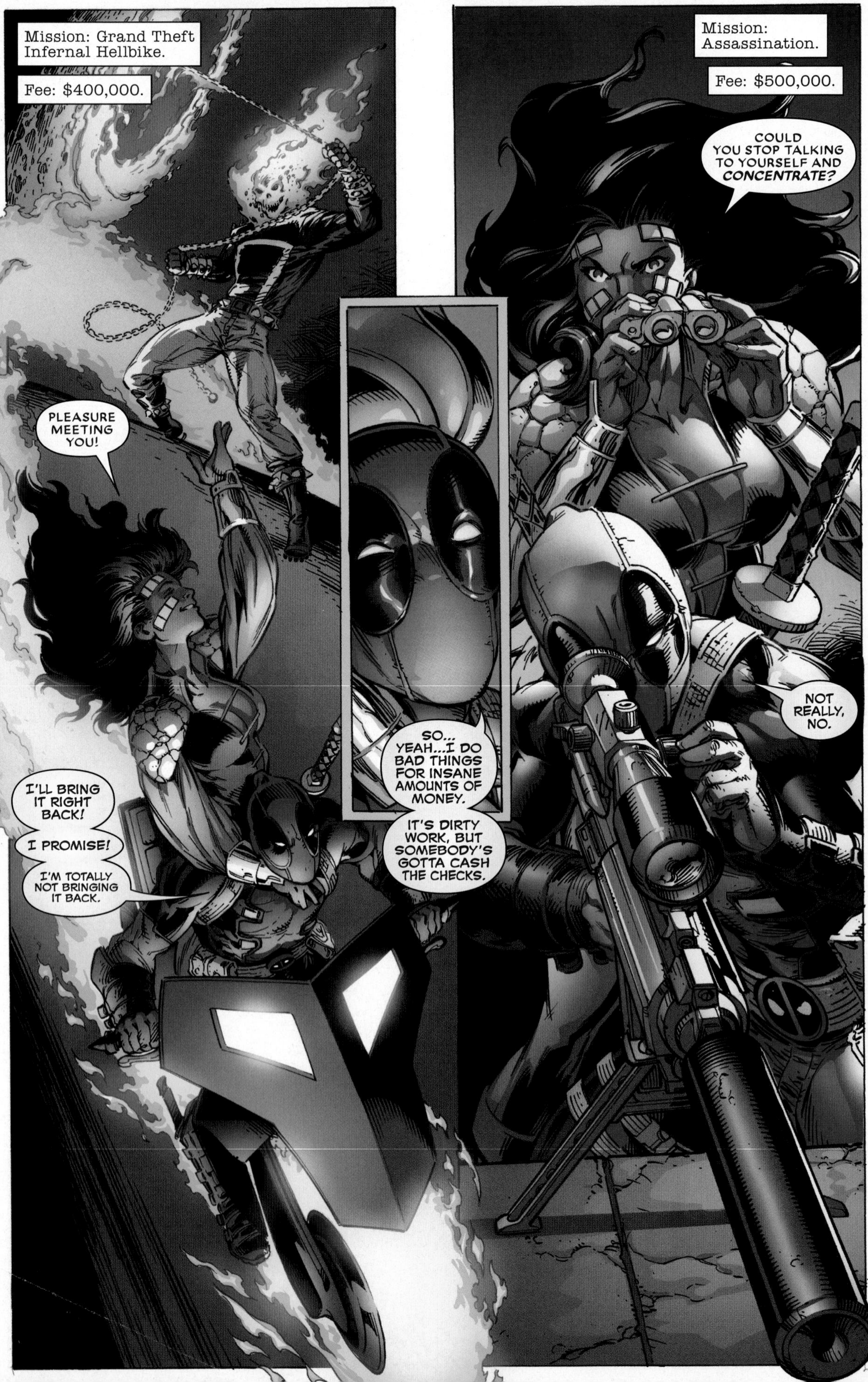
Mission: Grand Theft Infernal Hellbike.
Fee: $400,000.
PLEASURE MEETING YOU!
I'LL BRING IT RIGHT BACK!
I PROMISE!
I'M TOTALLY NOT BRINGING IT BACK.
SO... YEAH...I DO BAD THINGS FOR INSANE AMOUNTS OF MONEY.
IT'S DIRTY WORK, BUT SOMEBODY'S GOTTA CASH THE CHECKS.
Mission: Assassination.
Fee: $500,000.
COULD YOU STOP TALKING TO YOURSELF AND *CONCENTRATE?*
NOT REALLY, NO.

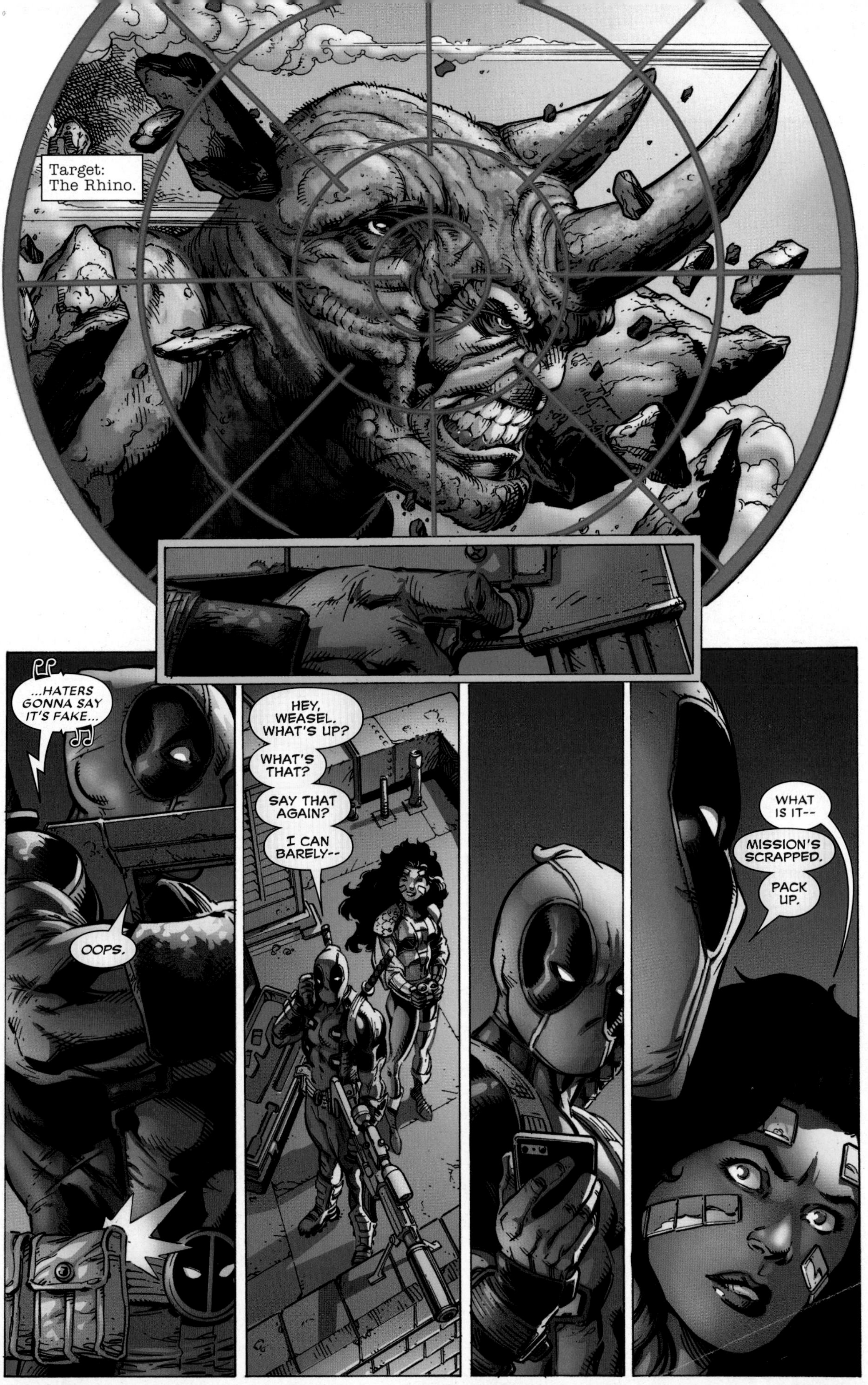

Target:
The Rhino.
...HATERS GONNA SAY IT'S FAKE...
OOPS.
HEY, WEASEL. WHAT'S UP?
WHAT'S THAT?
SAY THAT AGAIN?
I CAN BARELY--
WHAT IS IT--
MISSION'S SCRAPPED.
PACK UP.

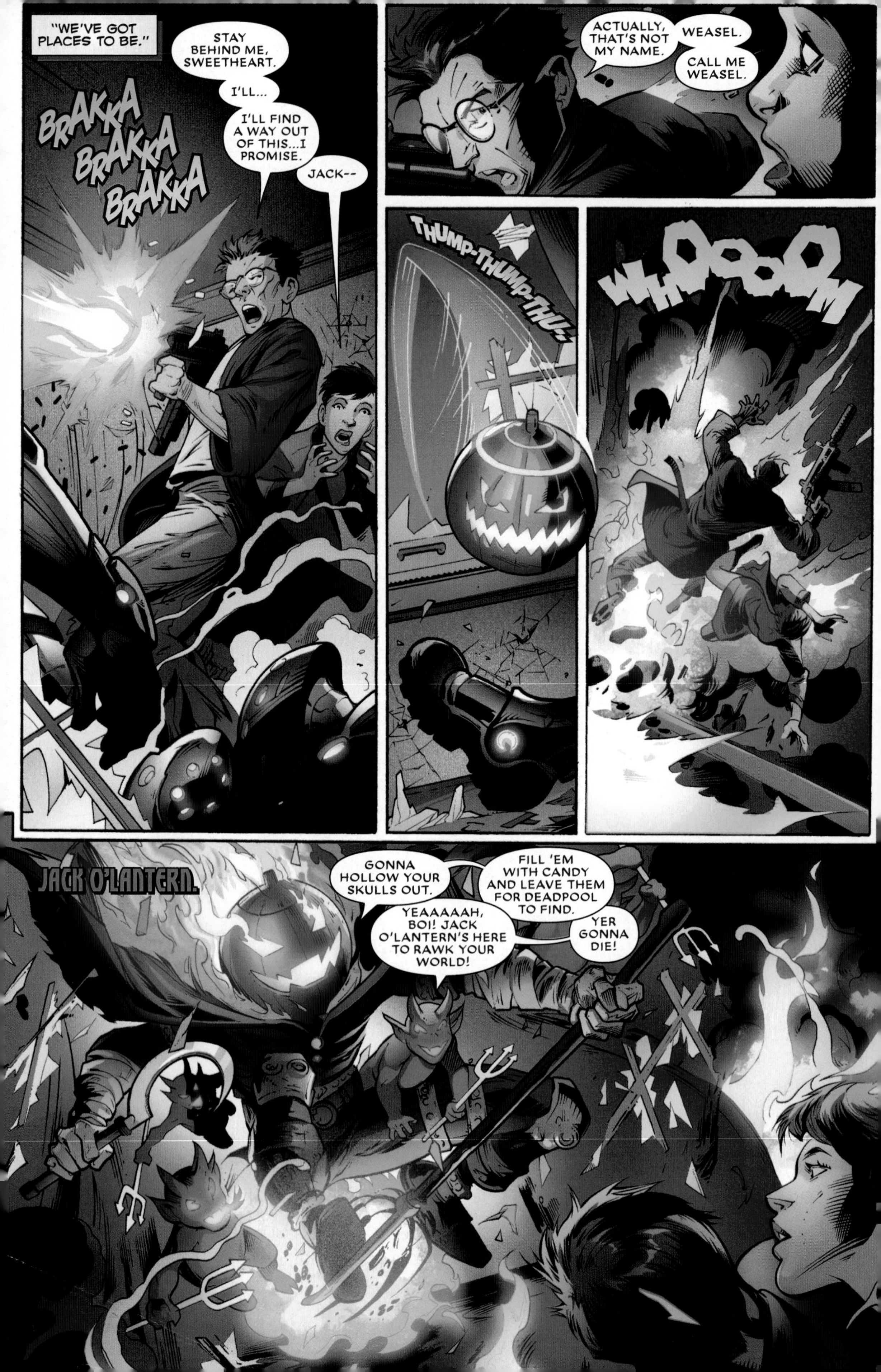
"WE'VE GOT PLACES TO BE."
STAY BEHIND ME, SWEETHEART.
I'LL...
I'LL FIND A WAY OUT OF THIS...I PROMISE.
JACK--
BRAKKA BRAKKA BRAKKA
ACTUALLY, THAT'S NOT MY NAME.
WEASEL.
CALL ME WEASEL.
THUMP-THUMP-THU--
WHOOOOM
JACK O'LANTERN.
GONNA HOLLOW YOUR SKULLS OUT.
FILL 'EM WITH CANDY AND LEAVE THEM FOR DEADPOOL TO FIND.
YEAAAAAH, BOI! JACK O'LANTERN'S HERE TO RAWK YOUR WORLD!
YER GONNA DIE!

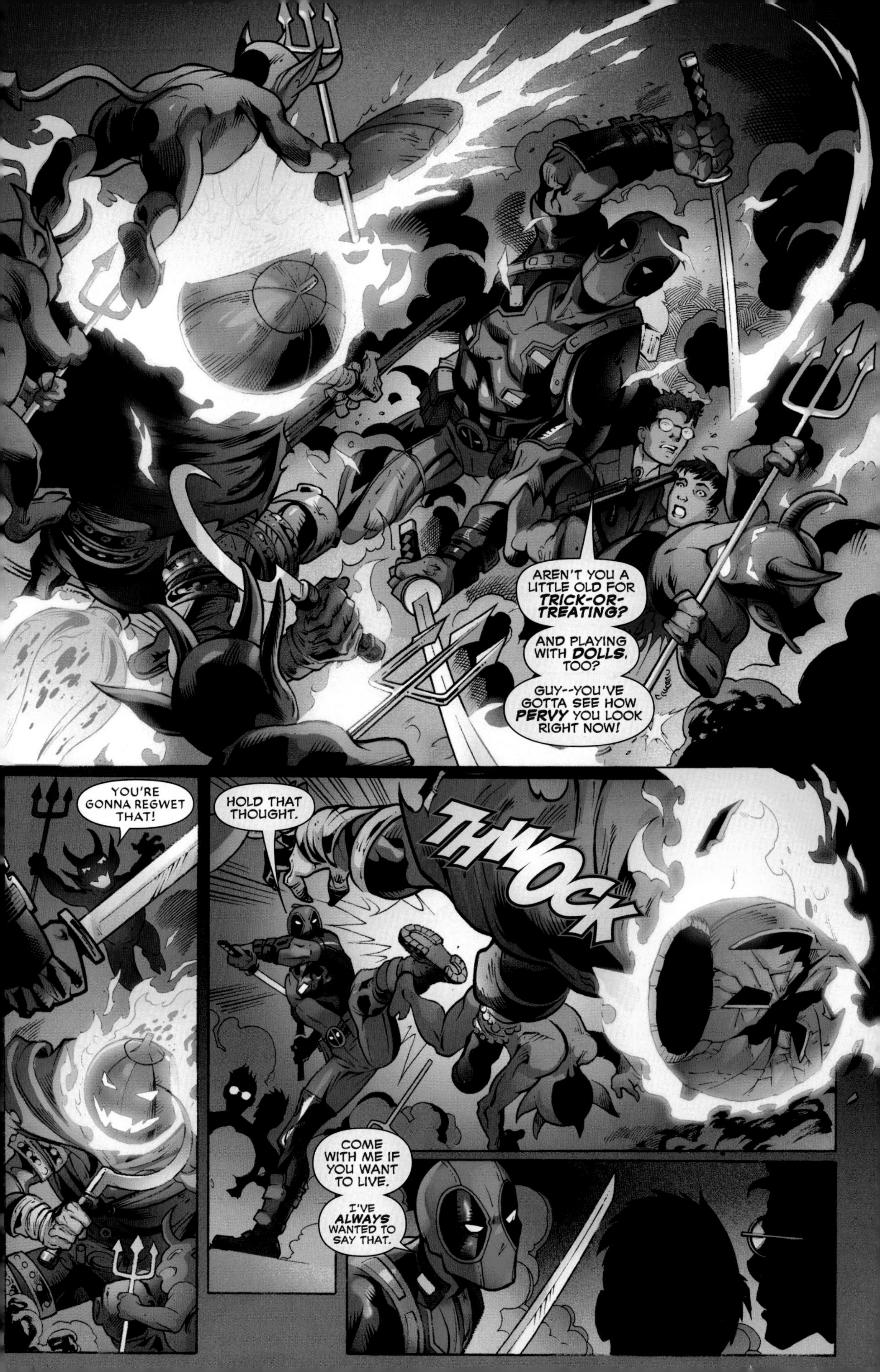
AREN'T YOU A LITTLE OLD FOR TRICK-OR-TREATING?
AND PLAYING WITH DOLLS, TOO?
GUY--YOU'VE GOTTA SEE HOW PERVY YOU LOOK RIGHT NOW!
YOU'RE GONNA REGWET THAT!
HOLD THAT THOUGHT.
THWOCK
COME WITH ME IF YOU WANT TO LIVE.
I'VE ALWAYS WANTED TO SAY THAT.

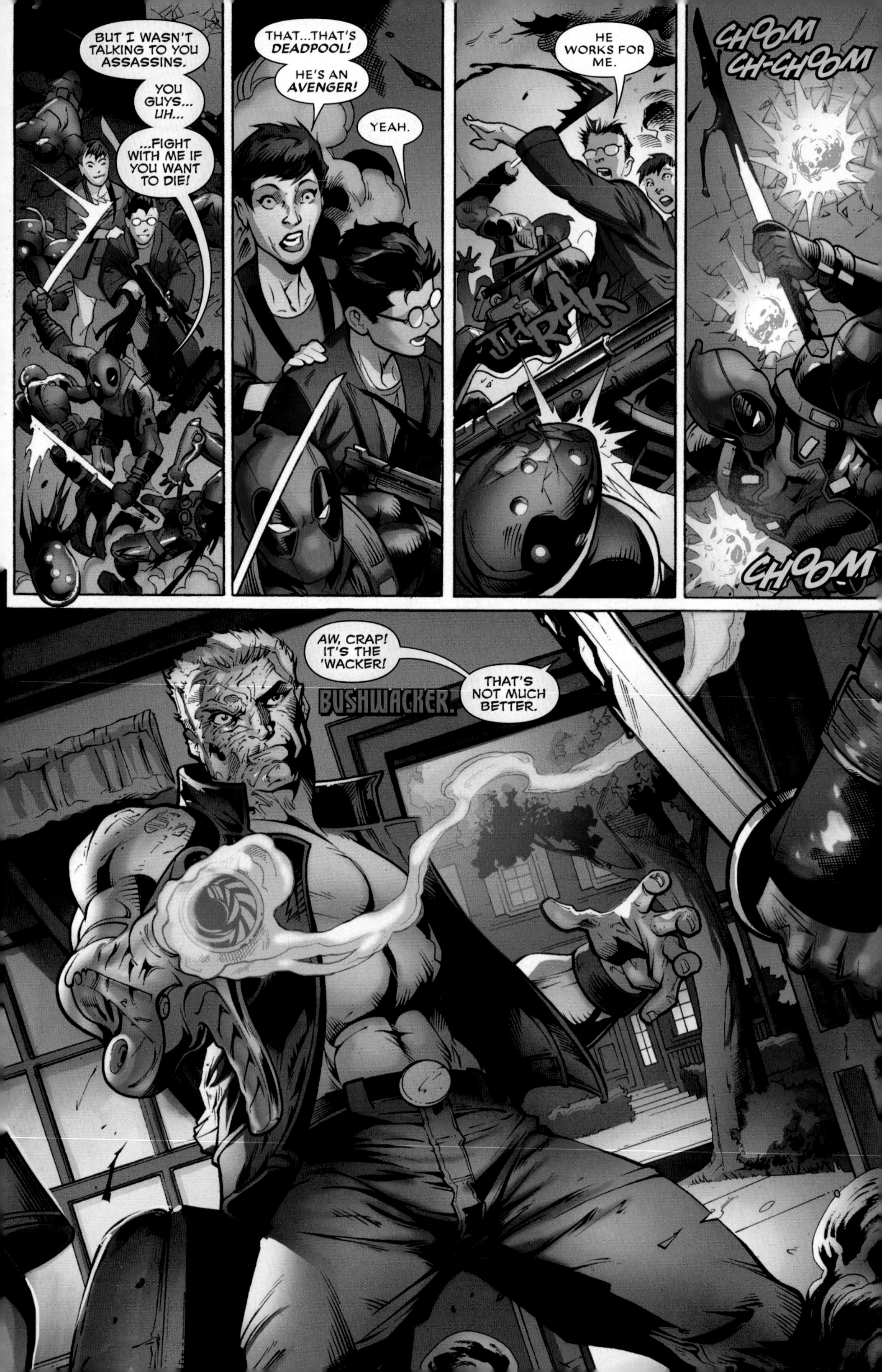

BUT I WASN'T TALKING TO YOU ASSASSINS.
YOU GUYS... UH...
...FIGHT WITH ME IF YOU WANT TO DIE!
THAT...THAT'S DEADPOOL!
HE'S AN AVENGER!
YEAH.
HE WORKS FOR ME.
THRAK
CHOOM CH-CHOOM
CHOOM
AW, CRAP! IT'S THE 'WACKER!
BUSHWACKER.
THAT'S NOT MUCH BETTER.

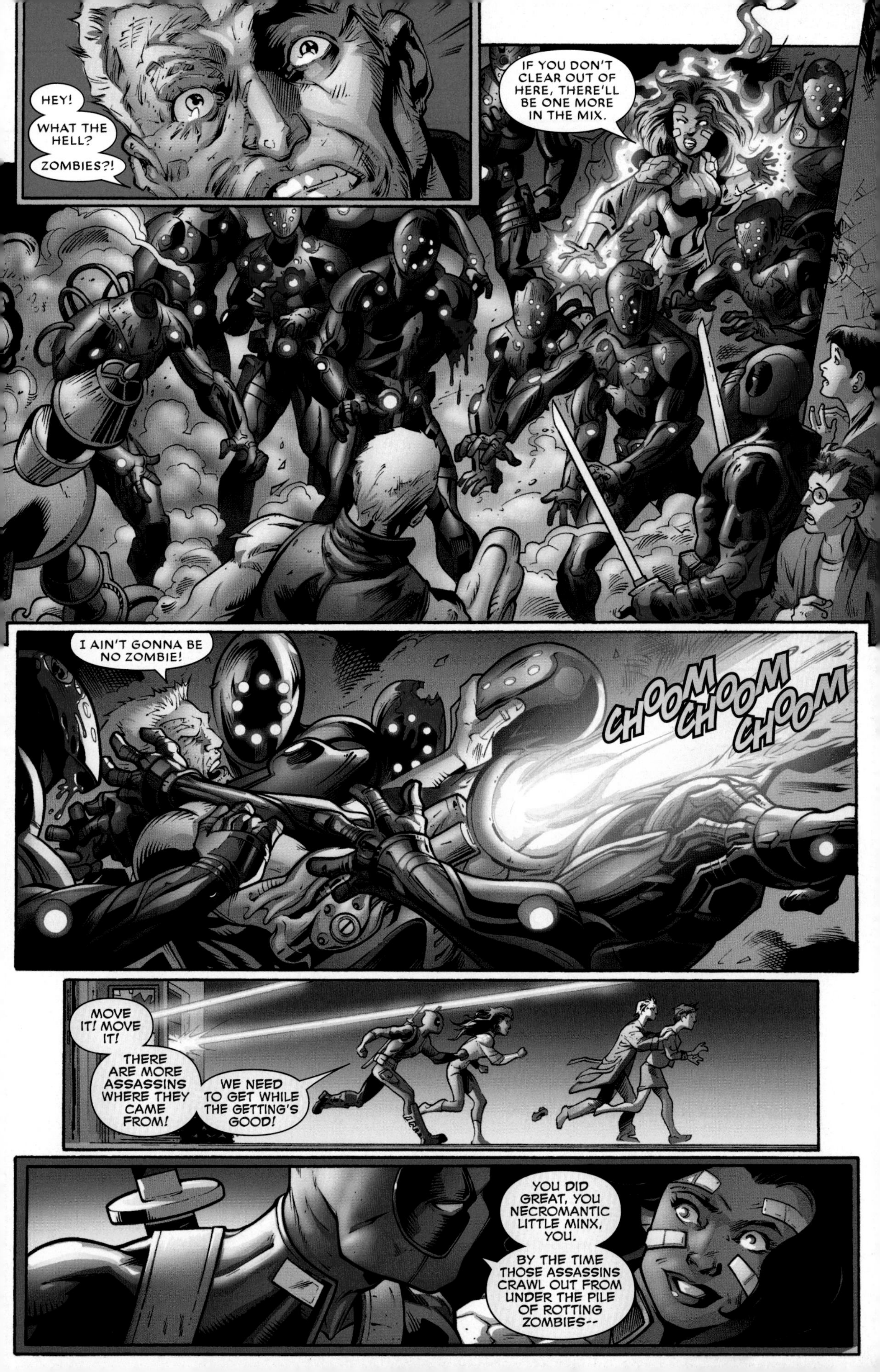
HEY!
WHAT THE HELL?
ZOMBIES?!
IF YOU DON'T CLEAR OUT OF HERE, THERE'LL BE ONE MORE IN THE MIX.
I AIN'T GONNA BE NO ZOMBIE!
CHOOM CHOOM CHOOM
MOVE IT! MOVE IT!
THERE ARE MORE ASSASSINS WHERE THEY CAME FROM!
WE NEED TO GET WHILE THE GETTING'S GOOD!
YOU DID GREAT, YOU NECROMANTIC LITTLE MINX, YOU.
BY THE TIME THOSE ASSASSINS CRAWL OUT FROM UNDER THE PILE OF ROTTING ZOMBIES--

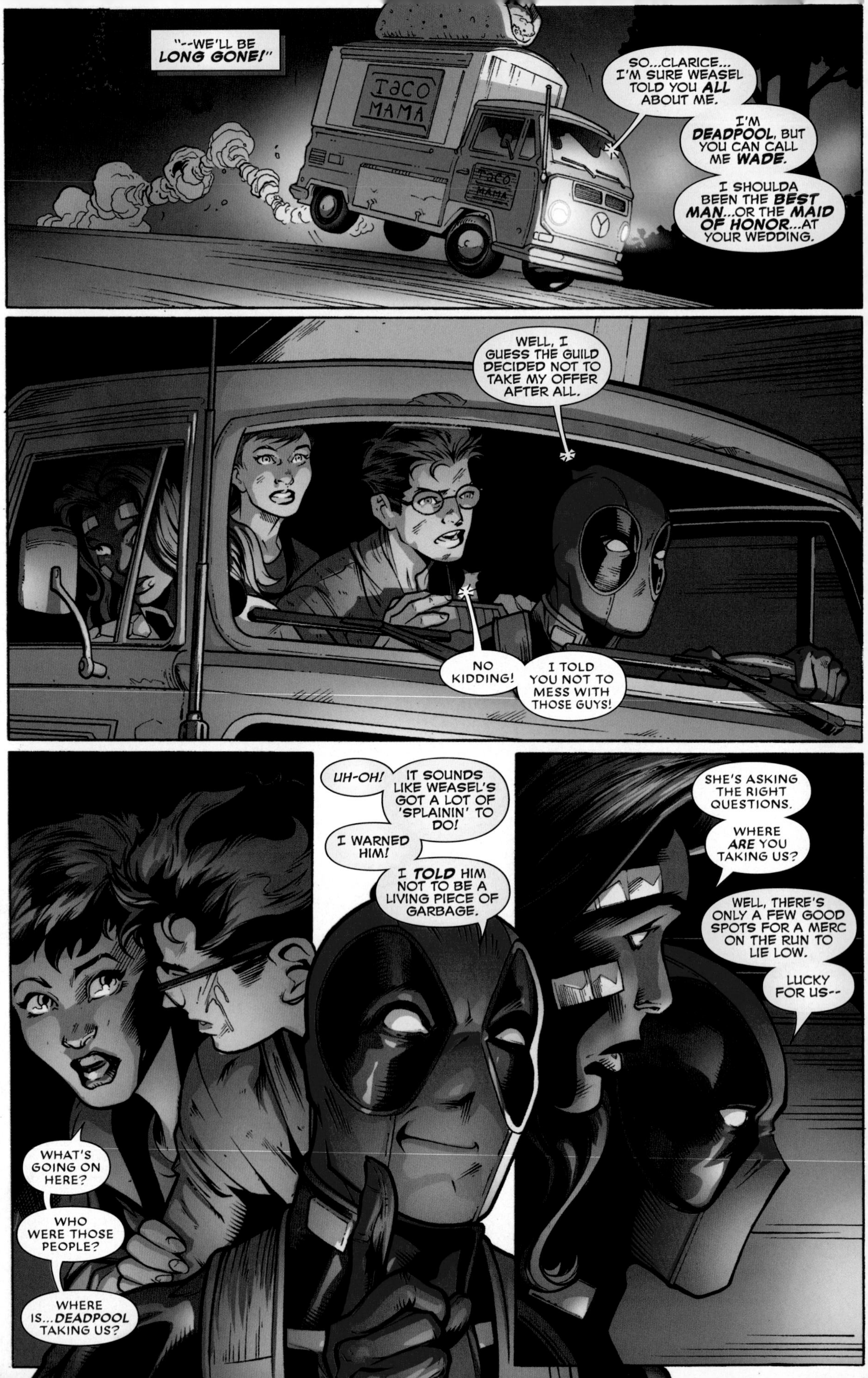
"--WE'LL BE LONG GONE!"
TACO MAMA
SO...CLARICE... I'M SURE WEASEL TOLD YOU ALL ABOUT ME.
I'M DEADPOOL, BUT YOU CAN CALL ME WADE.
I SHOULDA BEEN THE BEST MAN...OR THE MAID OF HONOR...AT YOUR WEDDING.
WELL, I GUESS THE GUILD DECIDED NOT TO TAKE MY OFFER AFTER ALL.
NO KIDDING!
I TOLD YOU NOT TO MESS WITH THOSE GUYS!
WHAT'S GOING ON HERE?
WHO WERE THOSE PEOPLE?
WHERE IS...DEADPOOL TAKING US?
UH-OH!
IT SOUNDS LIKE WEASEL'S GOT A LOT OF 'SPLAININ' TO DO!
I WARNED HIM!
I TOLD HIM NOT TO BE A LIVING PIECE OF GARBAGE.
SHE'S ASKING THE RIGHT QUESTIONS.
WHERE ARE YOU TAKING US?
WELL, THERE'S ONLY A FEW GOOD SPOTS FOR A MERC ON THE RUN TO LIE LOW.
LUCKY FOR US--

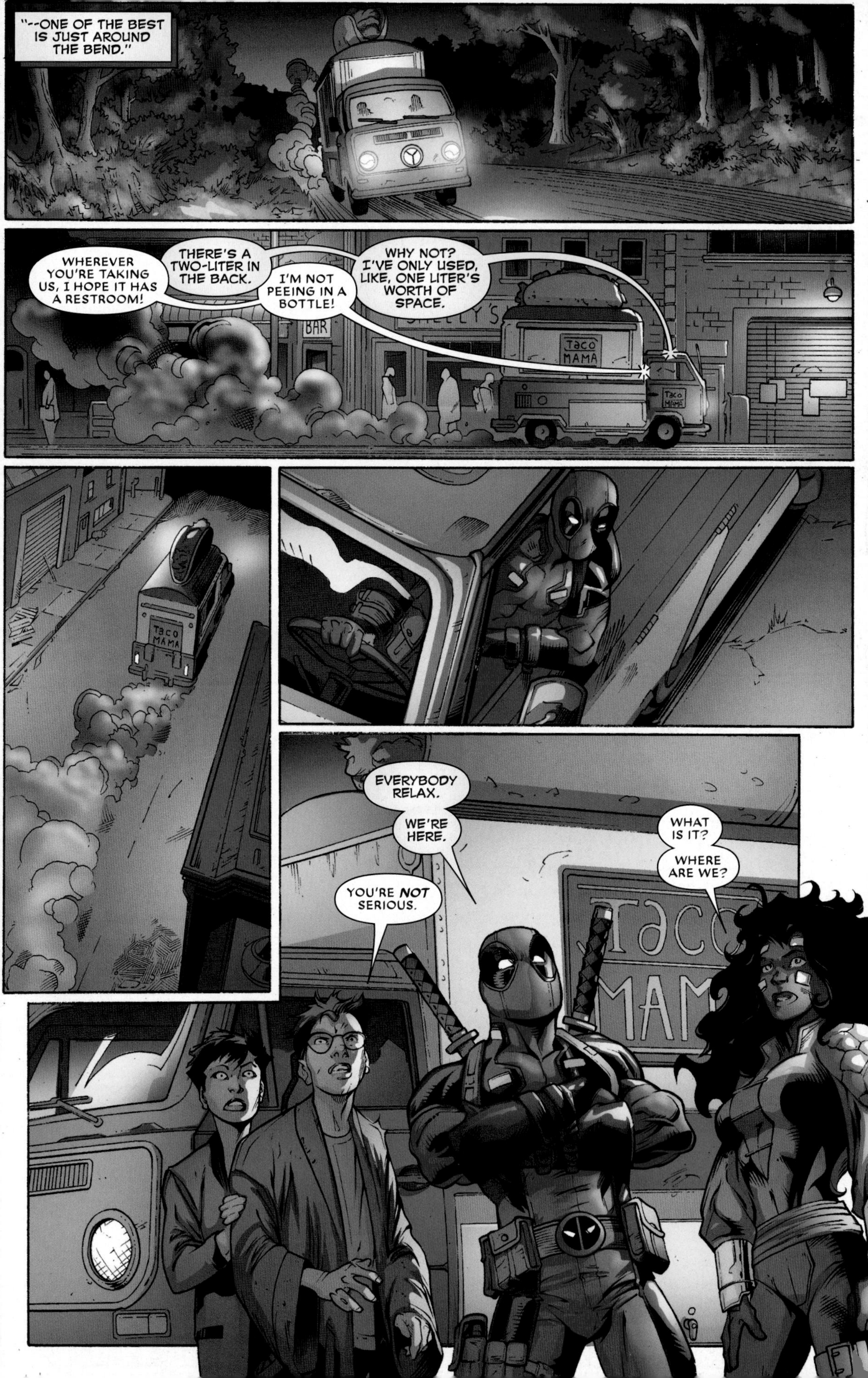
"--ONE OF THE BEST IS JUST AROUND THE BEND."
WHEREVER YOU'RE TAKING US, I HOPE IT HAS A RESTROOM!
THERE'S A TWO-LITER IN THE BACK.
I'M NOT PEEING IN A BOTTLE!
WHY NOT? I'VE ONLY USED, LIKE, ONE LITER'S WORTH OF SPACE.
SHELLY'S
BAR
TACO MAMA
TACO MAMA
TACO MAMA
EVERYBODY RELAX.
WE'RE HERE.
WHAT IS IT?
WHERE ARE WE?
YOU'RE *NOT* SERIOUS.
TACO MAMA

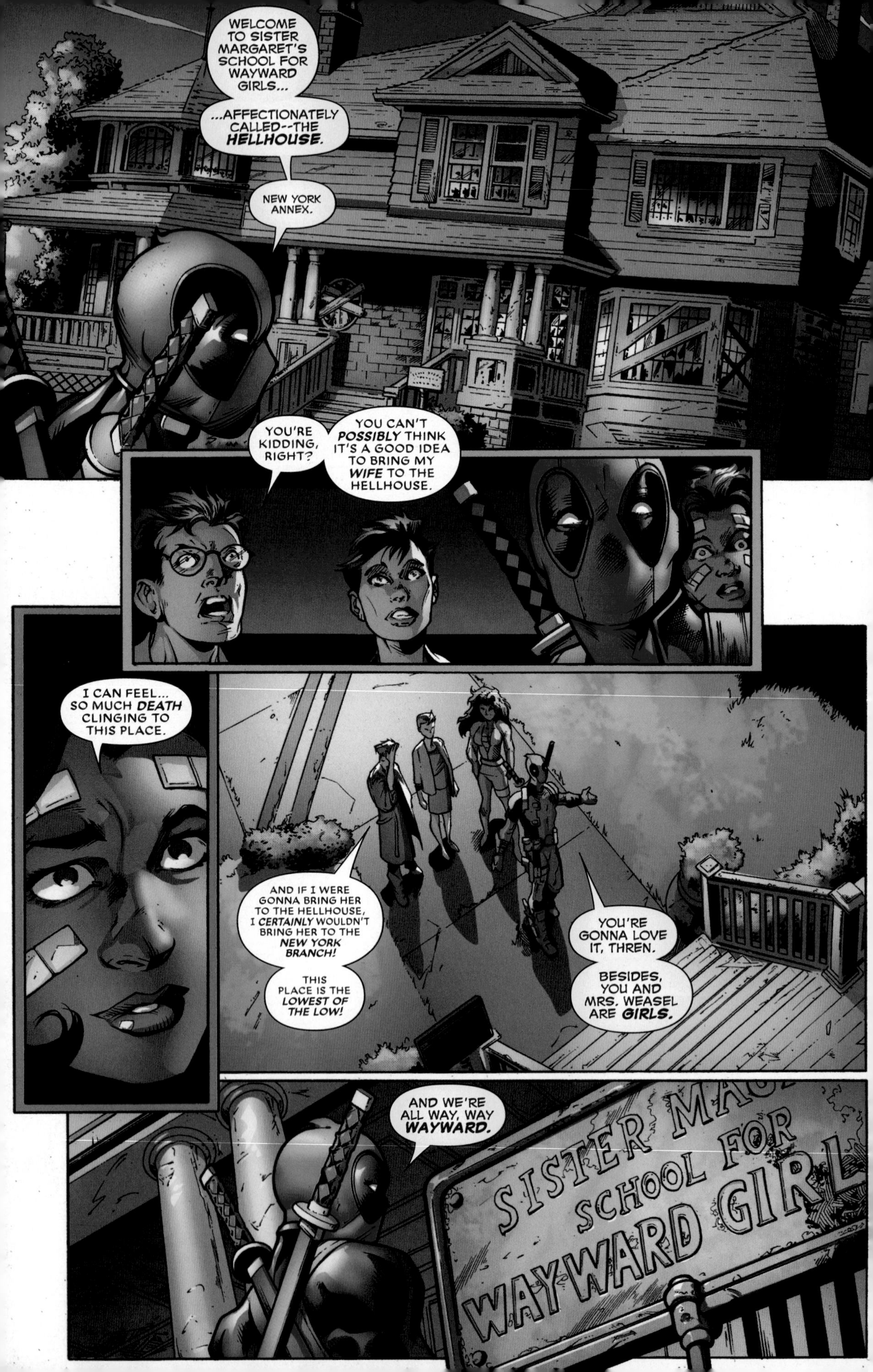
WELCOME TO SISTER MARGARET'S SCHOOL FOR WAYWARD GIRLS...
...AFFECTIONATELY CALLED--THE **HELLHOUSE**.
NEW YORK ANNEX.
YOU'RE KIDDING, RIGHT?
YOU CAN'T **POSSIBLY** THINK IT'S A GOOD IDEA TO BRING MY **WIFE** TO THE HELLHOUSE.
I CAN FEEL... SO MUCH **DEATH** CLINGING TO THIS PLACE.
AND IF I WERE GONNA BRING HER TO THE HELLHOUSE, I **CERTAINLY** WOULDN'T BRING HER TO THE **NEW YORK BRANCH!**
THIS PLACE IS THE **LOWEST OF THE LOW!**
YOU'RE GONNA LOVE IT, THREN.
BESIDES, YOU AND MRS. WEASEL ARE **GIRLS.**
AND WE'RE ALL WAY, WAY **WAYWARD.**
SISTER MA
SCHOOL FOR
WAYWARD GIRL

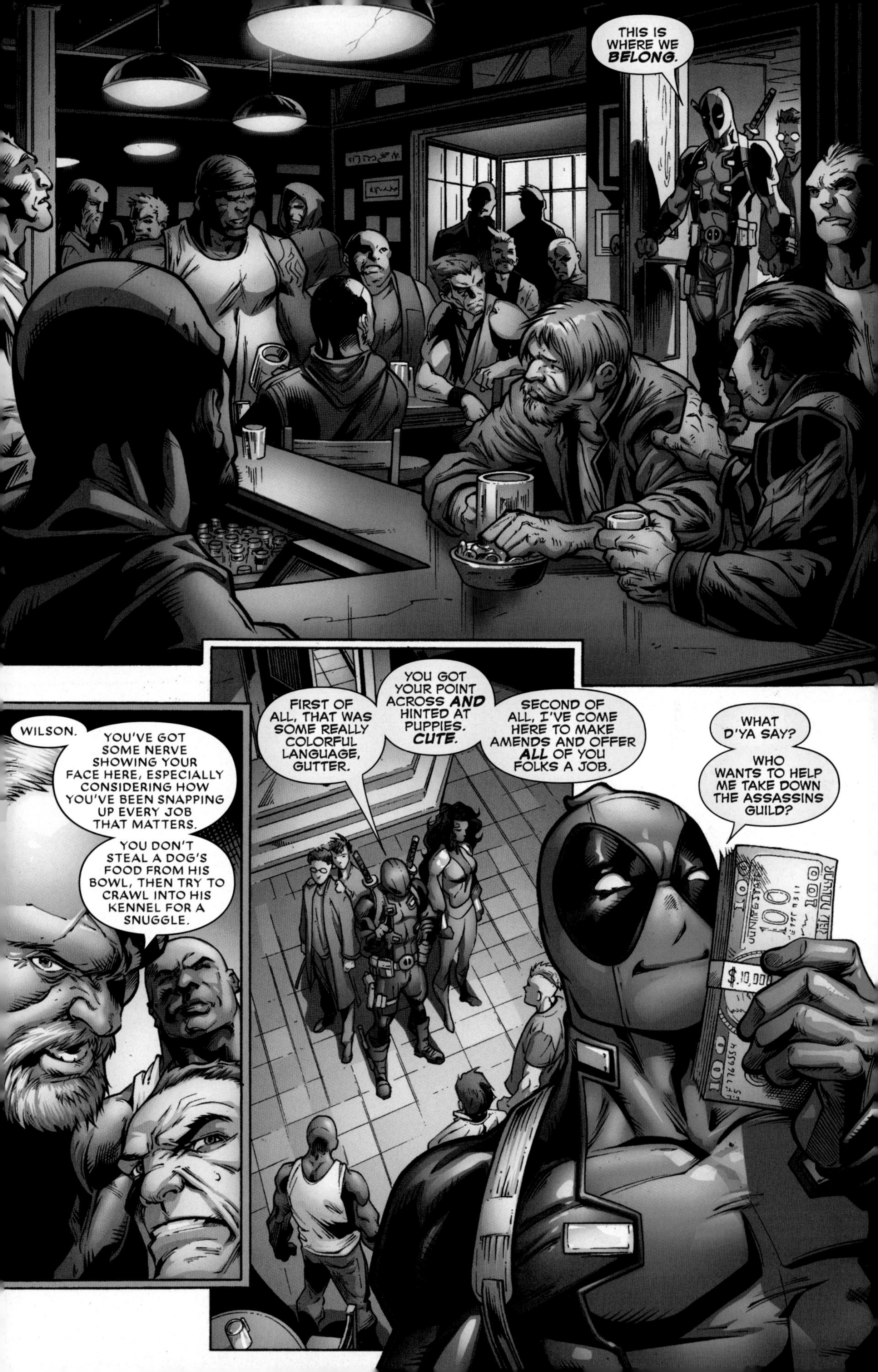
THIS IS WHERE WE BELONG.
WILSON.
YOU'VE GOT SOME NERVE SHOWING YOUR FACE HERE, ESPECIALLY CONSIDERING HOW YOU'VE BEEN SNAPPING UP EVERY JOB THAT MATTERS.
YOU DON'T STEAL A DOG'S FOOD FROM HIS BOWL, THEN TRY TO CRAWL INTO HIS KENNEL FOR A SNUGGLE.
FIRST OF ALL, THAT WAS SOME REALLY COLORFUL LANGUAGE, GUTTER.
YOU GOT YOUR POINT ACROSS AND HINTED AT PUPPIES. CUTE.
SECOND OF ALL, I'VE COME HERE TO MAKE AMENDS AND OFFER ALL OF YOU FOLKS A JOB.
WHAT D'YA SAY?
WHO WANTS TO HELP ME TAKE DOWN THE ASSASSINS GUILD?
$10,000

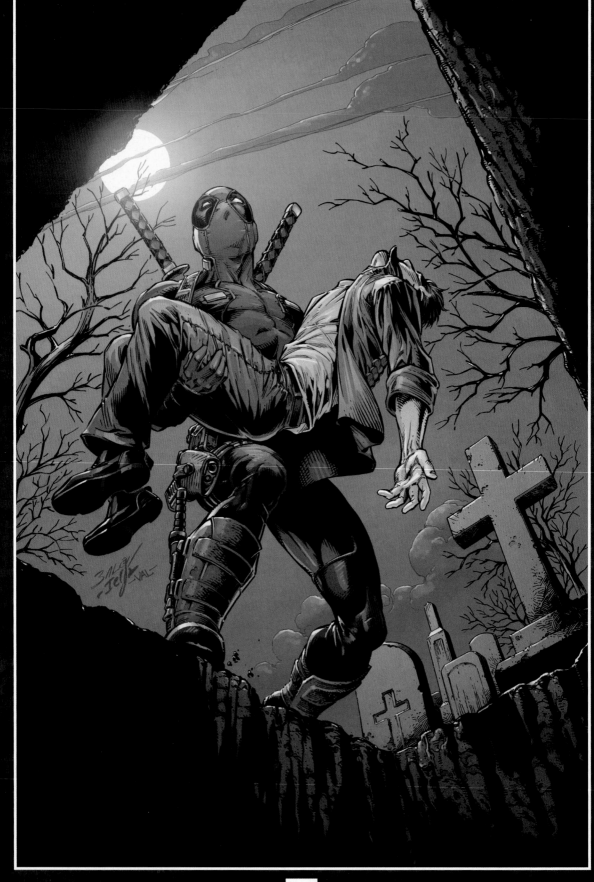

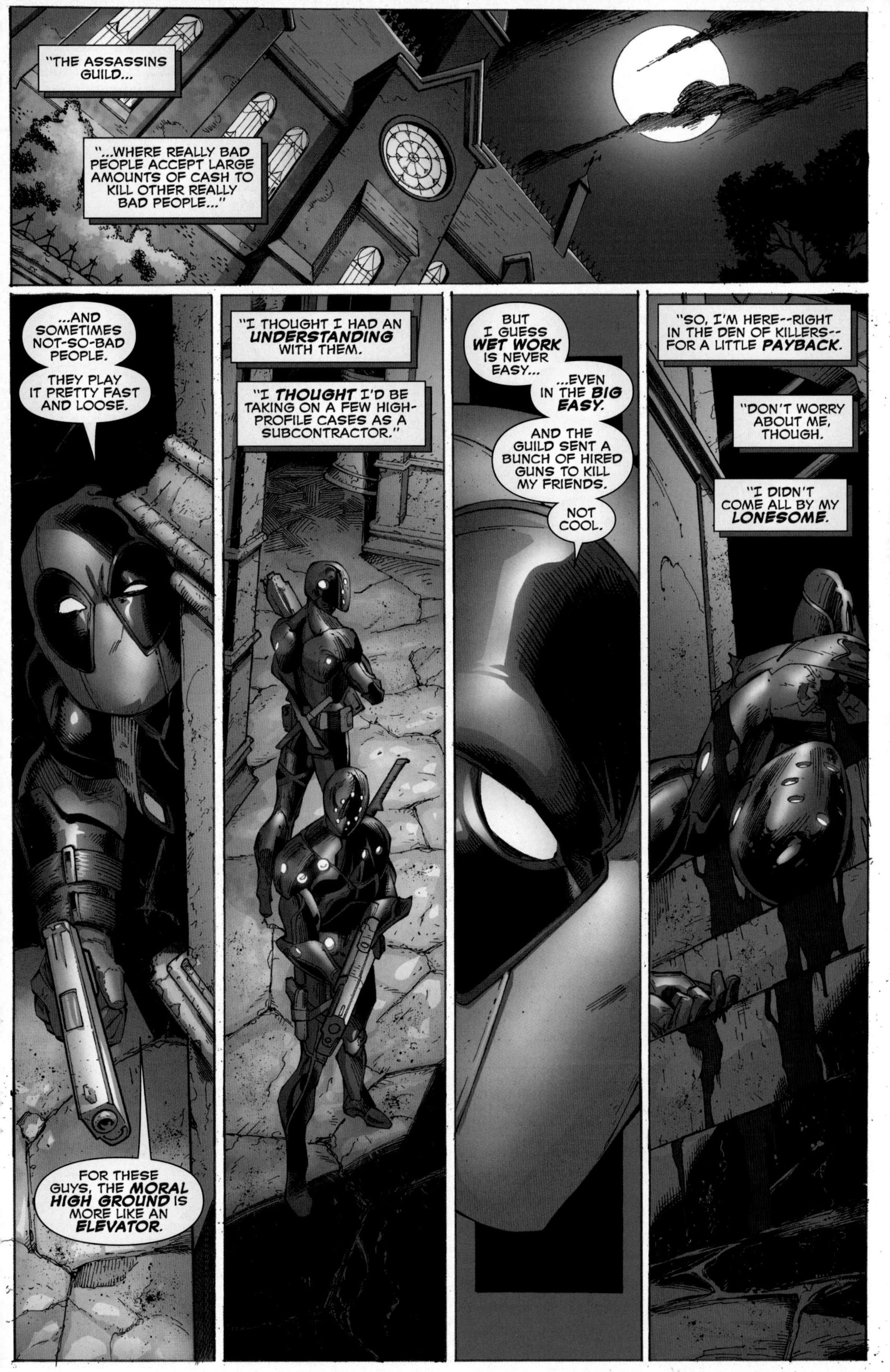
"THE ASSASSINS GUILD...
"...WHERE REALLY BAD PEOPLE ACCEPT LARGE AMOUNTS OF CASH TO KILL OTHER REALLY BAD PEOPLE..."
...AND SOMETIMES NOT-SO-BAD PEOPLE.
THEY PLAY IT PRETTY FAST AND LOOSE.
FOR THESE GUYS, THE MORAL HIGH GROUND IS MORE LIKE AN ELEVATOR.
"I THOUGHT I HAD AN UNDERSTANDING WITH THEM.
"I THOUGHT I'D BE TAKING ON A FEW HIGH-PROFILE CASES AS A SUBCONTRACTOR."
BUT I GUESS WET WORK IS NEVER EASY...
...EVEN IN THE BIG EASY.
AND THE GUILD SENT A BUNCH OF HIRED GUNS TO KILL MY FRIENDS.
NOT COOL.
"SO, I'M HERE--RIGHT IN THE DEN OF KILLERS--FOR A LITTLE PAYBACK.
"DON'T WORRY ABOUT ME, THOUGH.
"I DIDN'T COME ALL BY MY LONESOME.

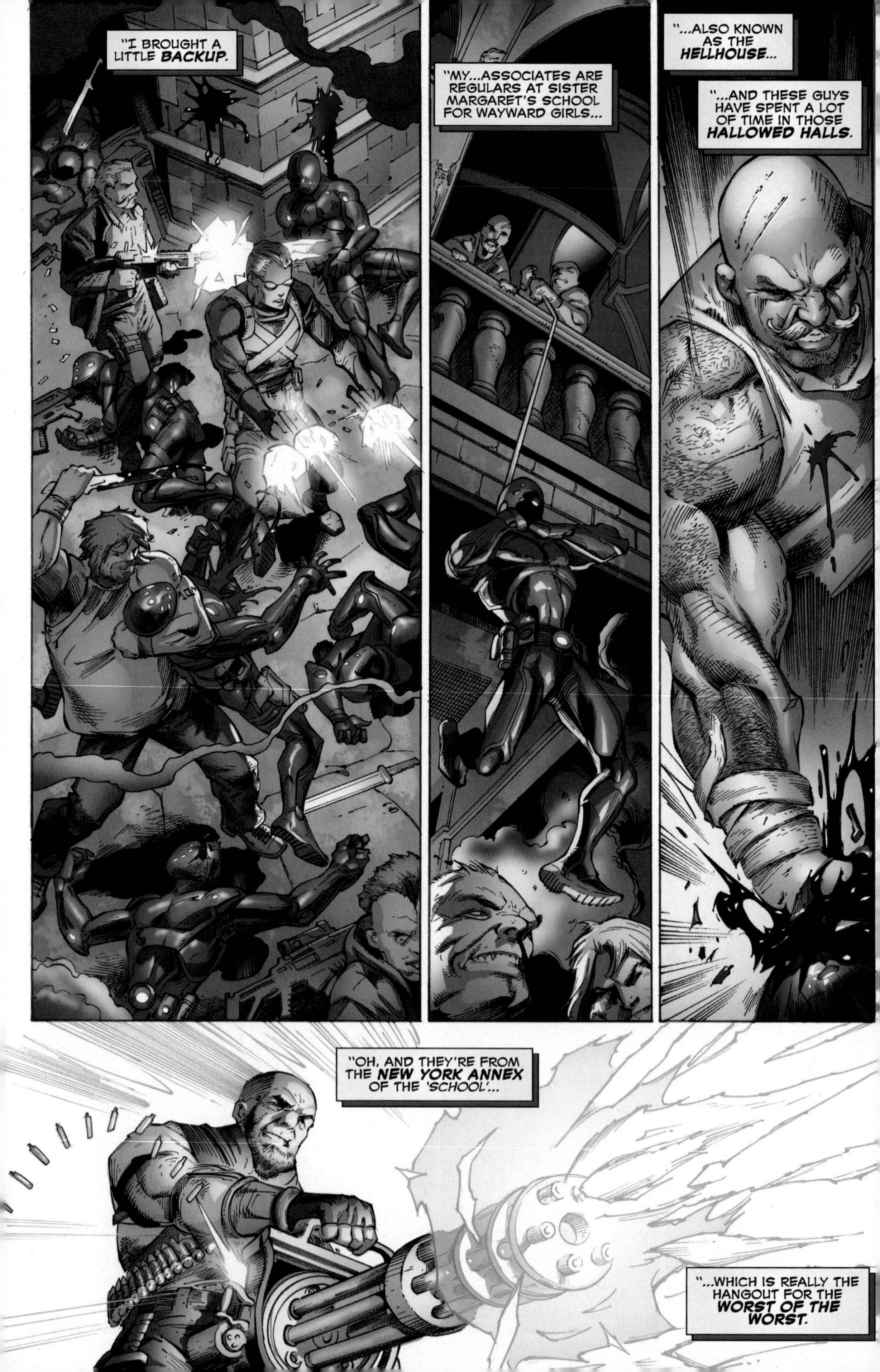
"I BROUGHT A LITTLE BACKUP.
"MY...ASSOCIATES ARE REGULARS AT SISTER MARGARET'S SCHOOL FOR WAYWARD GIRLS...
"...ALSO KNOWN AS THE HELLHOUSE...
"...AND THESE GUYS HAVE SPENT A LOT OF TIME IN THOSE HALLOWED HALLS.
"OH, AND THEY'RE FROM THE NEW YORK ANNEX OF THE 'SCHOOL'...
"...WHICH IS REALLY THE HANGOUT FOR THE WORST OF THE WORST.

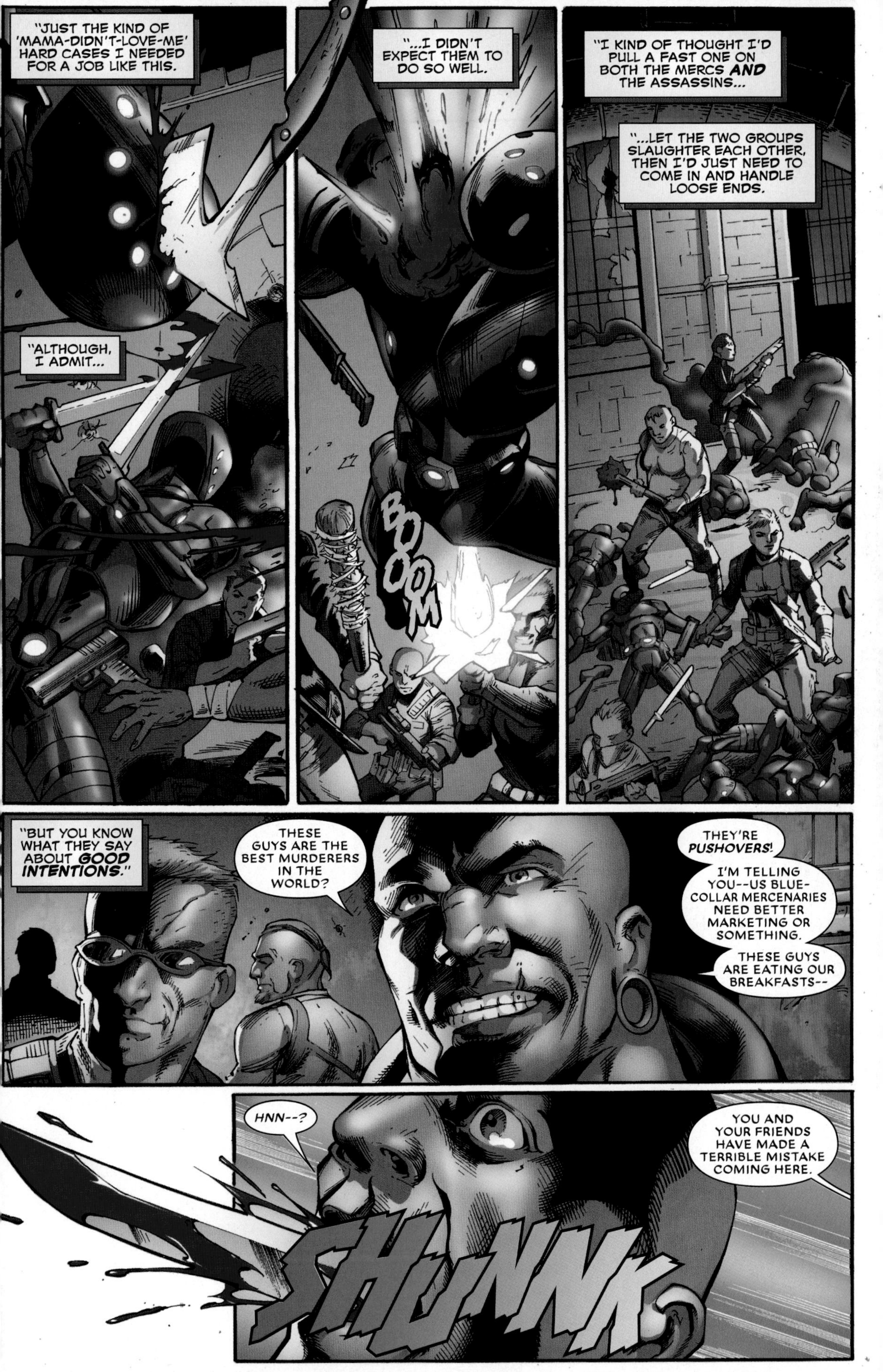
"JUST THE KIND OF 'MAMA-DIDN'T-LOVE-ME' HARD CASES I NEEDED FOR A JOB LIKE THIS.
"ALTHOUGH, I ADMIT...
"...I DIDN'T EXPECT THEM TO DO SO WELL.
BOOOOM
"I KIND OF THOUGHT I'D PULL A FAST ONE ON BOTH THE MERCS AND THE ASSASSINS...
"...LET THE TWO GROUPS SLAUGHTER EACH OTHER, THEN I'D JUST NEED TO COME IN AND HANDLE LOOSE ENDS.
"BUT YOU KNOW WHAT THEY SAY ABOUT GOOD INTENTIONS."
THESE GUYS ARE THE BEST MURDERERS IN THE WORLD?
THEY'RE PUSHOVERS!
I'M TELLING YOU--US BLUE-COLLAR MERCENARIES NEED BETTER MARKETING OR SOMETHING.
THESE GUYS ARE EATING OUR BREAKFASTS--
HNN--?
YOU AND YOUR FRIENDS HAVE MADE A TERRIBLE MISTAKE COMING HERE.
SHUNNK

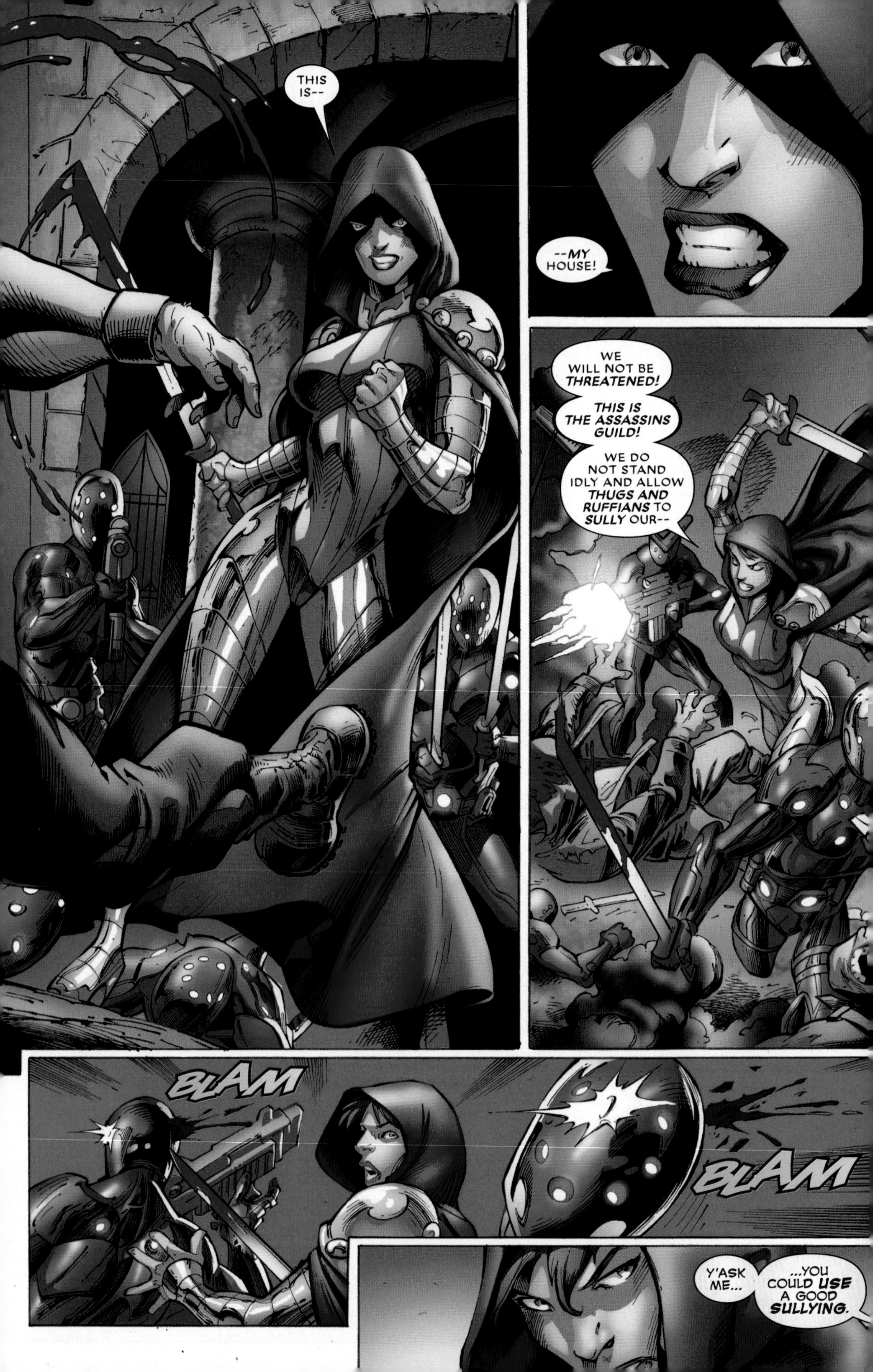

THIS IS--
--MY HOUSE!
WE WILL NOT BE THREATENED!
THIS IS THE ASSASSINS GUILD!
WE DO NOT STAND IDLY AND ALLOW THUGS AND RUFFIANS TO SULLY OUR--
BLAM
BLAM
Y'ASK ME...
...YOU COULD USE A GOOD SULLYING.

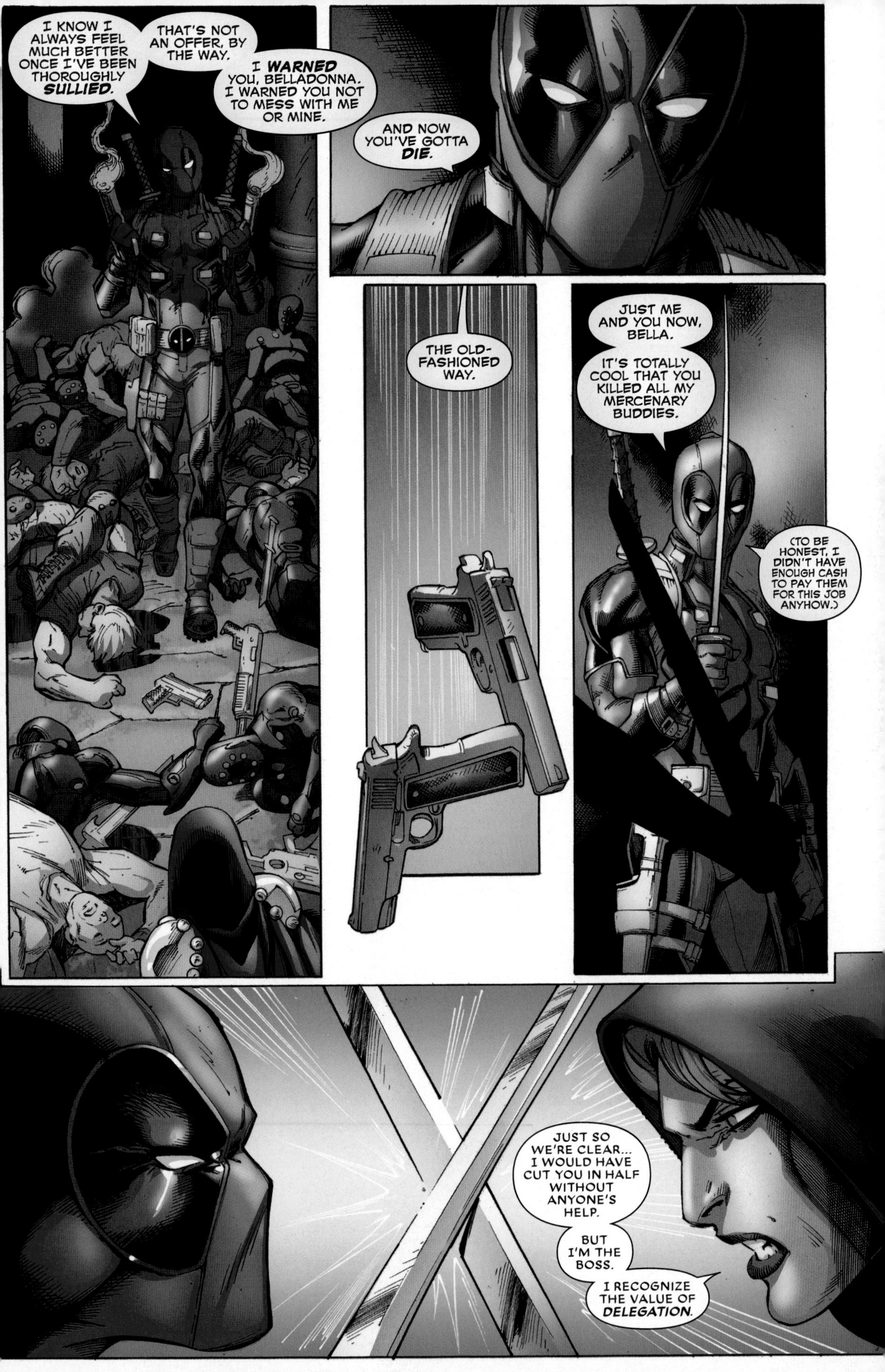

I KNOW I ALWAYS FEEL MUCH BETTER ONCE I'VE BEEN THOROUGHLY **SULLIED.**
THAT'S NOT AN OFFER, BY THE WAY.
I **WARNED** YOU, BELLADONNA. I WARNED YOU NOT TO MESS WITH ME OR MINE.
AND NOW YOU'VE GOTTA **DIE.**
THE OLD-FASHIONED WAY.
JUST ME AND YOU NOW, BELLA.
IT'S TOTALLY COOL THAT YOU KILLED ALL MY MERCENARY BUDDIES.
(TO BE HONEST, I DIDN'T HAVE ENOUGH CASH TO PAY THEM FOR THIS JOB ANYHOW.)
JUST SO WE'RE CLEAR... I WOULD HAVE CUT YOU IN HALF WITHOUT ANYONE'S HELP.
BUT I'M THE BOSS.
I RECOGNIZE THE VALUE OF **DELEGATION.**

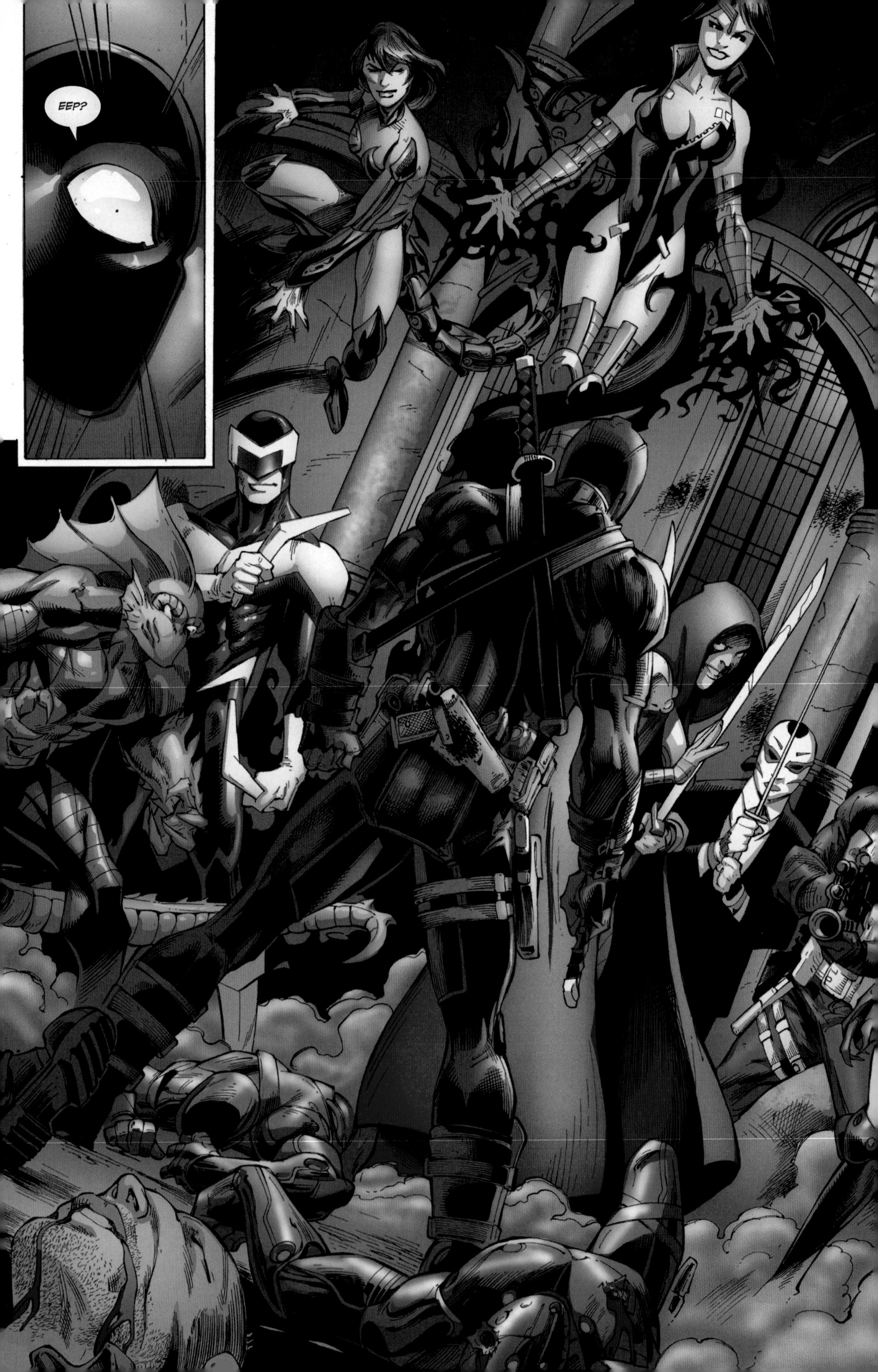
EEP?

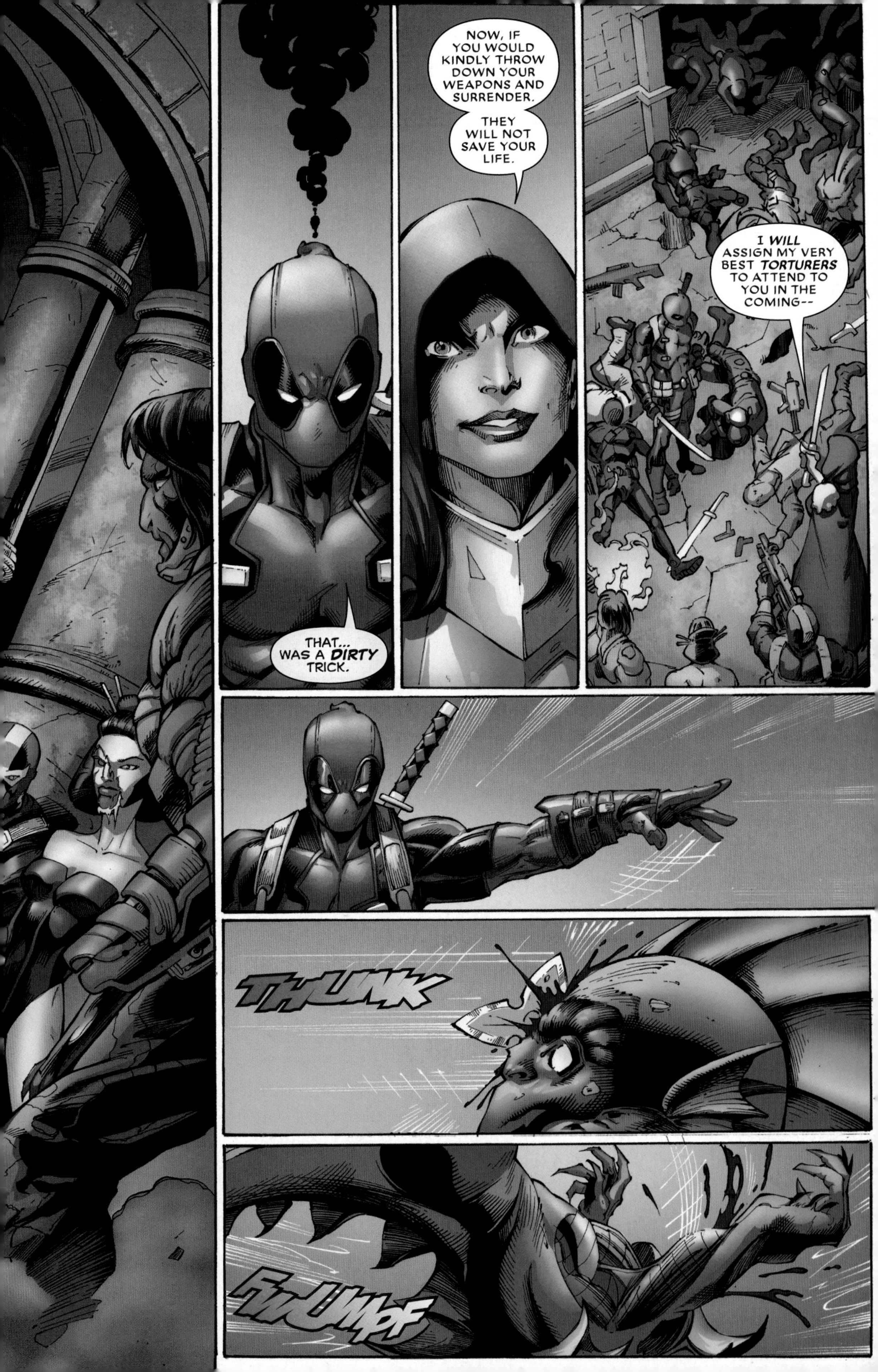
THAT... WAS A DIRTY TRICK.
NOW, IF YOU WOULD KINDLY THROW DOWN YOUR WEAPONS AND SURRENDER.
THEY WILL NOT SAVE YOUR LIFE.
I WILL ASSIGN MY VERY BEST TORTURERS TO ATTEND TO YOU IN THE COMING--
THUNK
FWUMPF

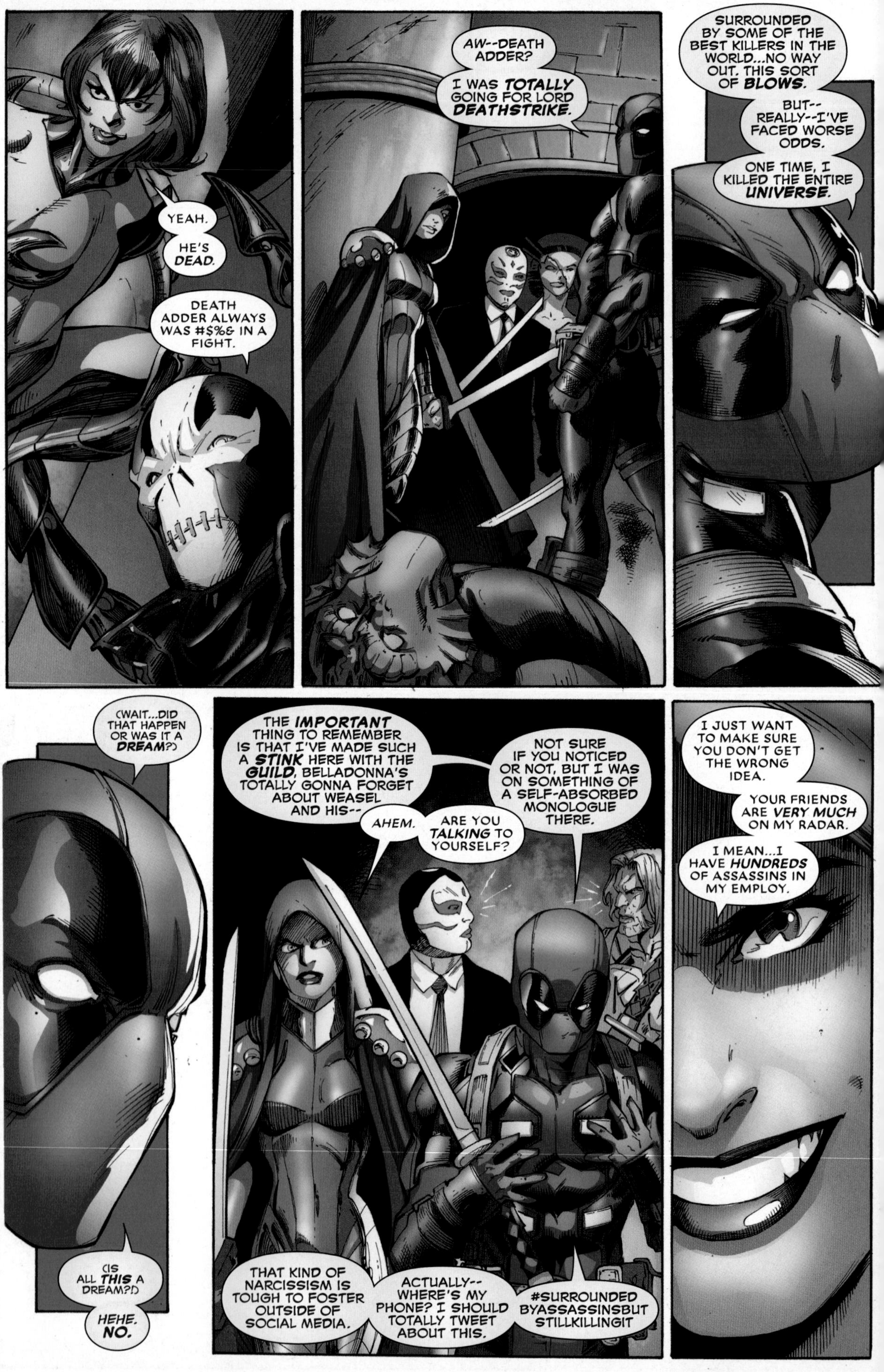
YEAH.
HE'S DEAD.
DEATH ADDER ALWAYS WAS #$%& IN A FIGHT.
AW--DEATH ADDER?
I WAS TOTALLY GOING FOR LORD DEATHSTRIKE.
SURROUNDED BY SOME OF THE BEST KILLERS IN THE WORLD...NO WAY OUT. THIS SORT OF BLOWS.
BUT--REALLY--I'VE FACED WORSE ODDS.
ONE TIME, I KILLED THE ENTIRE UNIVERSE.
(WAIT...DID THAT HAPPEN OR WAS IT A DREAM?)
(IS ALL THIS A DREAM?!)
HEHE. NO.
THE IMPORTANT THING TO REMEMBER IS THAT I'VE MADE SUCH A STINK HERE WITH THE GUILD, BELLADONNA'S TOTALLY GONNA FORGET ABOUT WEASEL AND HIS--
AHEM.
ARE YOU TALKING TO YOURSELF?
NOT SURE IF YOU NOTICED OR NOT, BUT I WAS ON SOMETHING OF A SELF-ABSORBED MONOLOGUE THERE.
THAT KIND OF NARCISSISM IS TOUGH TO FOSTER OUTSIDE OF SOCIAL MEDIA.
ACTUALLY--WHERE'S MY PHONE? I SHOULD TOTALLY TWEET ABOUT THIS.
#SURROUNDEDBYASSASSINSBUTSTILLKILLINGIT
I JUST WANT TO MAKE SURE YOU DON'T GET THE WRONG IDEA.
YOUR FRIENDS ARE VERY MUCH ON MY RADAR.
I MEAN...I HAVE HUNDREDS OF ASSASSINS IN MY EMPLOY.

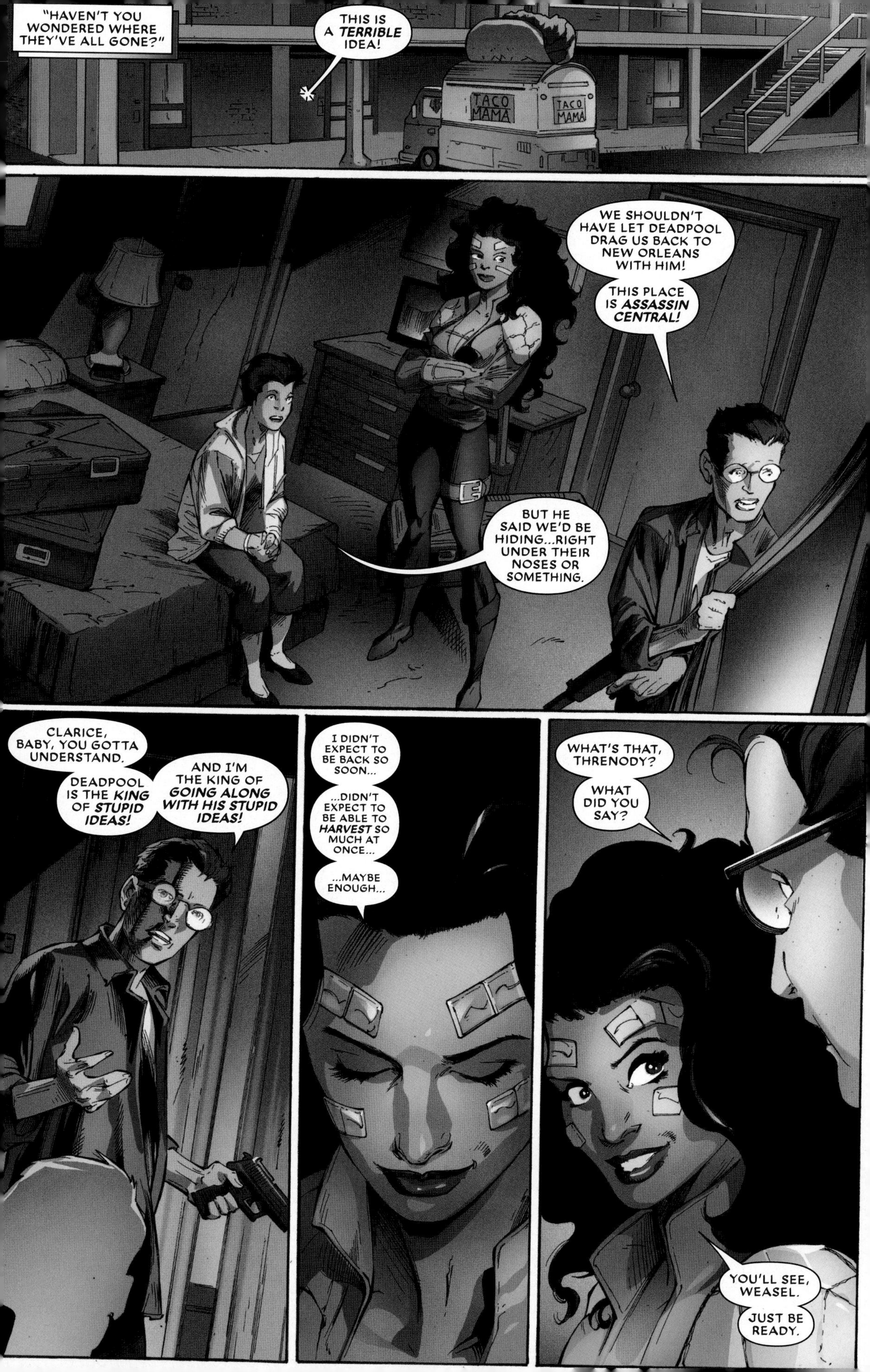
"HAVEN'T YOU WONDERED WHERE THEY'VE ALL GONE?"
THIS IS A TERRIBLE IDEA!
TACO MAMA
TACO MAMA
WE SHOULDN'T HAVE LET DEADPOOL DRAG US BACK TO NEW ORLEANS WITH HIM!
THIS PLACE IS ASSASSIN CENTRAL!
BUT HE SAID WE'D BE HIDING...RIGHT UNDER THEIR NOSES OR SOMETHING.
CLARICE, BABY, YOU GOTTA UNDERSTAND.
DEADPOOL IS THE KING OF STUPID IDEAS!
AND I'M THE KING OF GOING ALONG WITH HIS STUPID IDEAS!
I DIDN'T EXPECT TO BE BACK SO SOON...
...DIDN'T EXPECT TO BE ABLE TO HARVEST SO MUCH AT ONCE...
...MAYBE ENOUGH...
WHAT'S THAT, THRENODY?
WHAT DID YOU SAY?
YOU'LL SEE, WEASEL.
JUST BE READY.

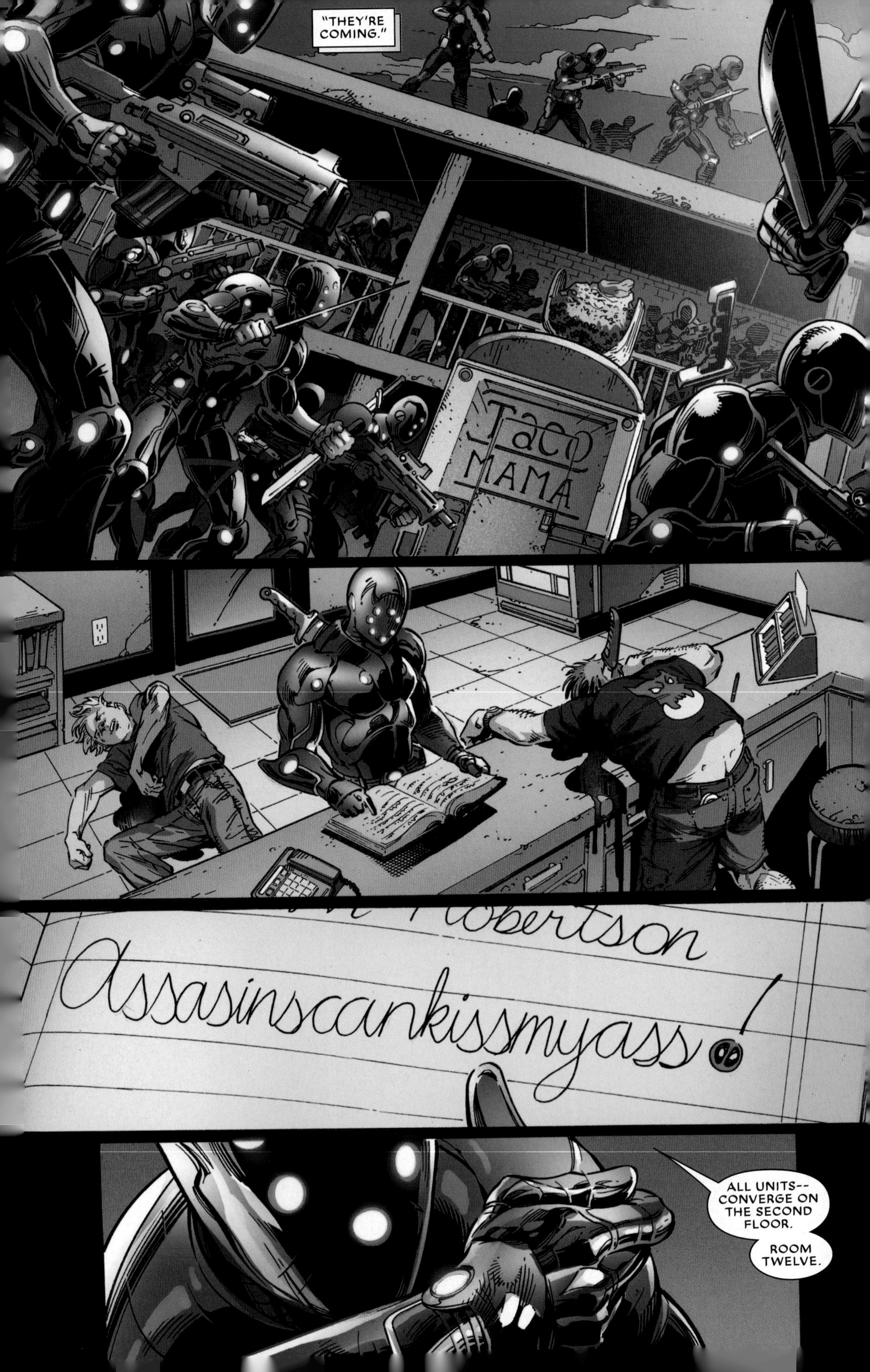
"THEY'RE COMING."
TACO MAMA
Robertson
Assasinscankissmyass!
ALL UNITS-- CONVERGE ON THE SECOND FLOOR.
ROOM TWELVE.

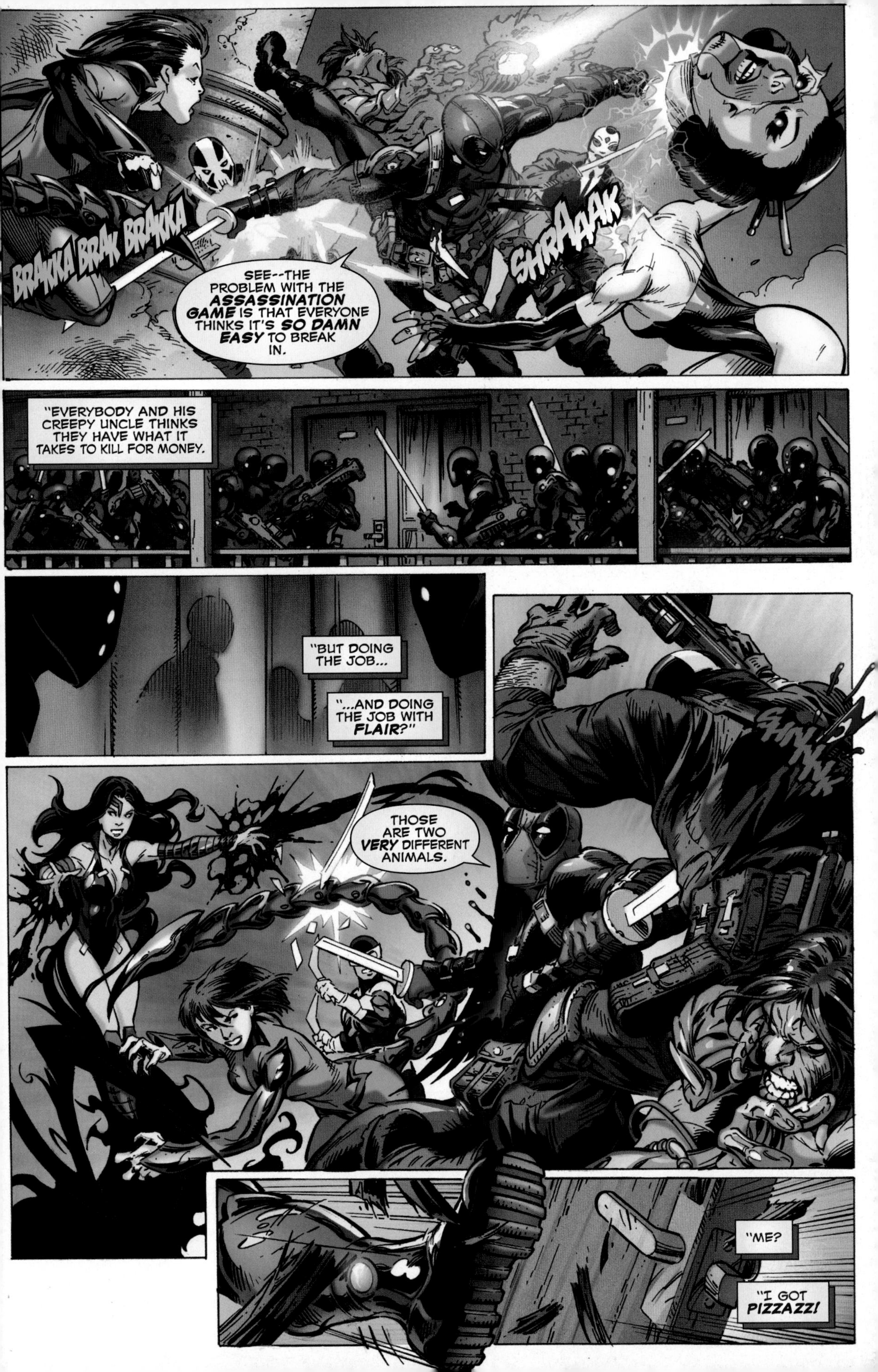
BRAKKA BRAK BRAKKA
SEE--THE PROBLEM WITH THE ASSASSINATION GAME IS THAT EVERYONE THINKS IT'S SO DAMN EASY TO BREAK IN.
SHRAAAK
"EVERYBODY AND HIS CREEPY UNCLE THINKS THEY HAVE WHAT IT TAKES TO KILL FOR MONEY.
"BUT DOING THE JOB...
"...AND DOING THE JOB WITH FLAIR?"
THOSE ARE TWO VERY DIFFERENT ANIMALS.
"ME?
"I GOT PIZZAZZ!

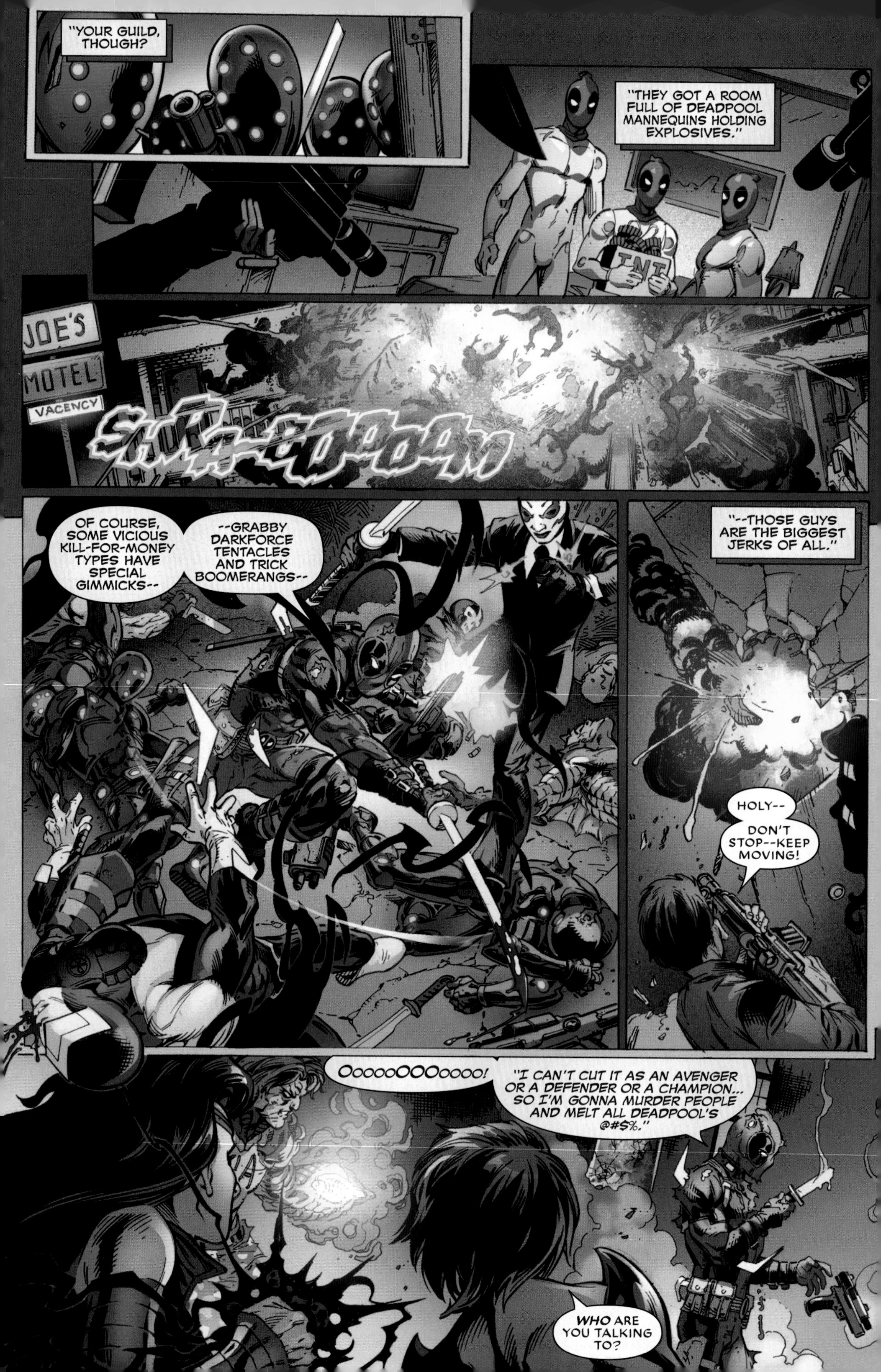
"YOUR GUILD, THOUGH?
"THEY GOT A ROOM FULL OF DEADPOOL MANNEQUINS HOLDING EXPLOSIVES."
TNT
JOE'S
MOTEL
VACANCY
SHRA-BOOOOM
OF COURSE, SOME VICIOUS KILL-FOR-MONEY TYPES HAVE SPECIAL GIMMICKS--
--GRABBY DARKFORCE TENTACLES AND TRICK BOOMERANGS--
"--THOSE GUYS ARE THE BIGGEST JERKS OF ALL."
HOLY--
DON'T STOP--KEEP MOVING!
OooooOOOoooo!
"I CAN'T CUT IT AS AN AVENGER OR A DEFENDER OR A CHAMPION... SO I'M GONNA MURDER PEOPLE AND MELT ALL DEADPOOL'S @#$%."
WHO ARE YOU TALKING TO?

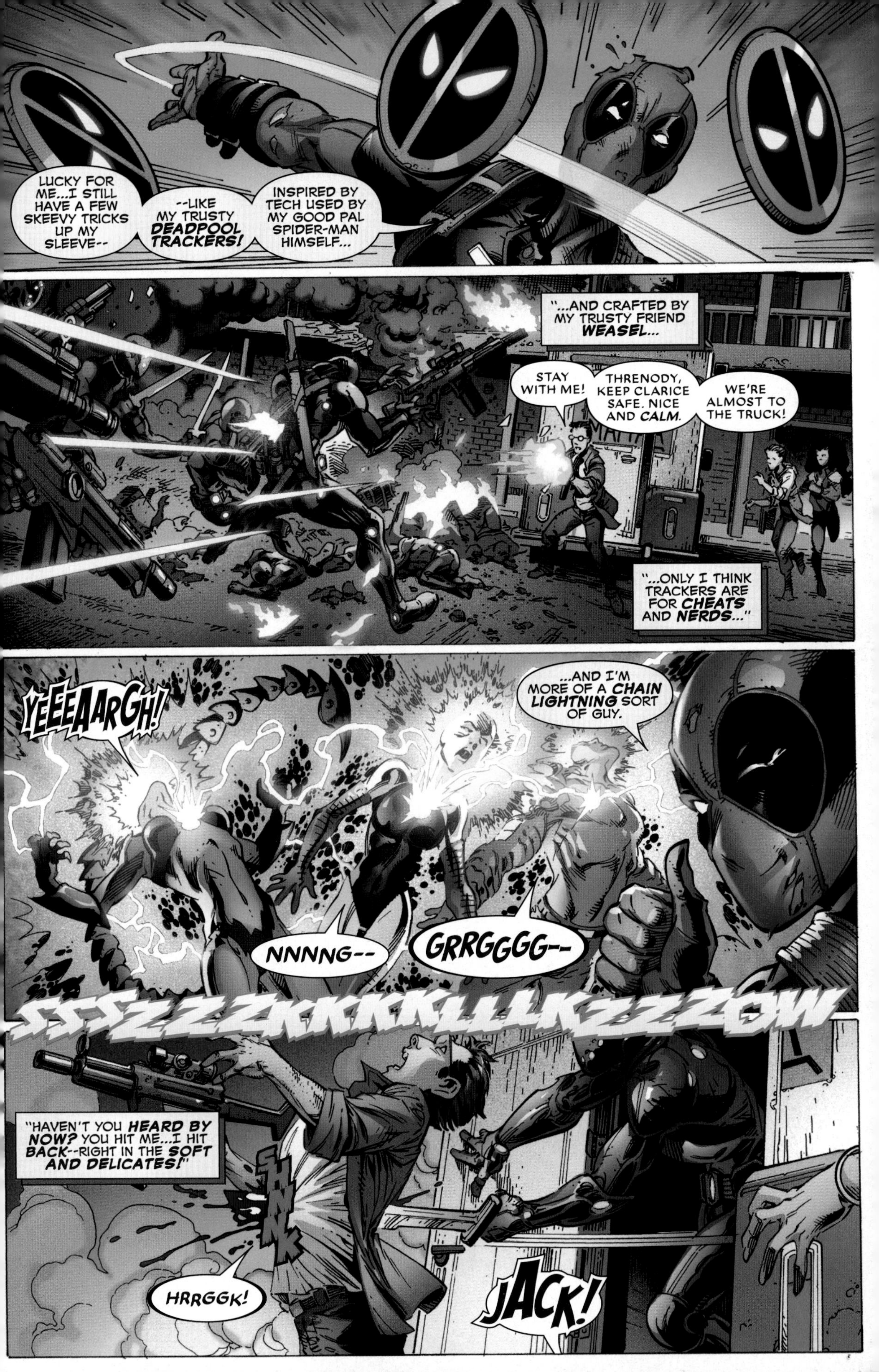

LUCKY FOR ME...I STILL HAVE A FEW SKEEVY TRICKS UP MY SLEEVE--
--LIKE MY TRUSTY DEADPOOL TRACKERS!
INSPIRED BY TECH USED BY MY GOOD PAL SPIDER-MAN HIMSELF...
"...AND CRAFTED BY MY TRUSTY FRIEND WEASEL...
STAY WITH ME!
THRENODY, KEEP CLARICE SAFE. NICE AND CALM.
WE'RE ALMOST TO THE TRUCK!
"...ONLY I THINK TRACKERS ARE FOR CHEATS AND NERDS..."
YEEEAARGH!
...AND I'M MORE OF A CHAIN LIGHTNING SORT OF GUY.
NNNNG--
GRRGGGG--
SSSZZZKKKKLLLLKZZZZOW
"HAVEN'T YOU HEARD BY NOW? YOU HIT ME...I HIT BACK--RIGHT IN THE SOFT AND DELICATES!"
SHNK
HRRGGK!
JACK!

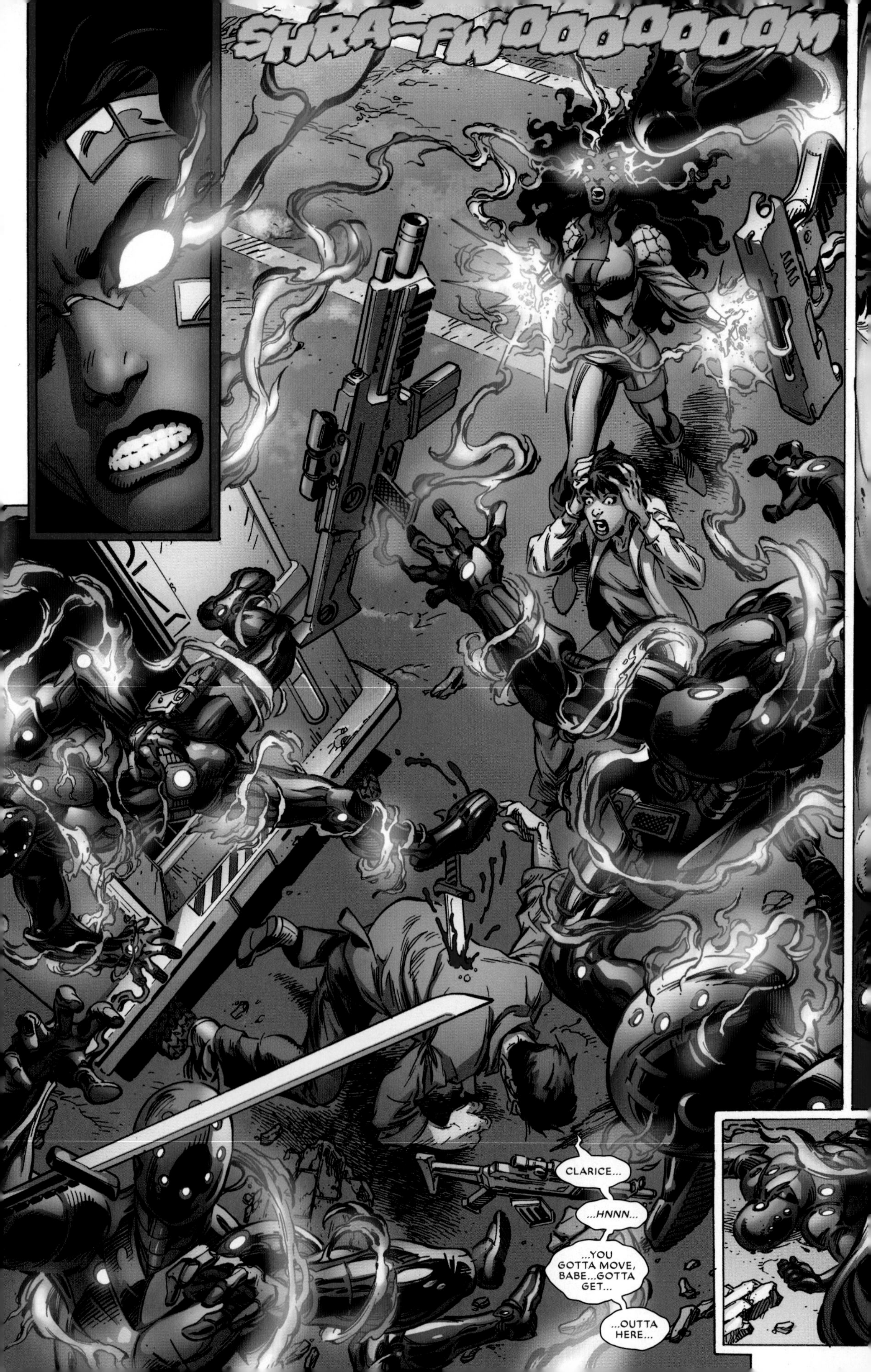
SHRA-FWOOOOOOOM
CLARICE...
...HNNN...
...YOU GOTTA MOVE, BABE...GOTTA GET...
...OUTTA HERE...

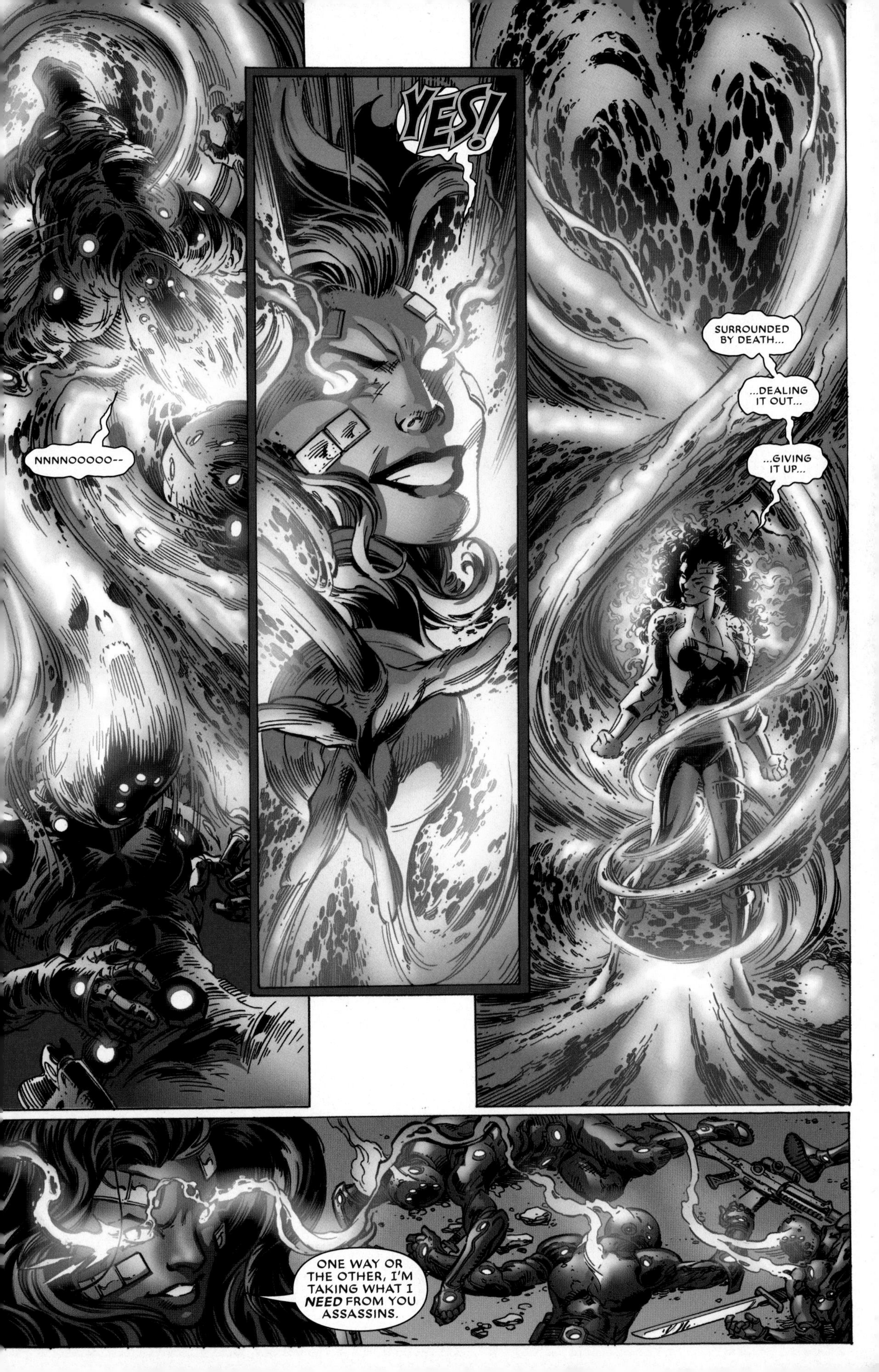
NNNNOOOOO--
YES!
SURROUNDED BY DEATH...
...DEALING IT OUT...
...GIVING IT UP...
ONE WAY OR THE OTHER, I'M TAKING WHAT I NEED FROM YOU ASSASSINS.

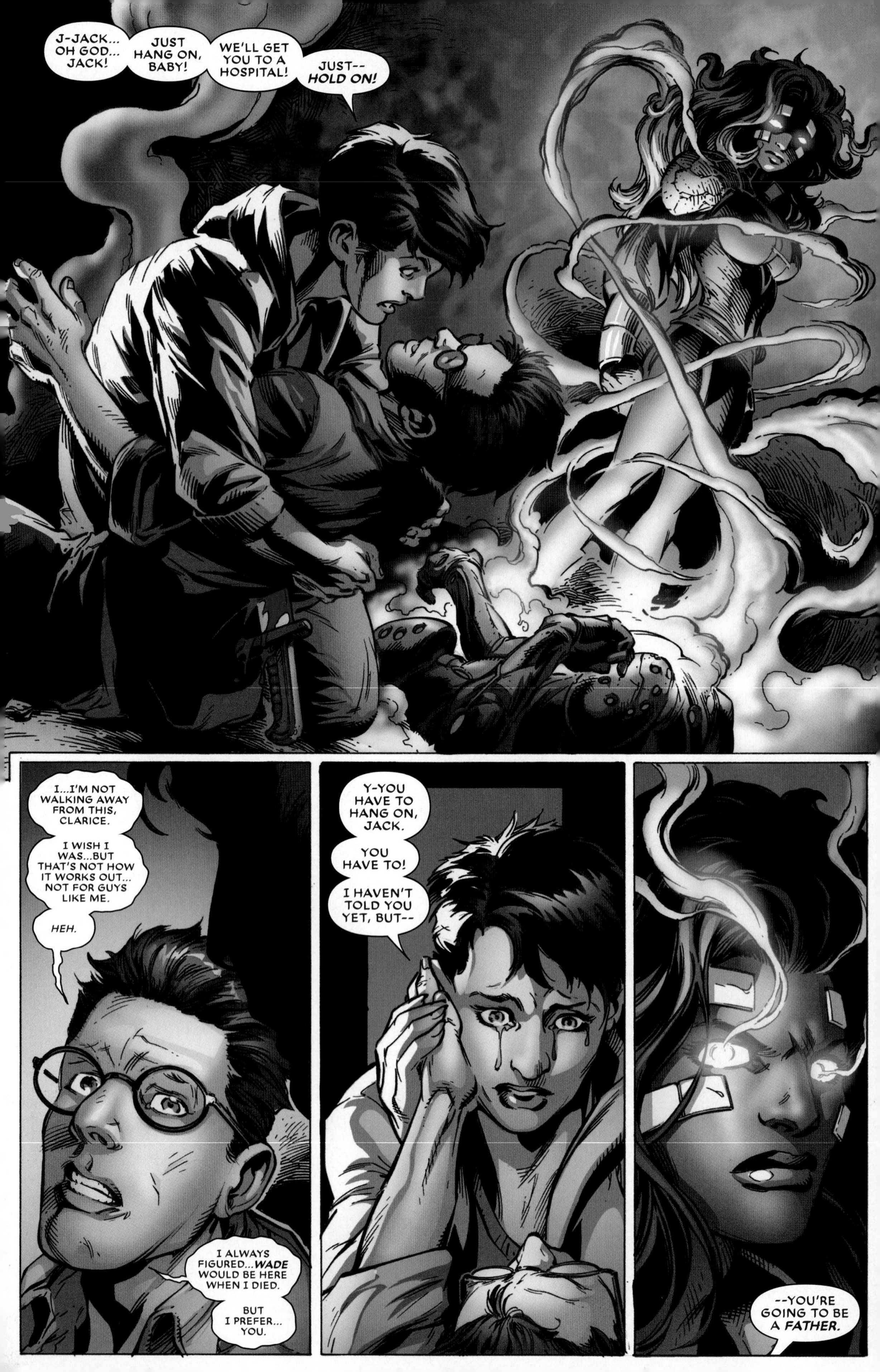
J-JACK... OH GOD... JACK!
JUST HANG ON, BABY!
WE'LL GET YOU TO A HOSPITAL!
JUST-- *HOLD ON!*
I...I'M NOT WALKING AWAY FROM THIS, CLARICE.
I WISH I WAS...BUT THAT'S NOT HOW IT WORKS OUT... NOT FOR GUYS LIKE ME.
HEH.
I ALWAYS FIGURED...*WADE* WOULD BE HERE WHEN I DIED.
BUT I PREFER... YOU.
Y-YOU HAVE TO HANG ON, JACK.
YOU HAVE TO!
I HAVEN'T TOLD YOU YET, BUT--
--YOU'RE GOING TO BE A *FATHER.*

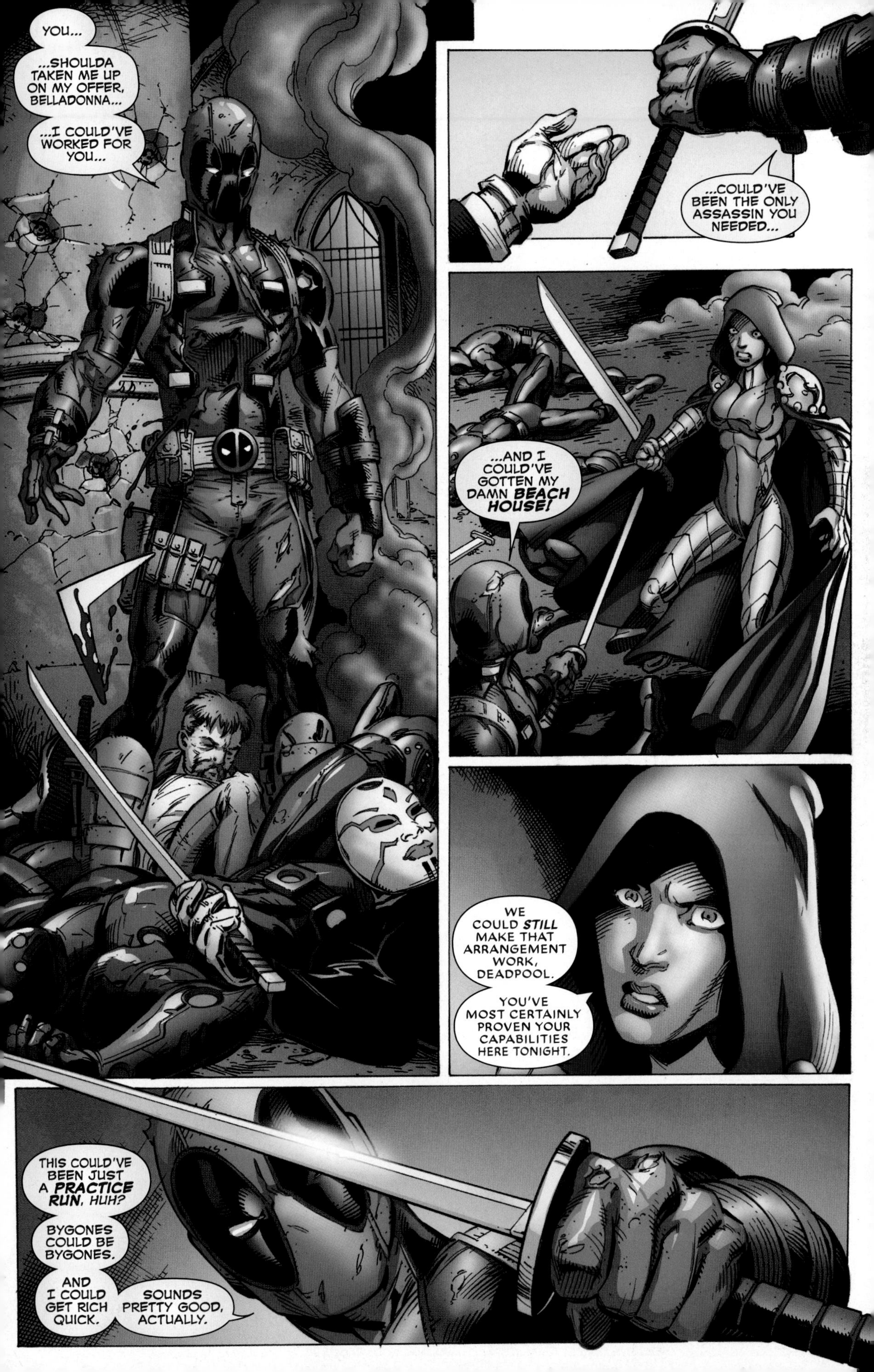
YOU...
...SHOULDA TAKEN ME UP ON MY OFFER, BELLADONNA...
...I COULD'VE WORKED FOR YOU...
...COULD'VE BEEN THE ONLY ASSASSIN YOU NEEDED...
...AND I COULD'VE GOTTEN MY DAMN BEACH HOUSE!
WE COULD STILL MAKE THAT ARRANGEMENT WORK, DEADPOOL.
YOU'VE MOST CERTAINLY PROVEN YOUR CAPABILITIES HERE TONIGHT.
THIS COULD'VE BEEN JUST A PRACTICE RUN, HUH?
BYGONES COULD BE BYGONES.
AND I COULD GET RICH QUICK.
SOUNDS PRETTY GOOD, ACTUALLY.

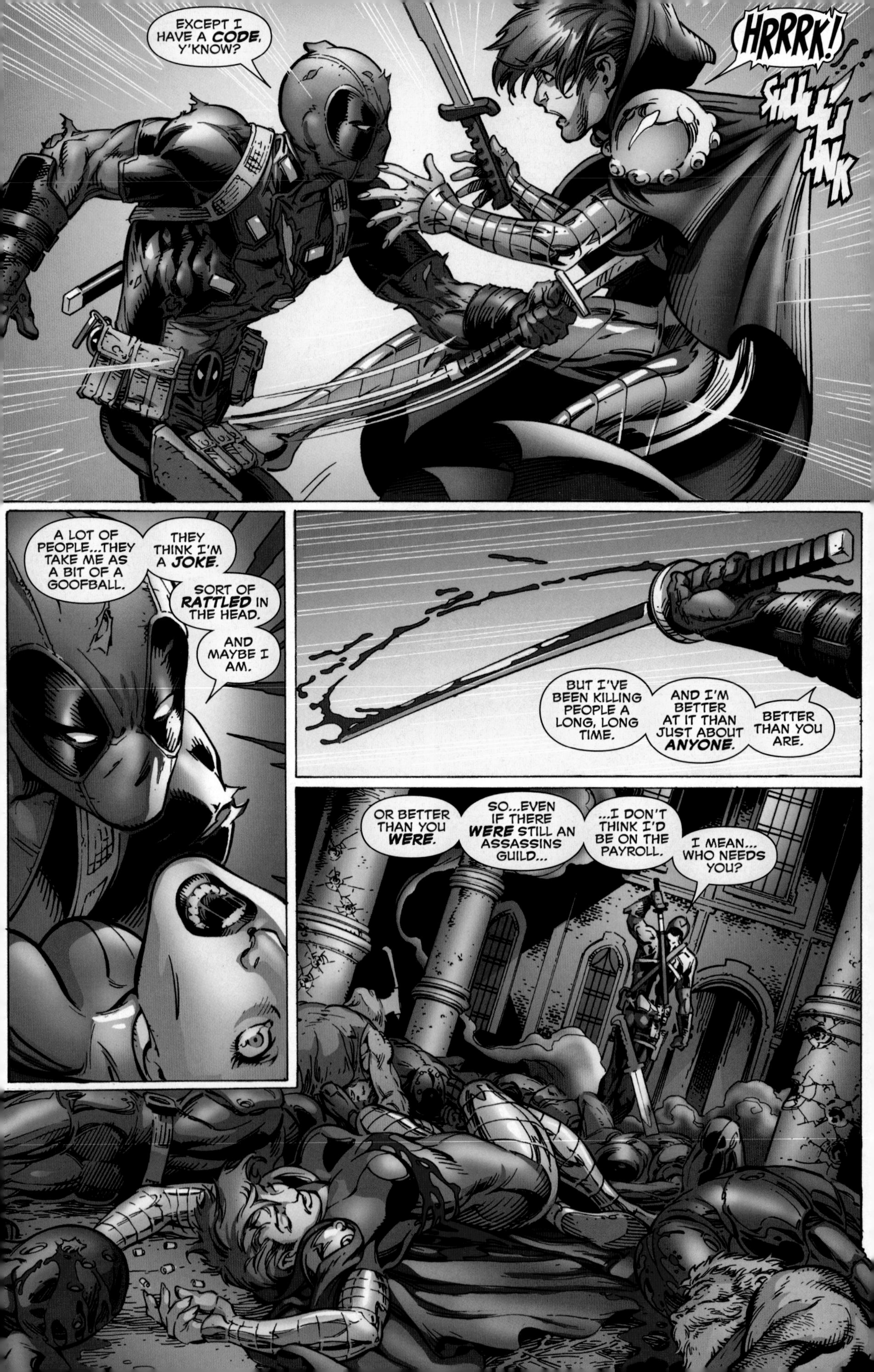
EXCEPT I HAVE A CODE, Y'KNOW?
HRRRK!
SHULUNK
A LOT OF PEOPLE...THEY TAKE ME AS A BIT OF A GOOFBALL.
THEY THINK I'M A JOKE.
SORT OF RATTLED IN THE HEAD.
AND MAYBE I AM.
BUT I'VE BEEN KILLING PEOPLE A LONG, LONG TIME.
AND I'M BETTER AT IT THAN JUST ABOUT ANYONE.
BETTER THAN YOU ARE.
OR BETTER THAN YOU WERE.
SO...EVEN IF THERE WERE STILL AN ASSASSINS GUILD...
...I DON'T THINK I'D BE ON THE PAYROLL.
I MEAN... WHO NEEDS YOU?

"AFTER ALL, WEASEL IS MY CO-PILOT."

MOTEL 7

WEASEL!

YOU...

...YOU'VE GOT A SWORD STUCK IN YOU!

≠GASP≠

WEASEL?

YOU'RE A--

W-WADE...

...WADE... THRENODY...

...SHE TOOK CLARICE, WADE...

...SHE TOOK HER...AND YOU HAVE TO FIND HER...

...I ALWAYS KNEW...

...I'D DIE... LOOKING AT...

...YOUR UGLY MUG...

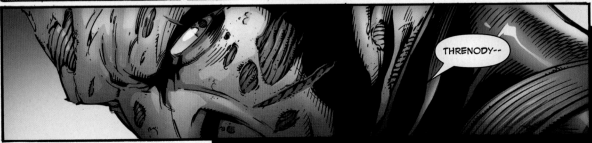

THRENODY--

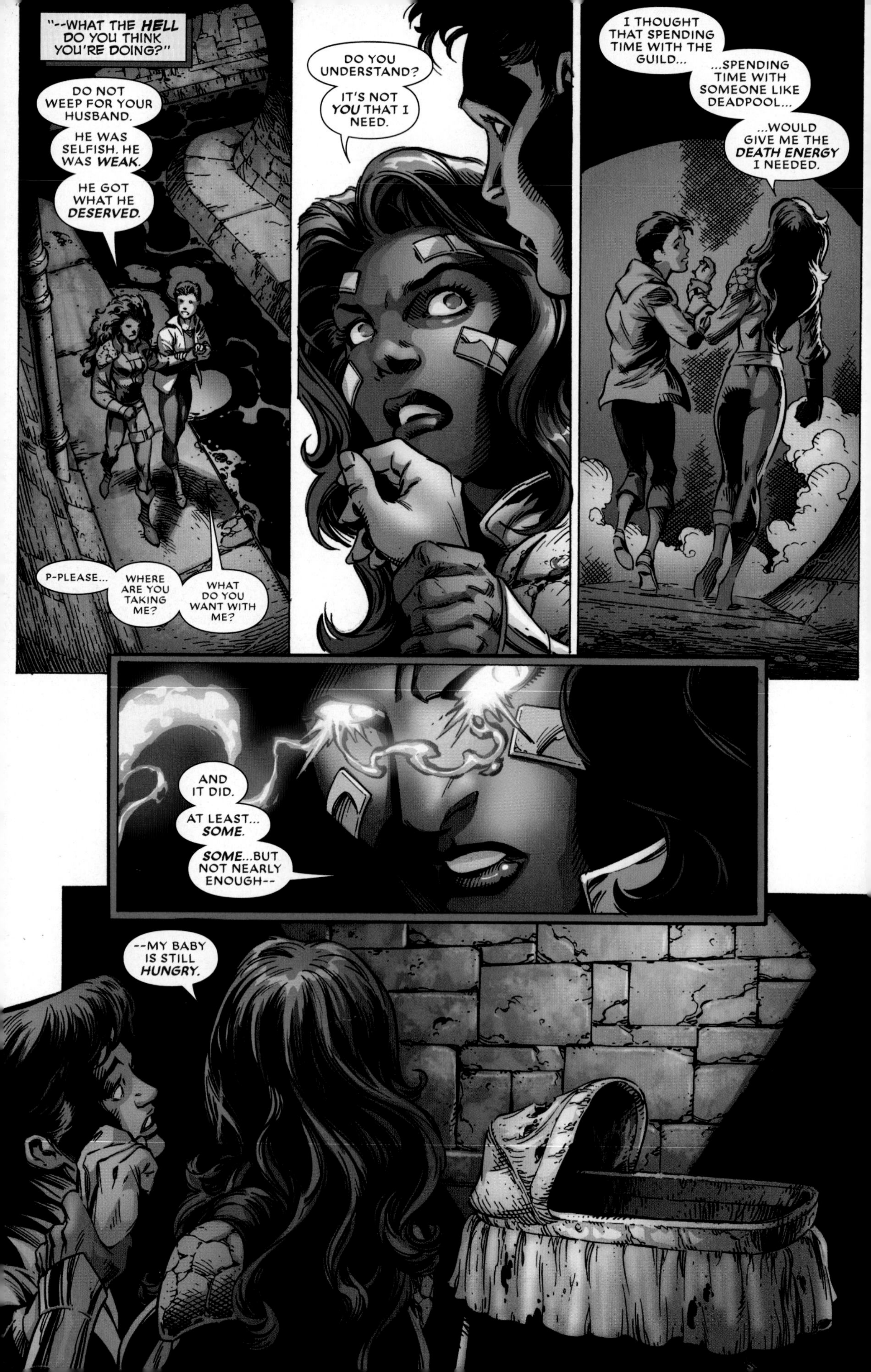
"--WHAT THE HELL DO YOU THINK YOU'RE DOING?"
DO NOT WEEP FOR YOUR HUSBAND.
HE WAS SELFISH. HE WAS WEAK.
HE GOT WHAT HE DESERVED.
P-PLEASE...
WHERE ARE YOU TAKING ME?
WHAT DO YOU WANT WITH ME?
DO YOU UNDERSTAND?
IT'S NOT YOU THAT I NEED.
I THOUGHT THAT SPENDING TIME WITH THE GUILD...
...SPENDING TIME WITH SOMEONE LIKE DEADPOOL...
...WOULD GIVE ME THE DEATH ENERGY I NEEDED.
AND IT DID.
AT LEAST... SOME.
SOME...BUT NOT NEARLY ENOUGH--
--MY BABY IS STILL HUNGRY.

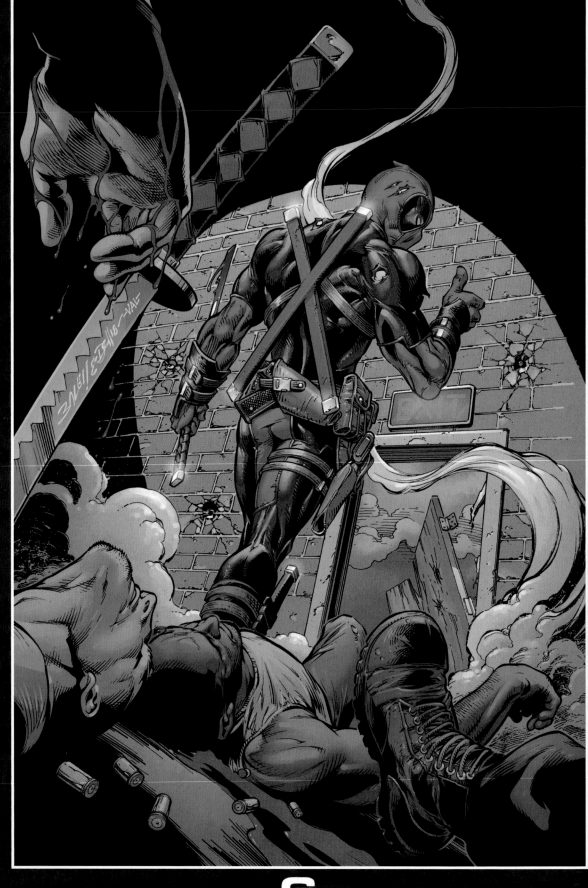

6

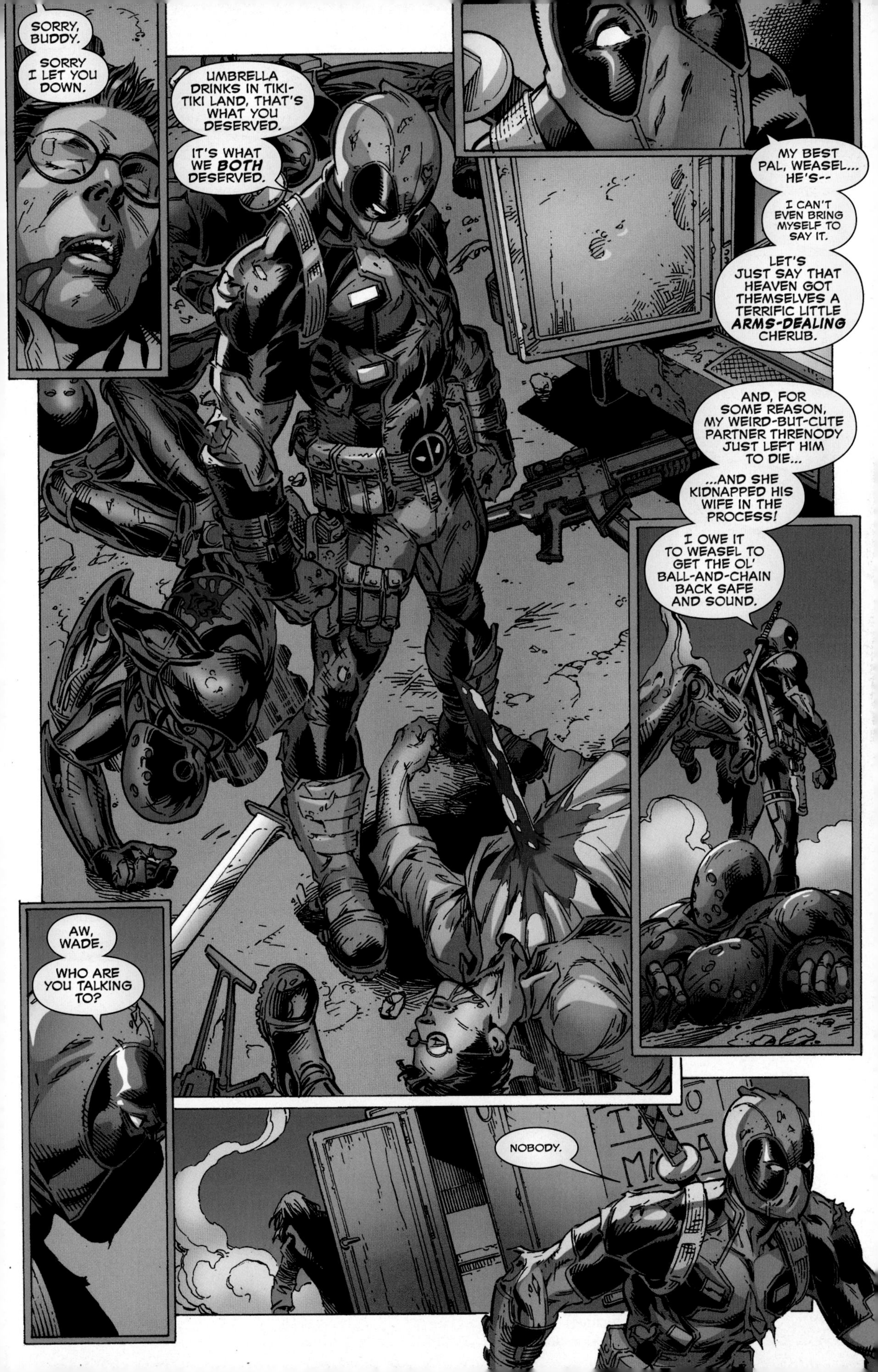
SORRY, BUDDY.
SORRY I LET YOU DOWN.
UMBRELLA DRINKS IN TIKI-TIKI LAND, THAT'S WHAT YOU DESERVED.
IT'S WHAT WE BOTH DESERVED.
MY BEST PAL, WEASEL... HE'S--
I CAN'T EVEN BRING MYSELF TO SAY IT.
LET'S JUST SAY THAT HEAVEN GOT THEMSELVES A TERRIFIC LITTLE ARMS-DEALING CHERUB.
AND, FOR SOME REASON, MY WEIRD-BUT-CUTE PARTNER THRENODY JUST LEFT HIM TO DIE...
...AND SHE KIDNAPPED HIS WIFE IN THE PROCESS!
I OWE IT TO WEASEL TO GET THE OL' BALL-AND-CHAIN BACK SAFE AND SOUND.
AW, WADE.
WHO ARE YOU TALKING TO?
NOBODY.
TACO MA

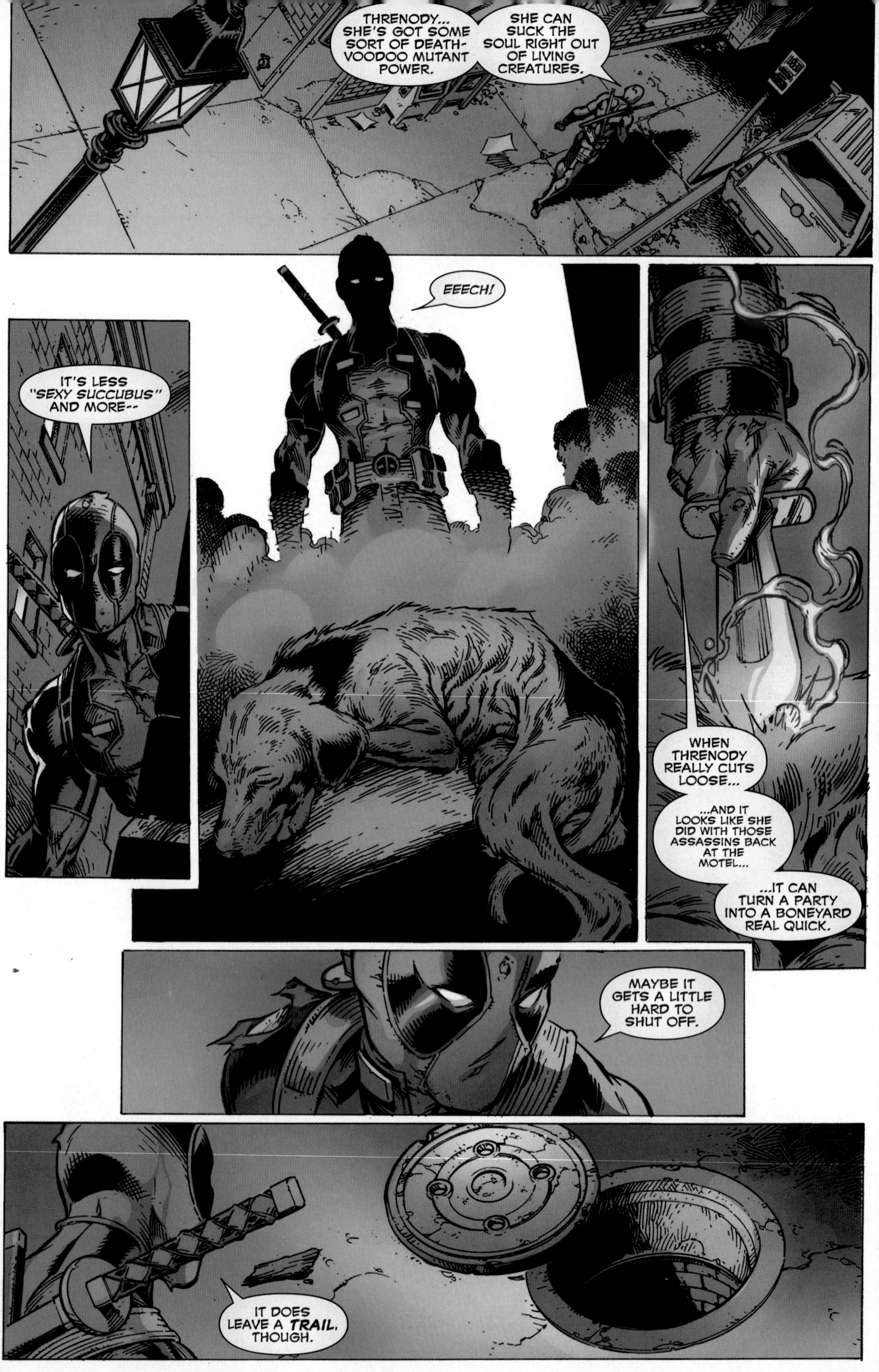
THRENODY... SHE'S GOT SOME SORT OF DEATH-VOODOO MUTANT POWER.
SHE CAN SUCK THE SOUL RIGHT OUT OF LIVING CREATURES.
IT'S LESS "SEXY SUCCUBUS" AND MORE--
EEECH!
WHEN THRENODY REALLY CUTS LOOSE...
...AND IT LOOKS LIKE SHE DID WITH THOSE ASSASSINS BACK AT THE MOTEL...
...IT CAN TURN A PARTY INTO A BONEYARD REAL QUICK.
MAYBE IT GETS A LITTLE HARD TO SHUT OFF.
IT DOES LEAVE A TRAIL, THOUGH.

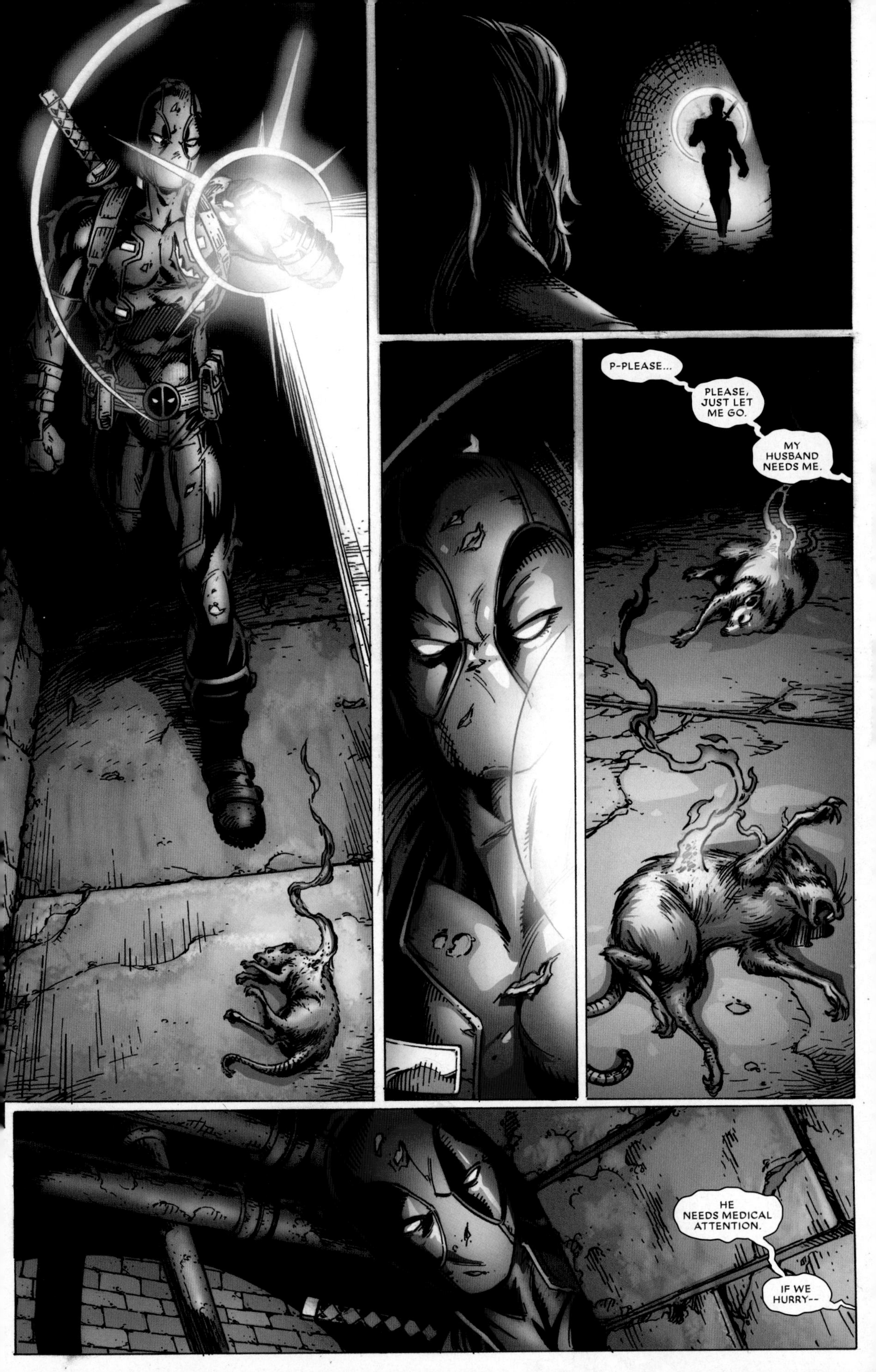
P-PLEASE...
PLEASE, JUST LET ME GO.
MY HUSBAND NEEDS ME.
HE NEEDS MEDICAL ATTENTION.
IF WE HURRY--

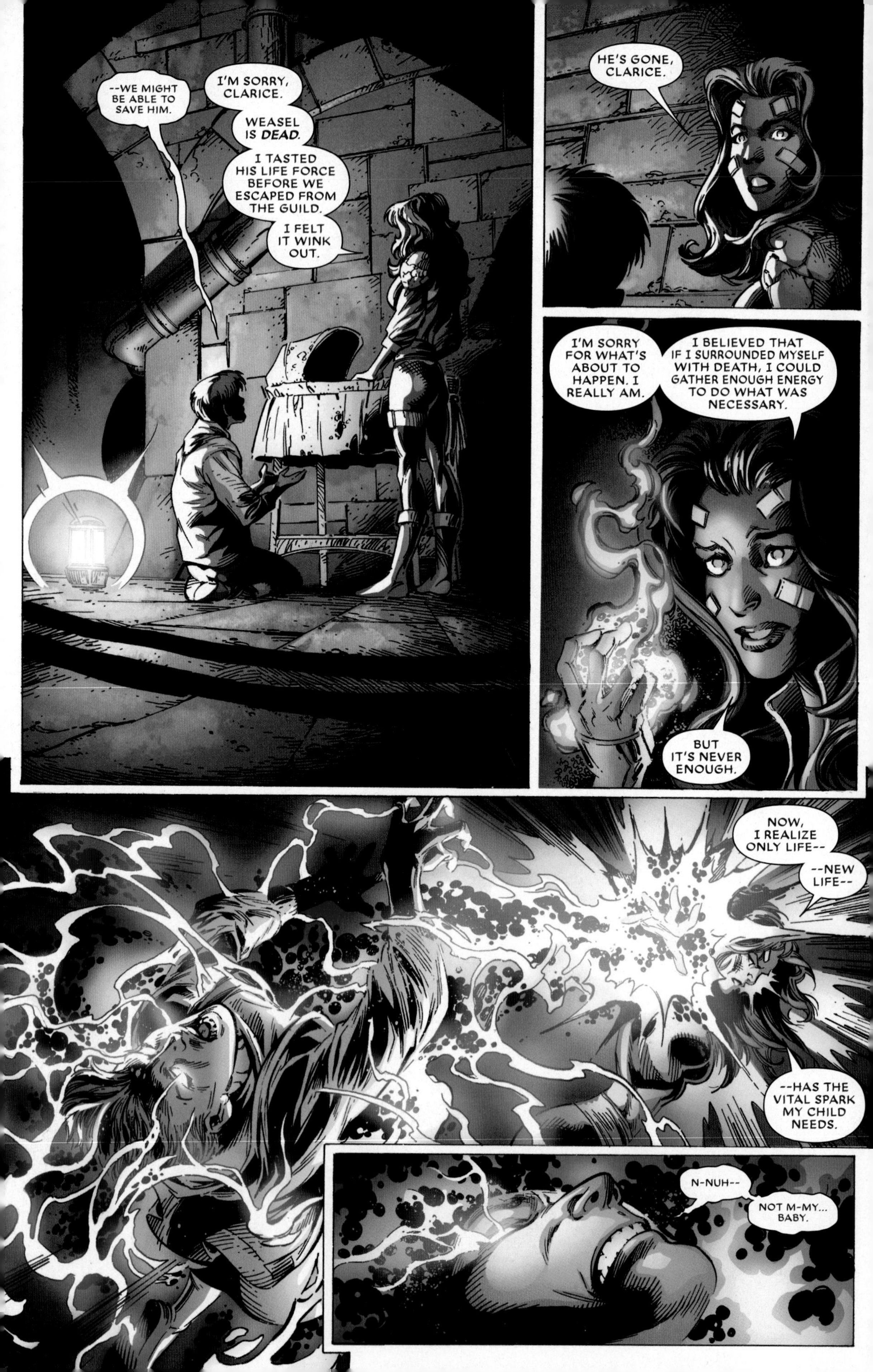
--WE MIGHT BE ABLE TO SAVE HIM.
I'M SORRY, CLARICE.
WEASEL IS *DEAD*.
I TASTED HIS LIFE FORCE BEFORE WE ESCAPED FROM THE GUILD.
I FELT IT WINK OUT.
HE'S GONE, CLARICE.
I'M SORRY FOR WHAT'S ABOUT TO HAPPEN. I REALLY AM.
I BELIEVED THAT IF I SURROUNDED MYSELF WITH DEATH, I COULD GATHER ENOUGH ENERGY TO DO WHAT WAS NECESSARY.
BUT IT'S NEVER ENOUGH.
NOW, I REALIZE ONLY LIFE--
--NEW LIFE--
--HAS THE VITAL SPARK MY CHILD NEEDS.
N-NUH--
NOT M-MY... BABY.

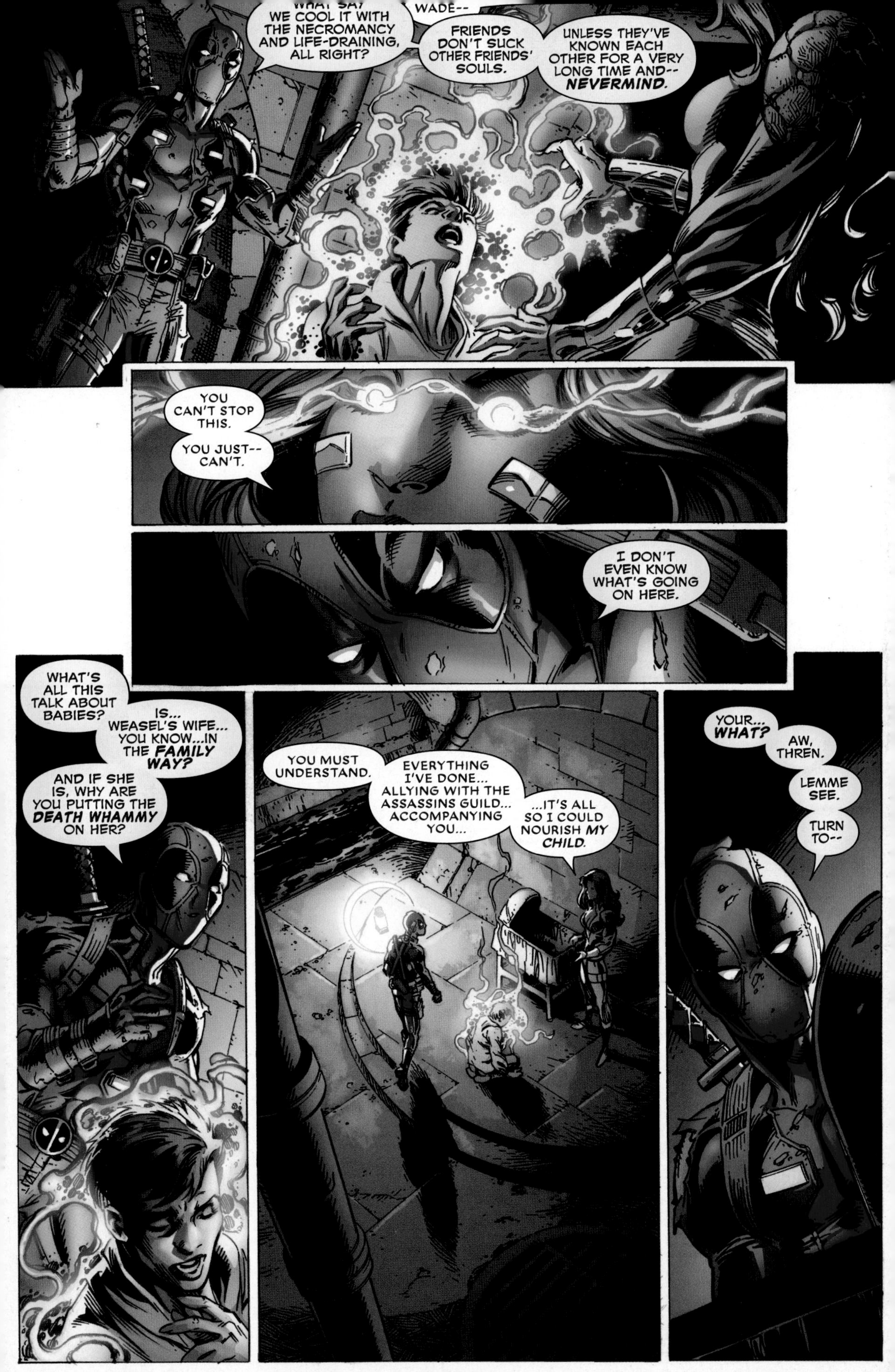
WHAT SAY WE COOL IT WITH THE NECROMANCY AND LIFE-DRAINING, ALL RIGHT?
WADE--
FRIENDS DON'T SUCK OTHER FRIENDS' SOULS.
UNLESS THEY'VE KNOWN EACH OTHER FOR A VERY LONG TIME AND-- NEVERMIND.
YOU CAN'T STOP THIS.
YOU JUST-- CAN'T.
I DON'T EVEN KNOW WHAT'S GOING ON HERE.
WHAT'S ALL THIS TALK ABOUT BABIES?
IS... WEASEL'S WIFE... YOU KNOW...IN THE FAMILY WAY?
AND IF SHE IS, WHY ARE YOU PUTTING THE DEATH WHAMMY ON HER?
YOU MUST UNDERSTAND.
EVERYTHING I'VE DONE... ALLYING WITH THE ASSASSINS GUILD... ACCOMPANYING YOU...
...IT'S ALL SO I COULD NOURISH MY CHILD.
YOUR... WHAT?
AW, THREN.
LEMME SEE.
TURN TO--

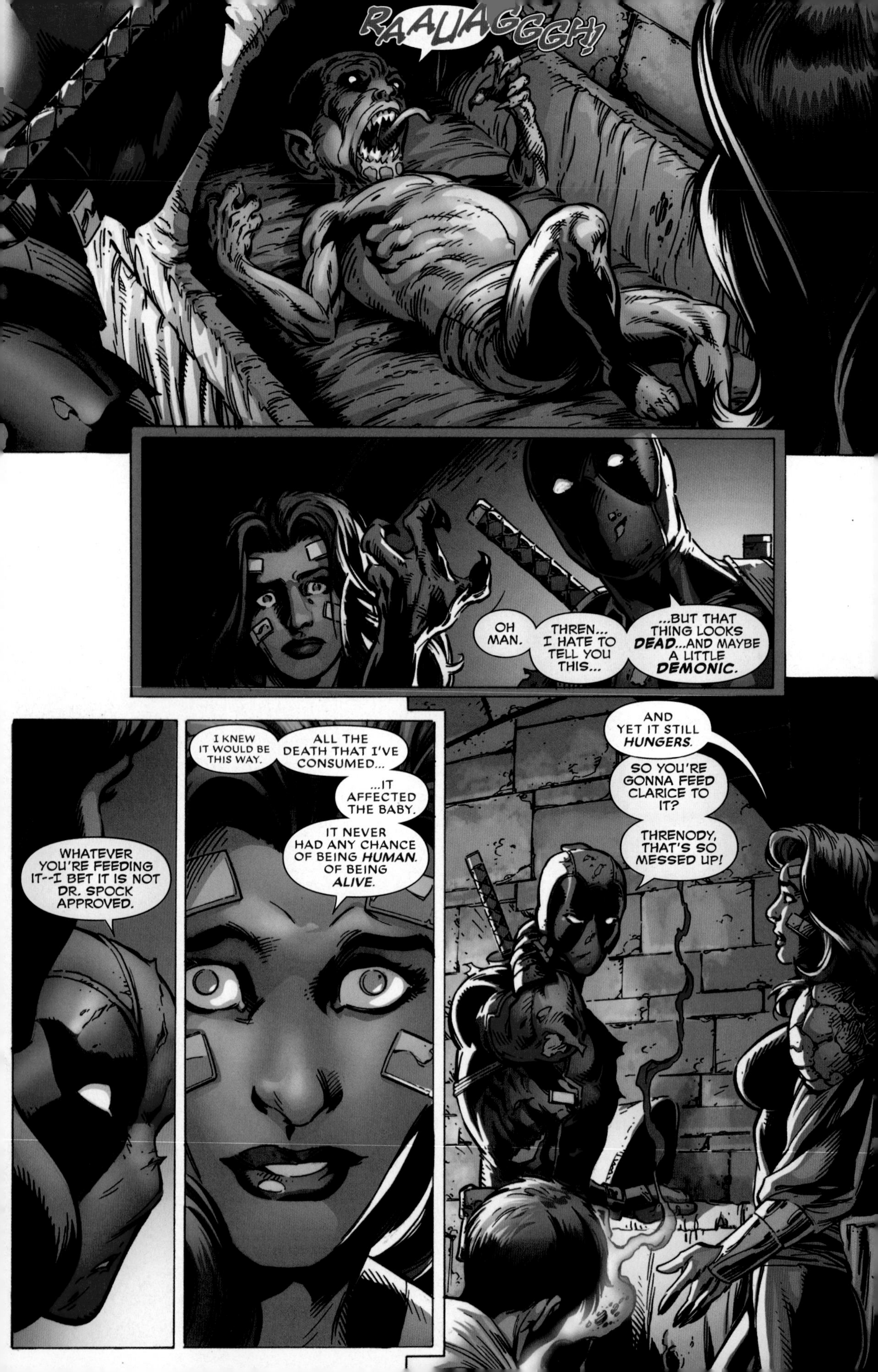
RAAUAGGGH!
OH MAN.
THREN... I HATE TO TELL YOU THIS...
...BUT THAT THING LOOKS DEAD...AND MAYBE A LITTLE DEMONIC.
WHATEVER YOU'RE FEEDING IT--I BET IT IS NOT DR. SPOCK APPROVED.
I KNEW IT WOULD BE THIS WAY.
ALL THE DEATH THAT I'VE CONSUMED...
...IT AFFECTED THE BABY.
IT NEVER HAD ANY CHANCE OF BEING HUMAN. OF BEING ALIVE.
AND YET IT STILL HUNGERS.
SO YOU'RE GONNA FEED CLARICE TO IT?
THRENODY, THAT'S SO MESSED UP!

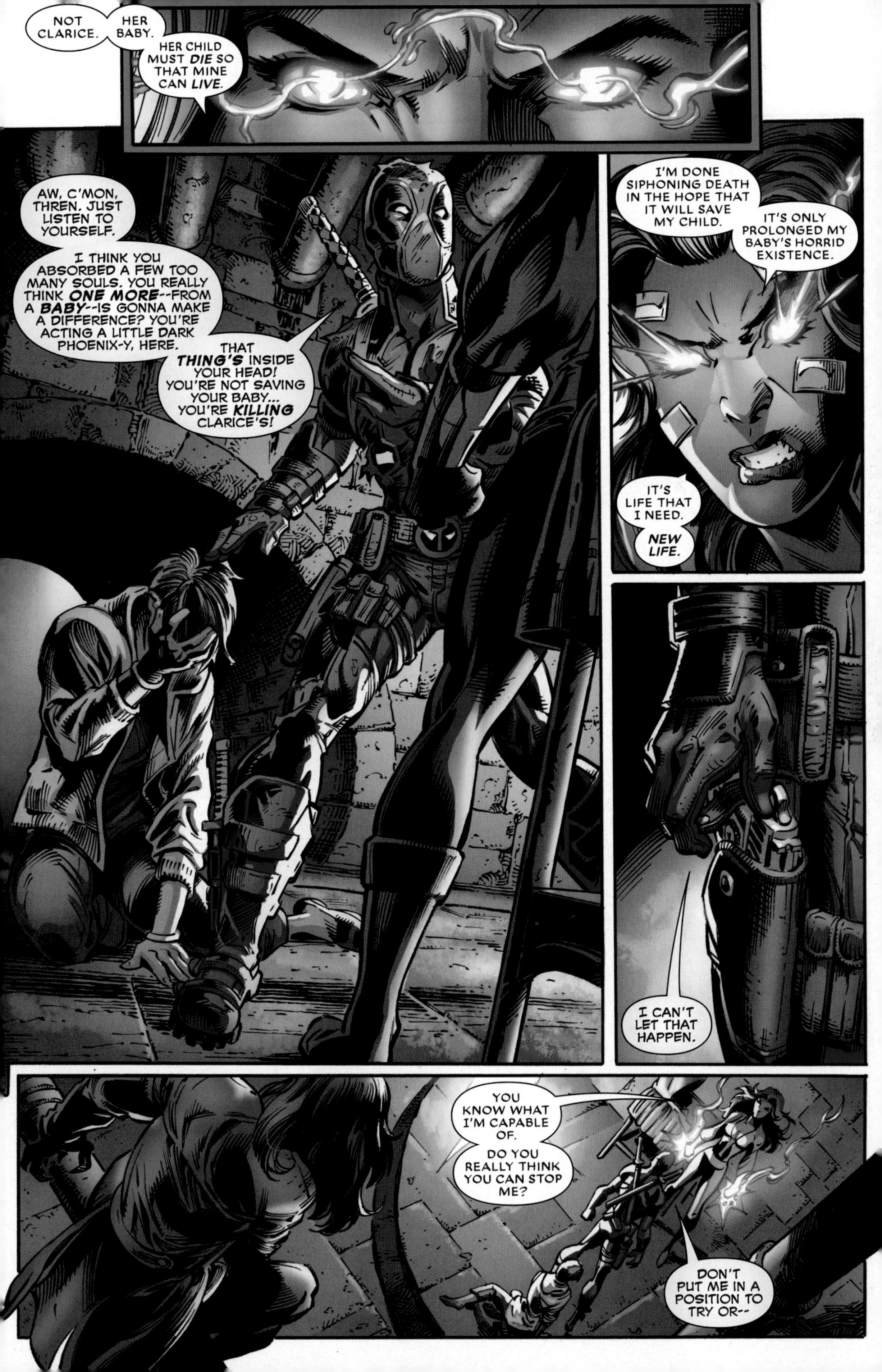

NOT CLARICE.
HER BABY.
HER CHILD MUST *DIE* SO THAT MINE CAN *LIVE.*
AW, C'MON, THREN. JUST LISTEN TO YOURSELF.
I THINK YOU ABSORBED A FEW TOO MANY SOULS. YOU REALLY THINK ***ONE MORE***--FROM A ***BABY***--IS GONNA MAKE A DIFFERENCE? YOU'RE ACTING A LITTLE DARK PHOENIX-Y, HERE.
THAT ***THING'S*** INSIDE YOUR HEAD! YOU'RE NOT SAVING YOUR BABY... YOU'RE ***KILLING*** CLARICE'S!
I'M DONE SIPHONING DEATH IN THE HOPE THAT IT WILL SAVE MY CHILD.
IT'S ONLY PROLONGED MY BABY'S HORRID EXISTENCE.
IT'S LIFE THAT I NEED.
NEW LIFE.
I CAN'T LET THAT HAPPEN.
YOU KNOW WHAT I'M CAPABLE OF.
DO YOU REALLY THINK YOU CAN STOP ME?
DON'T PUT ME IN A POSITION TO TRY OR--

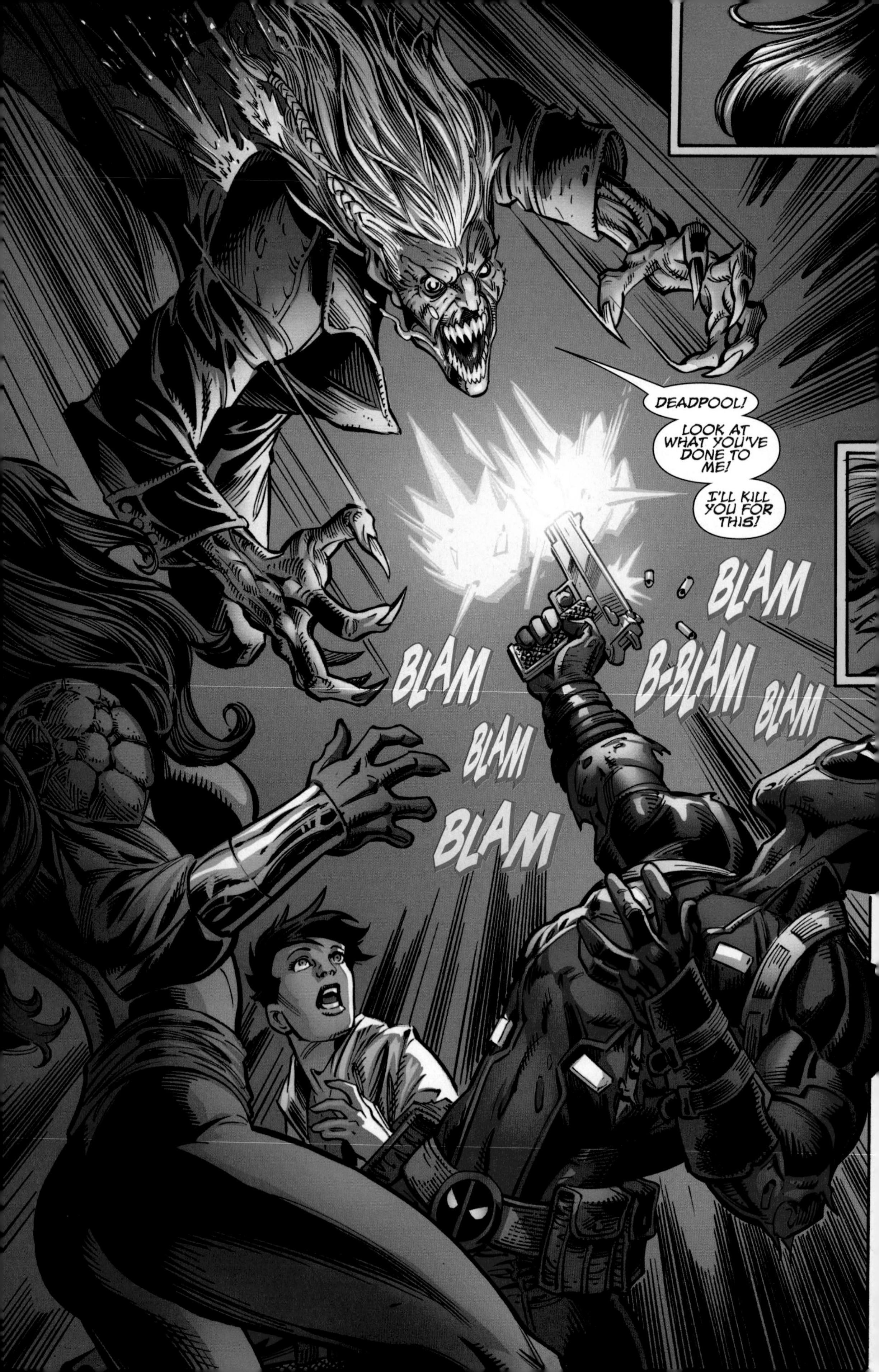
DEADPOOL!
LOOK AT WHAT YOU'VE DONE TO ME!
I'LL KILL YOU FOR THIS!
BLAM
BLAM
B-BLAM
BLAM
BLAM
BLAM

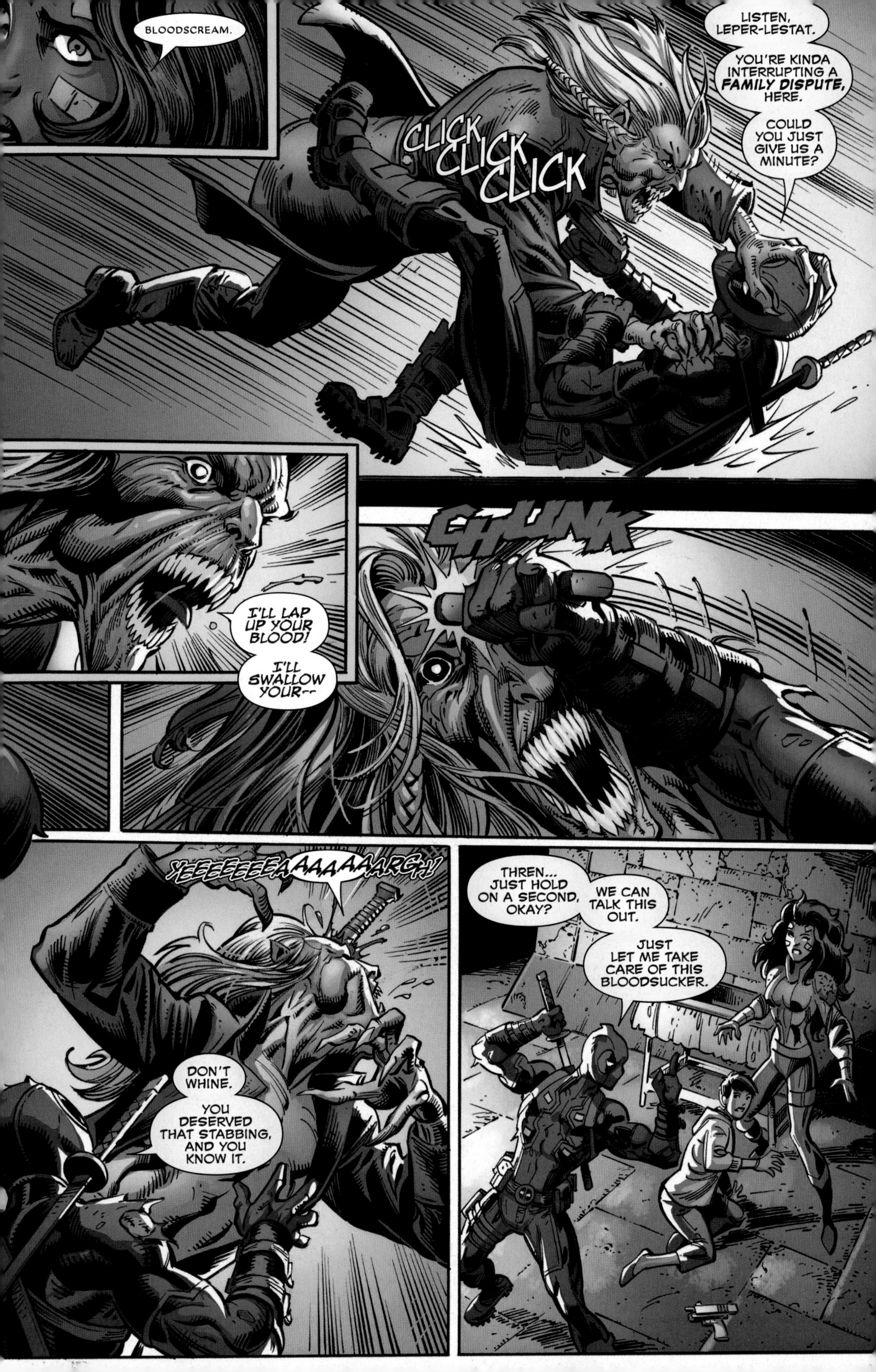
BLOODSCREAM.
LISTEN, LEPER-LESTAT.
YOU'RE KINDA INTERRUPTING A FAMILY DISPUTE, HERE.
COULD YOU JUST GIVE US A MINUTE?
CLICK CLICK CLICK
I'LL LAP UP YOUR BLOOD!
I'LL SWALLOW YOUR--
CHUNK
YEEEEEEEEAAAAAAARGH!
DON'T WHINE.
YOU DESERVED THAT STABBING, AND YOU KNOW IT.
THREN... JUST HOLD ON A SECOND, OKAY?
WE CAN TALK THIS OUT.
JUST LET ME TAKE CARE OF THIS BLOODSUCKER.

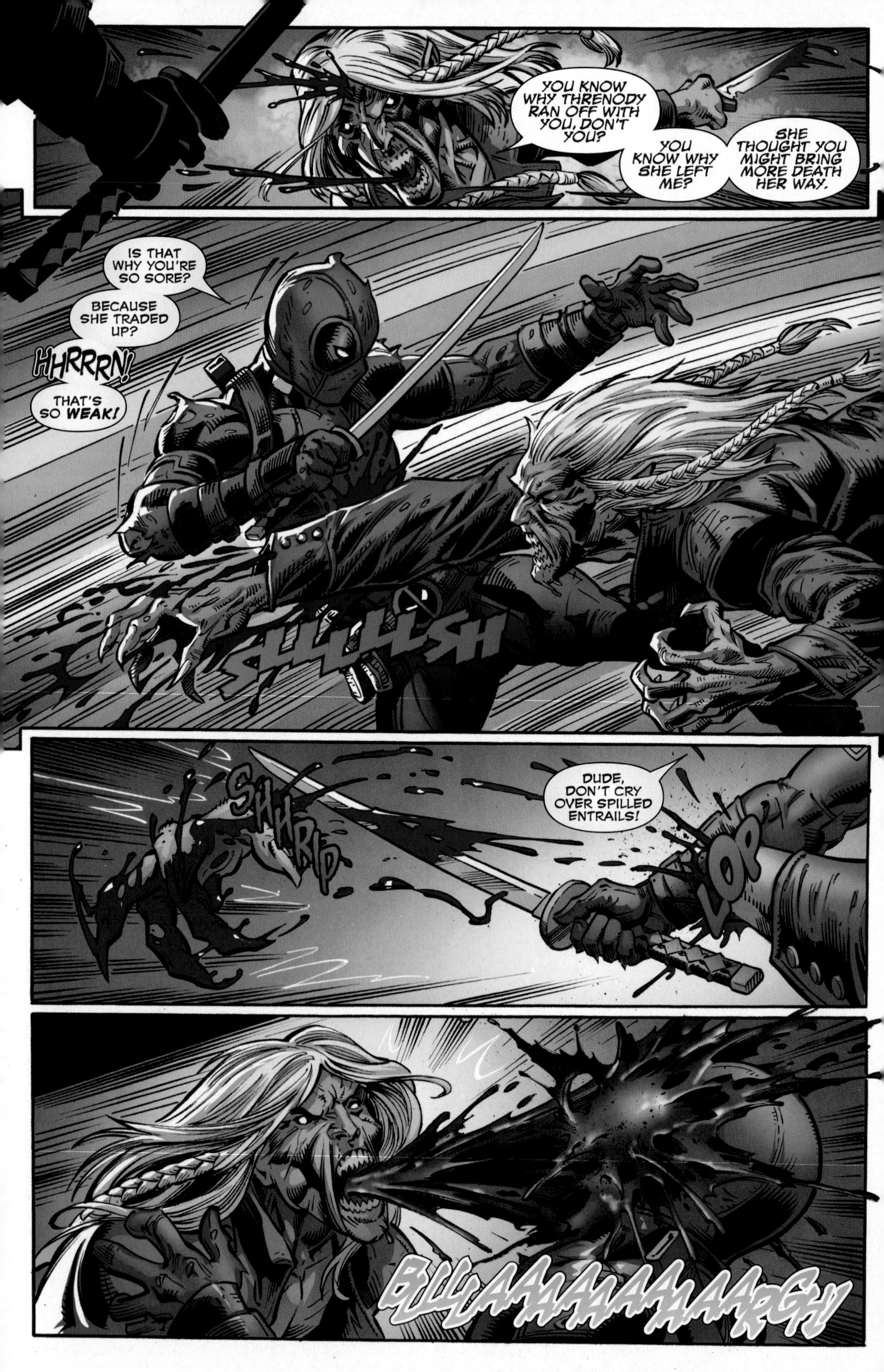
YOU KNOW WHY THRENODY RAN OFF WITH YOU, DON'T YOU?
YOU KNOW WHY SHE LEFT ME?
SHE THOUGHT YOU MIGHT BRING MORE DEATH HER WAY.
IS THAT WHY YOU'RE SO SORE?
BECAUSE SHE TRADED UP?
HHRRRN!
THAT'S SO WEAK!
SHLLLLSH
SHHRIP
DUDE, DON'T CRY OVER SPILLED ENTRAILS!
LOP
BULLAAAAAAAAARGH!

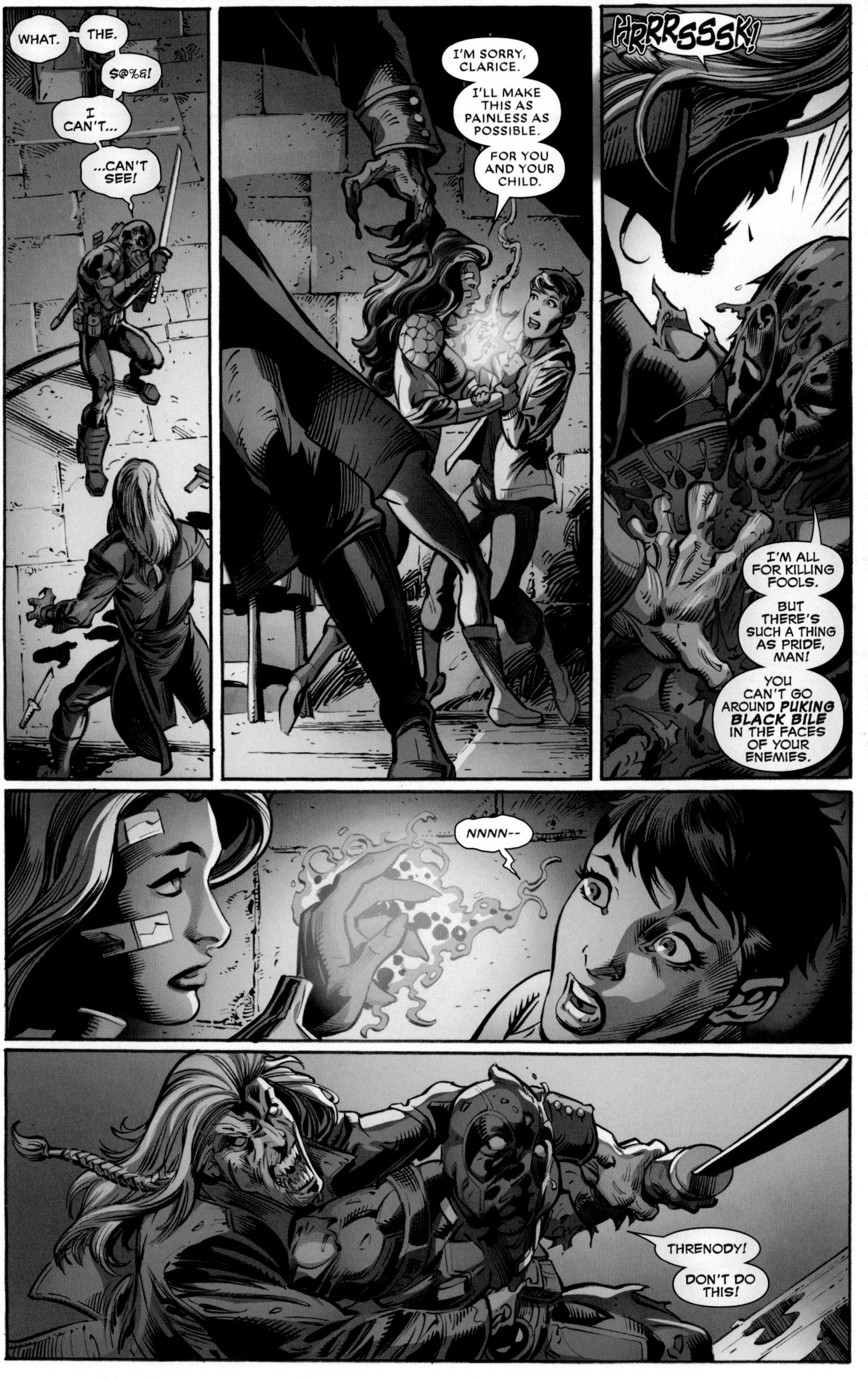
WHAT.
THE.
$@%&!
I CAN'T...
...CAN'T SEE!
I'M SORRY, CLARICE.
I'LL MAKE THIS AS PAINLESS AS POSSIBLE.
FOR YOU AND YOUR CHILD.
HRRRSSSK!
I'M ALL FOR KILLING FOOLS.
BUT THERE'S SUCH A THING AS PRIDE, MAN!
YOU CAN'T GO AROUND PUKING BLACK BILE IN THE FACES OF YOUR ENEMIES.
NNNN--
THRENODY!
DON'T DO THIS!

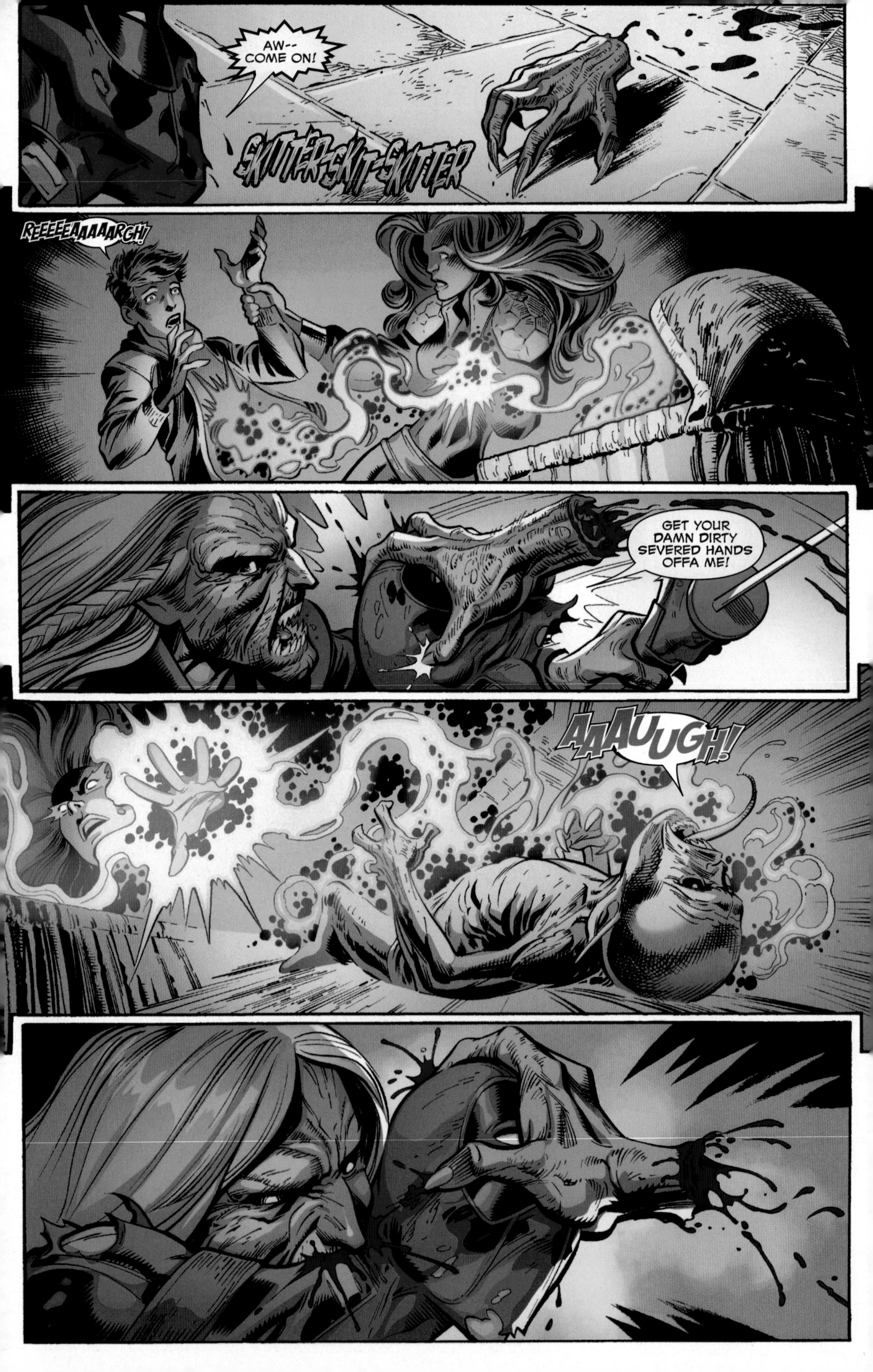
AW-- COME ON!
SKITTER-SKIT-SKITTER
REEEEEAAAAARGH!
GET YOUR DAMN DIRTY SEVERED HANDS OFFA ME!
AAAAUUGH!

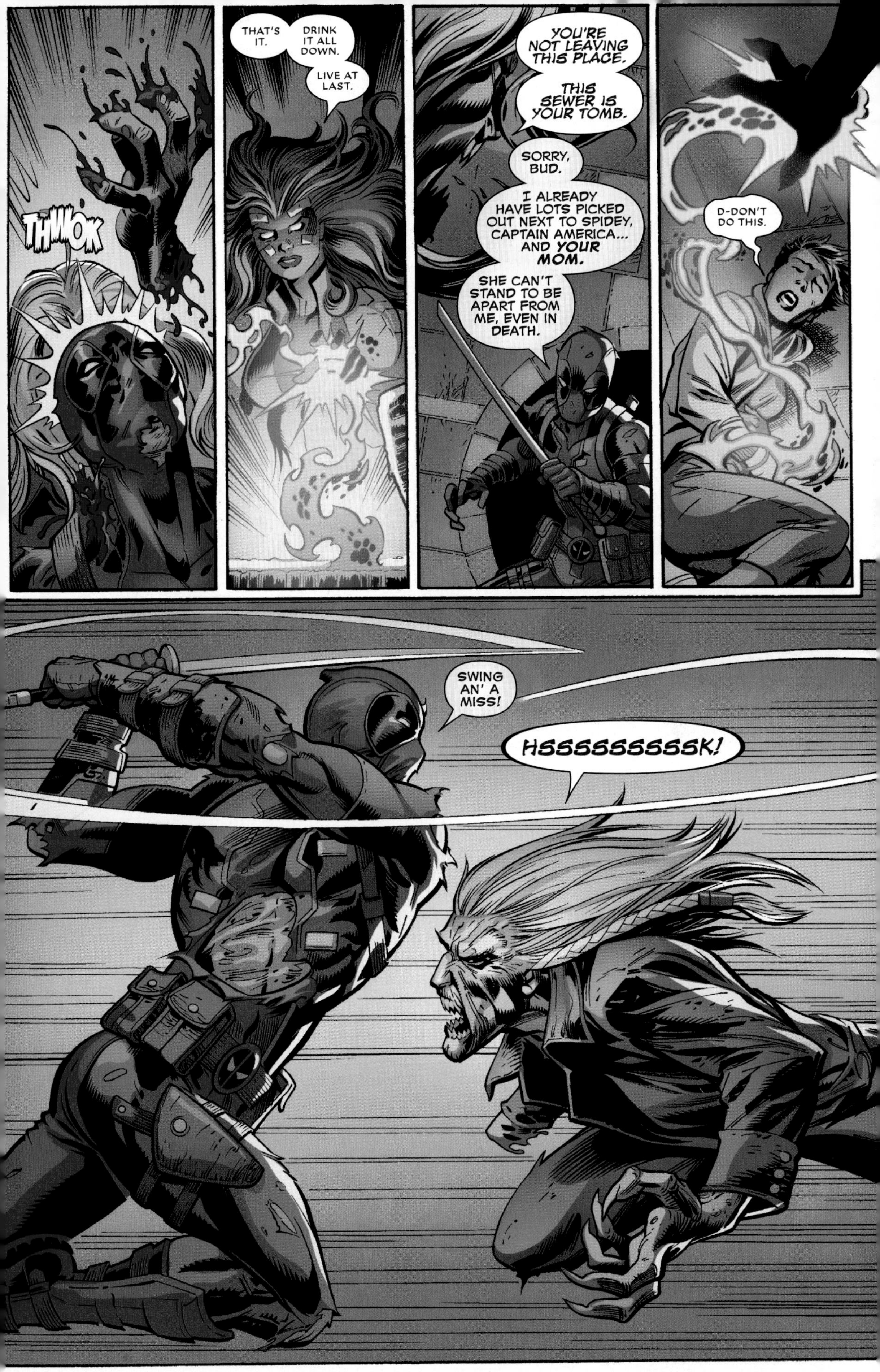
THWOK
THAT'S IT.
DRINK IT ALL DOWN.
LIVE AT LAST.
YOU'RE NOT LEAVING THIS PLACE.
THIS SEWER IS YOUR TOMB.
SORRY, BUD.
I ALREADY HAVE LOTS PICKED OUT NEXT TO SPIDEY, CAPTAIN AMERICA... AND YOUR MOM.
SHE CAN'T STAND TO BE APART FROM ME, EVEN IN DEATH.
D-DON'T DO THIS.
SWING AN' A MISS!
HSSSSSSSSSK!

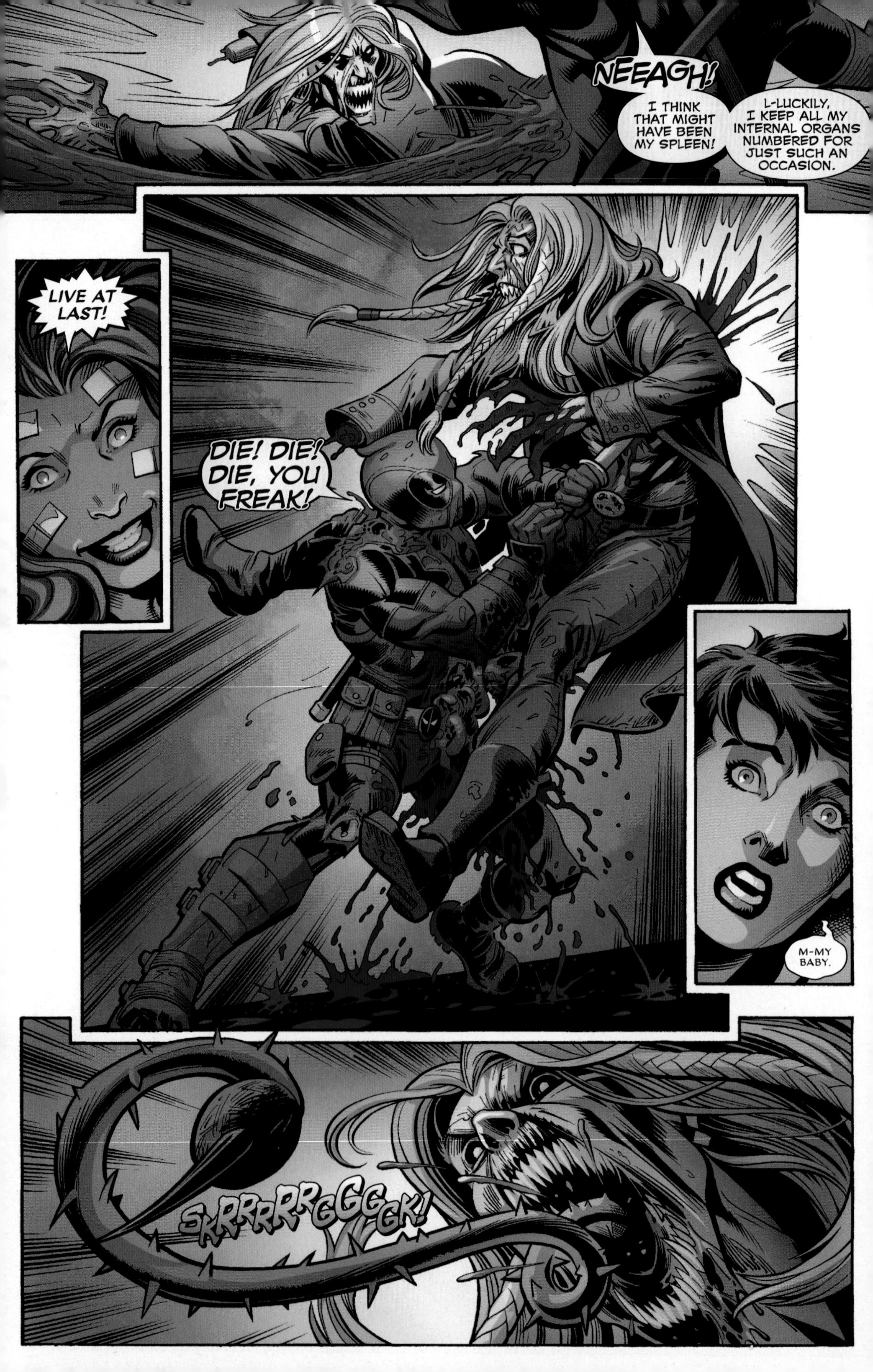
NEEAGH!
I THINK THAT MIGHT HAVE BEEN MY SPLEEN!
L-LUCKILY, I KEEP ALL MY INTERNAL ORGANS NUMBERED FOR JUST SUCH AN OCCASION.
LIVE AT LAST!
DIE! DIE! DIE, YOU FREAK!
M-MY BABY.
SKRRRRRRGGGGK!

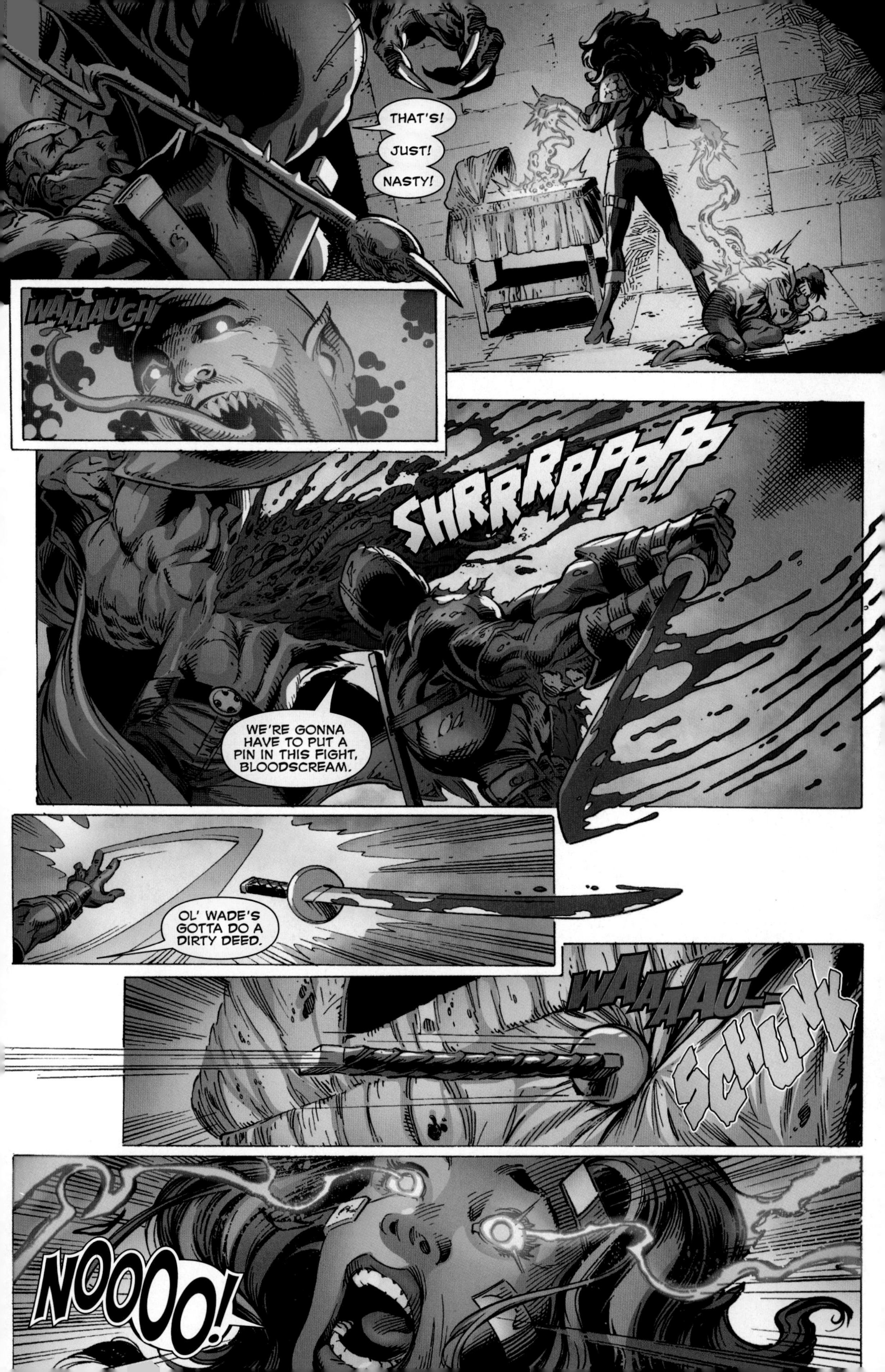
THAT'S!
JUST!
NASTY!
WAAAAUGH!
SHRRRRPPPB
WE'RE GONNA HAVE TO PUT A PIN IN THIS FIGHT, BLOODSCREAM.
OL' WADE'S GOTTA DO A DIRTY DEED.
WAAAAU--
SCHUNK
NOOOO!

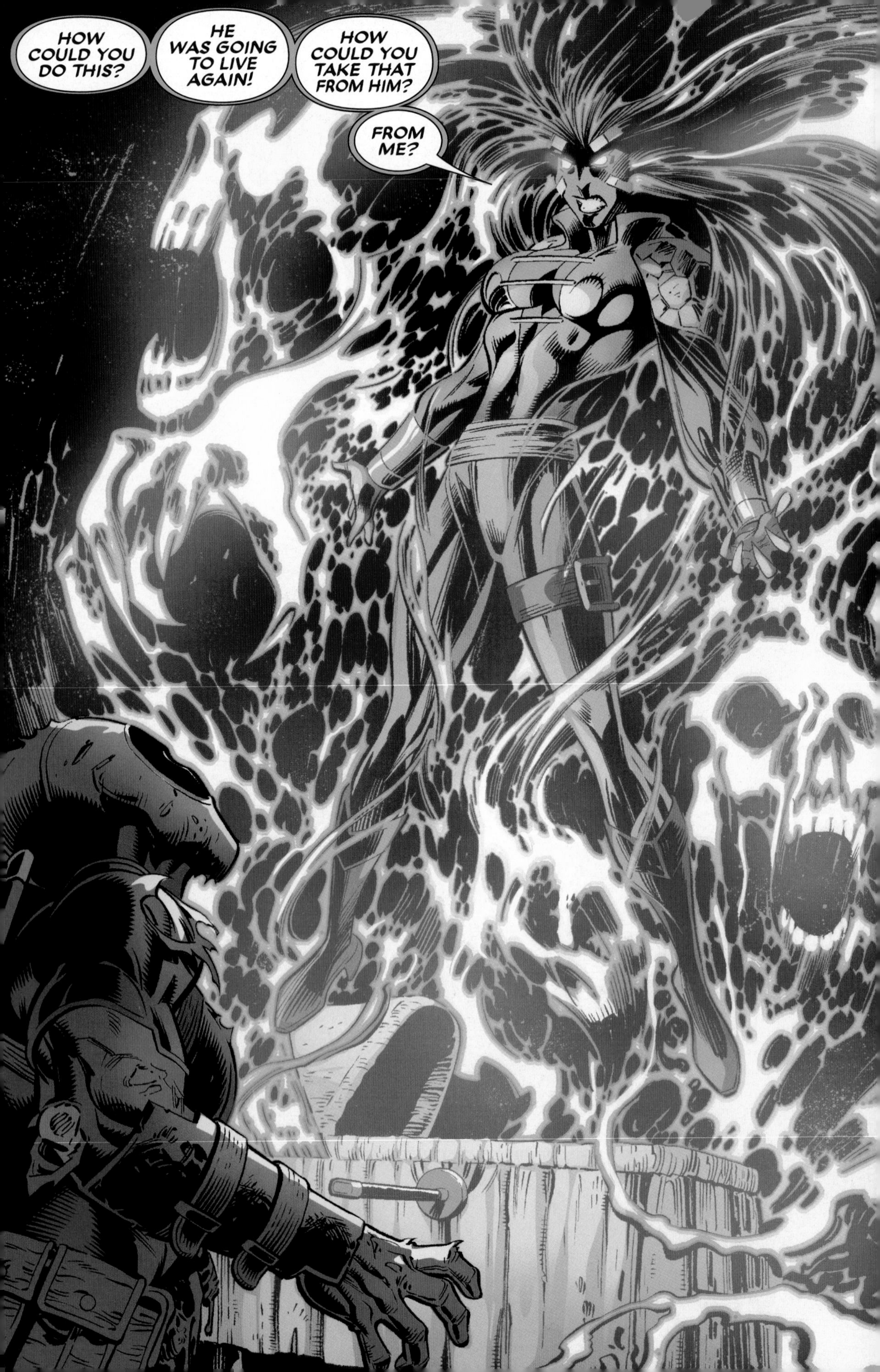
HOW COULD YOU DO THIS?
HE WAS GOING TO LIVE AGAIN!
HOW COULD YOU TAKE THAT FROM HIM?
FROM ME?

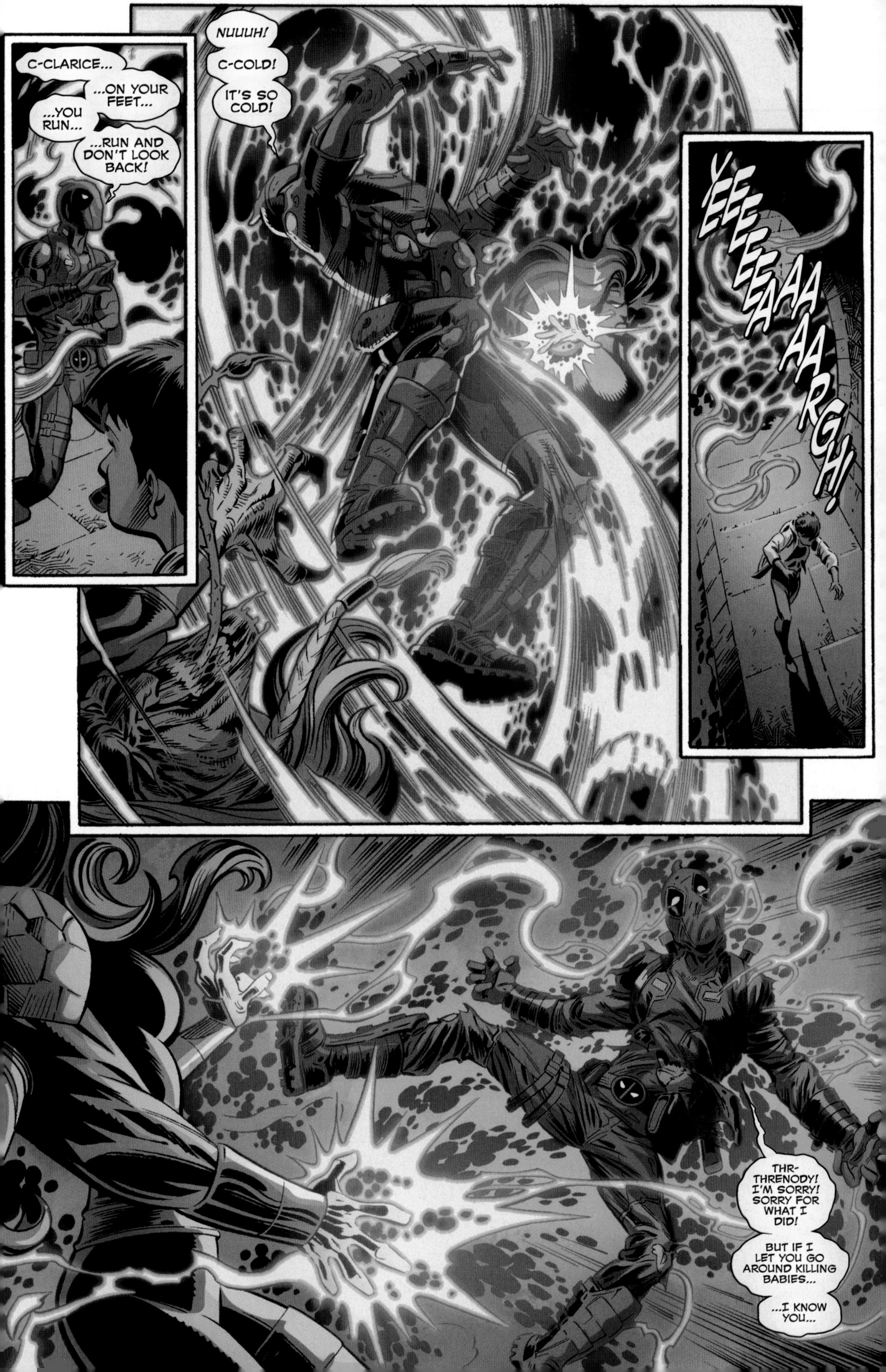
C-CLARICE...
...ON YOUR FEET...
...YOU RUN...
...RUN AND DON'T LOOK BACK!
NUUUH!
C-COLD!
IT'S SO COLD!
YEEEEEAAAAARGH!
THR-THRENODY! I'M SORRY! SORRY FOR WHAT I DID!
BUT IF I LET YOU GO AROUND KILLING BABIES...
...I KNOW YOU...

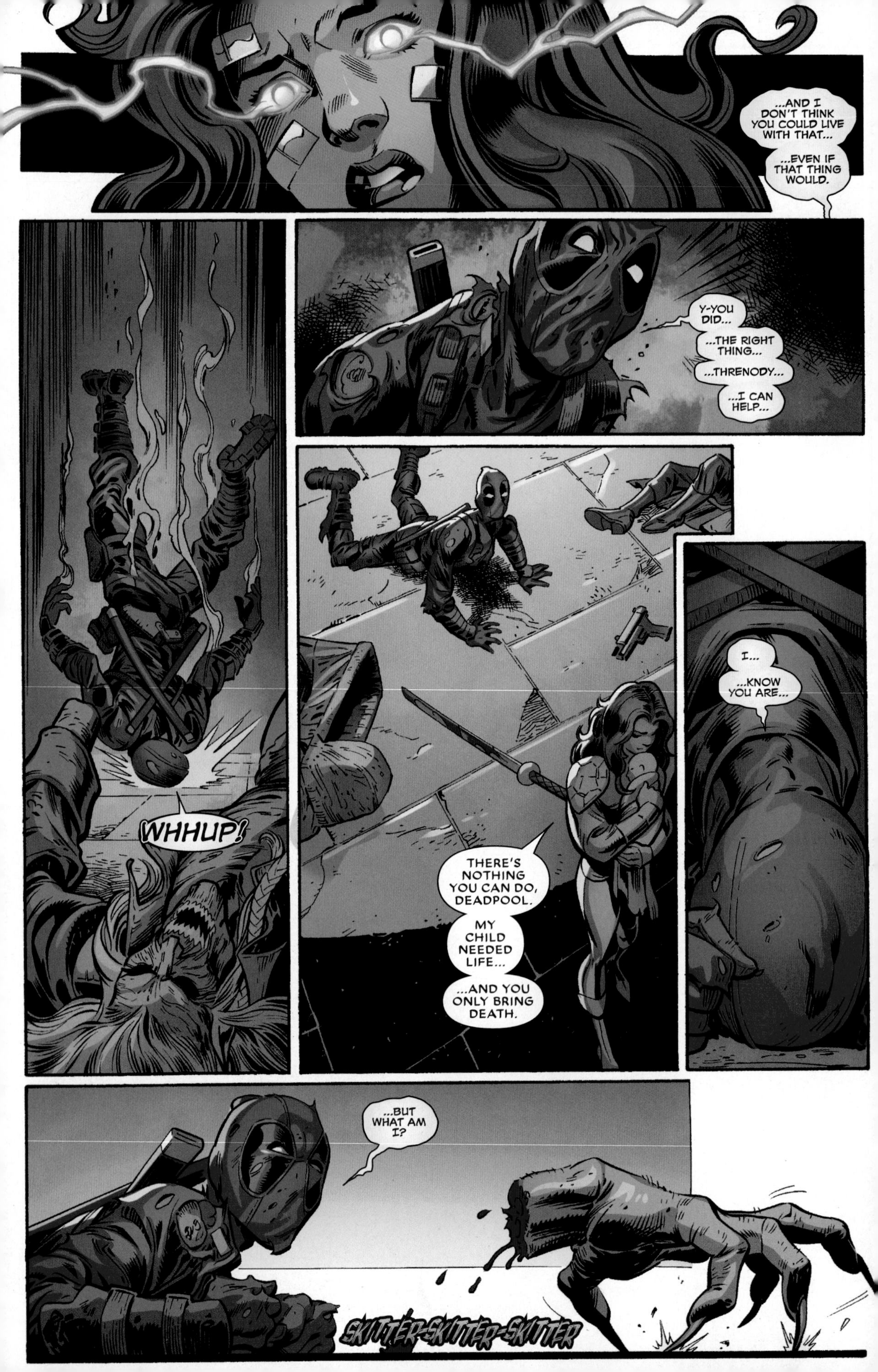
...AND I DON'T THINK YOU COULD LIVE WITH THAT...
...EVEN IF THAT THING WOULD.
WHHUP!
Y-YOU DID...
...THE RIGHT THING...
...THRENODY...
...I CAN HELP...
THERE'S NOTHING YOU CAN DO, DEADPOOL.
MY CHILD NEEDED LIFE...
...AND YOU ONLY BRING DEATH.
I...
...KNOW YOU ARE...
...BUT WHAT AM I?
SKITTER-SKITTER-SKITTER

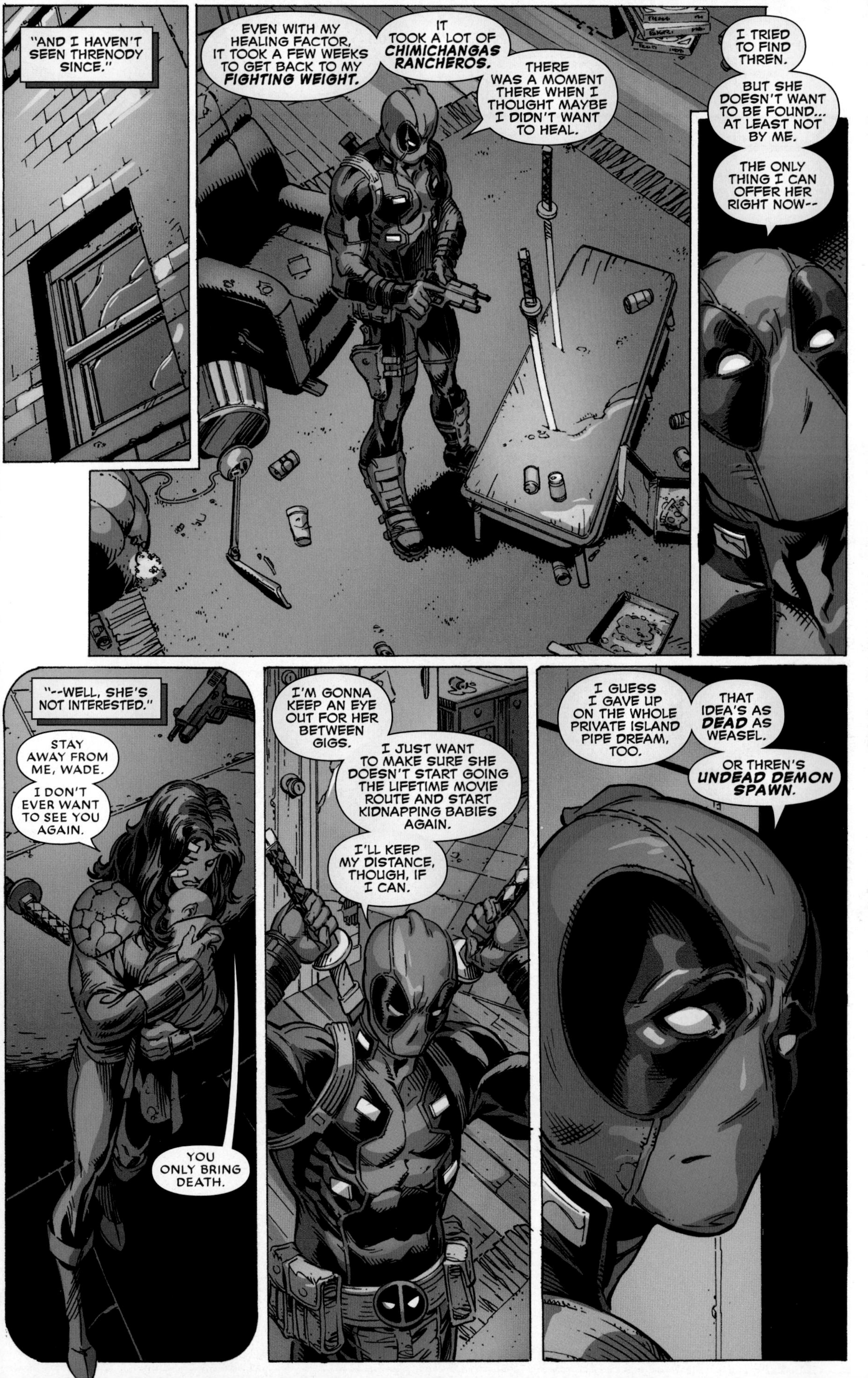

"AND I HAVEN'T SEEN THRENODY SINCE."
EVEN WITH MY HEALING FACTOR, IT TOOK A FEW WEEKS TO GET BACK TO MY FIGHTING WEIGHT.
IT TOOK A LOT OF CHIMICHANGAS RANCHEROS.
THERE WAS A MOMENT THERE WHEN I THOUGHT MAYBE I DIDN'T WANT TO HEAL.
I TRIED TO FIND THREN.
BUT SHE DOESN'T WANT TO BE FOUND... AT LEAST NOT BY ME.
THE ONLY THING I CAN OFFER HER RIGHT NOW--
"--WELL, SHE'S NOT INTERESTED."
STAY AWAY FROM ME, WADE.
I DON'T EVER WANT TO SEE YOU AGAIN.
YOU ONLY BRING DEATH.
I'M GONNA KEEP AN EYE OUT FOR HER BETWEEN GIGS.
I JUST WANT TO MAKE SURE SHE DOESN'T START GOING THE LIFETIME MOVIE ROUTE AND START KIDNAPPING BABIES AGAIN.
I'LL KEEP MY DISTANCE, THOUGH, IF I CAN.
I GUESS I GAVE UP ON THE WHOLE PRIVATE ISLAND PIPE DREAM, TOO.
THAT IDEA'S AS DEAD AS WEASEL.
OR THREN'S UNDEAD DEMON SPAWN.

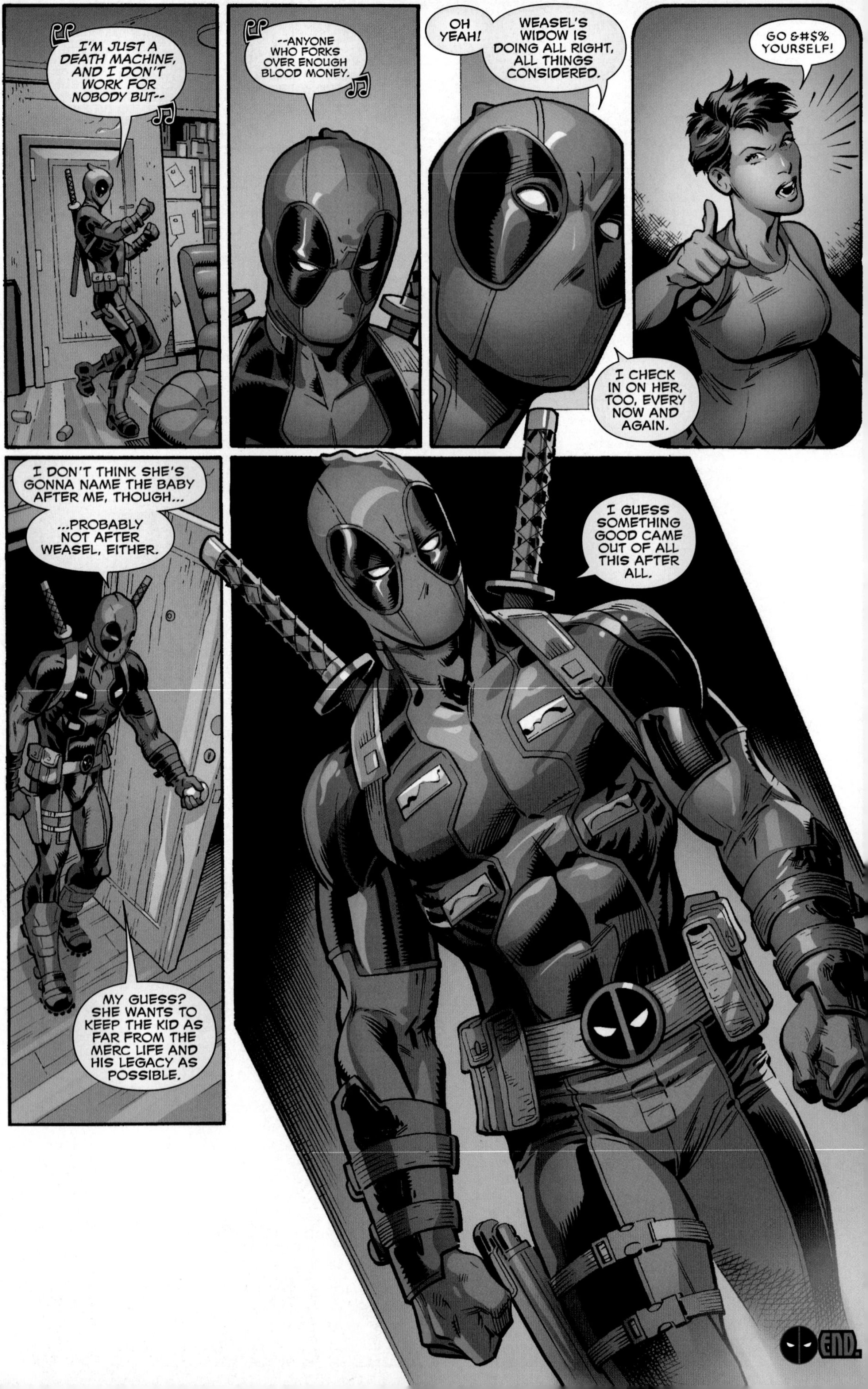
I'M JUST A DEATH MACHINE, AND I DON'T WORK FOR NOBODY BUT--
--ANYONE WHO FORKS OVER ENOUGH BLOOD MONEY.
OH YEAH!
WEASEL'S WIDOW IS DOING ALL RIGHT, ALL THINGS CONSIDERED.
GO &#$% YOURSELF!
I CHECK IN ON HER, TOO, EVERY NOW AND AGAIN.
I DON'T THINK SHE'S GONNA NAME THE BABY AFTER ME, THOUGH...
...PROBABLY NOT AFTER WEASEL, EITHER.
MY GUESS? SHE WANTS TO KEEP THE KID AS FAR FROM THE MERC LIFE AND HIS LEGACY AS POSSIBLE.
I GUESS SOMETHING GOOD CAME OUT OF ALL THIS AFTER ALL.
END.

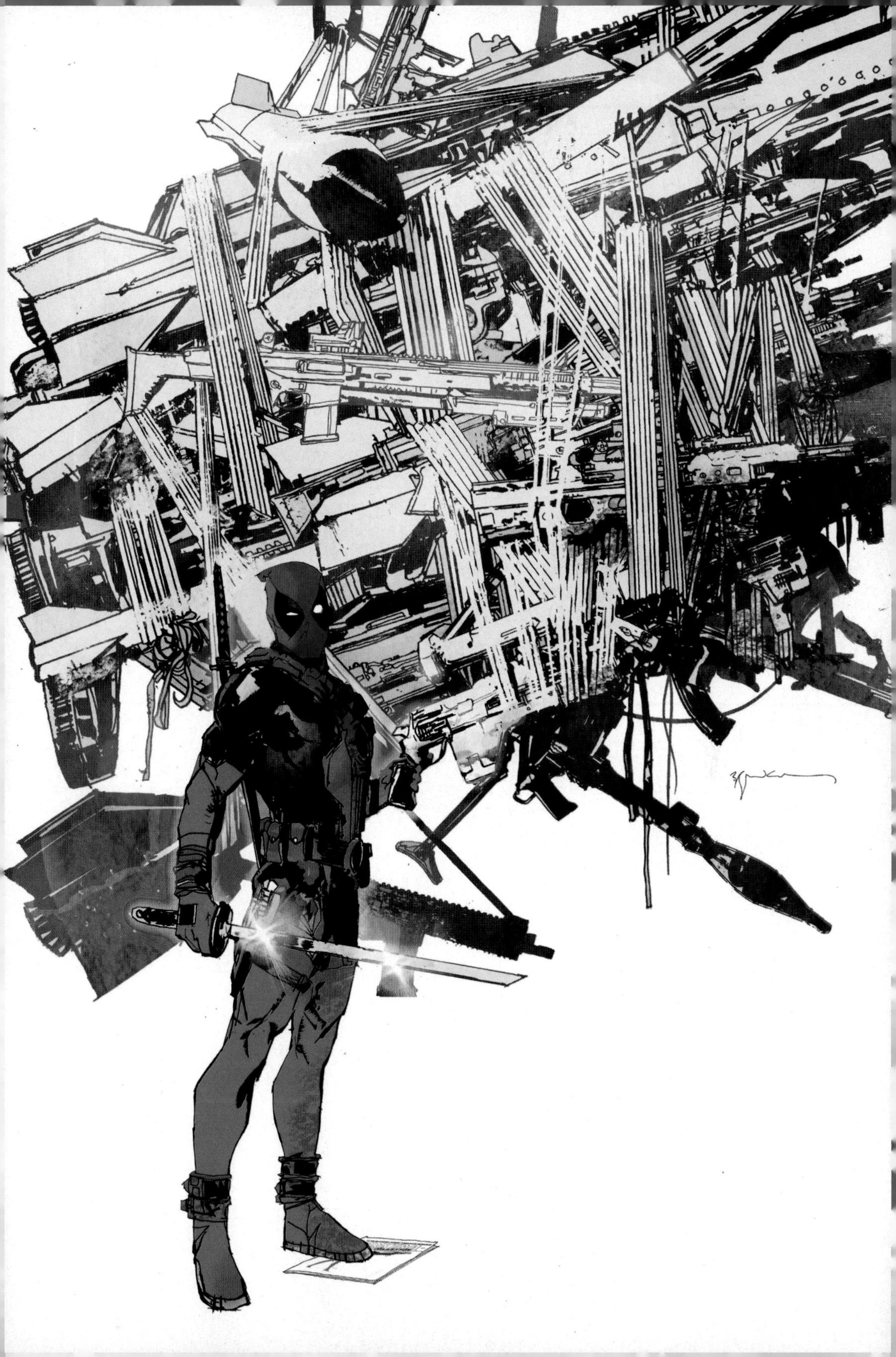

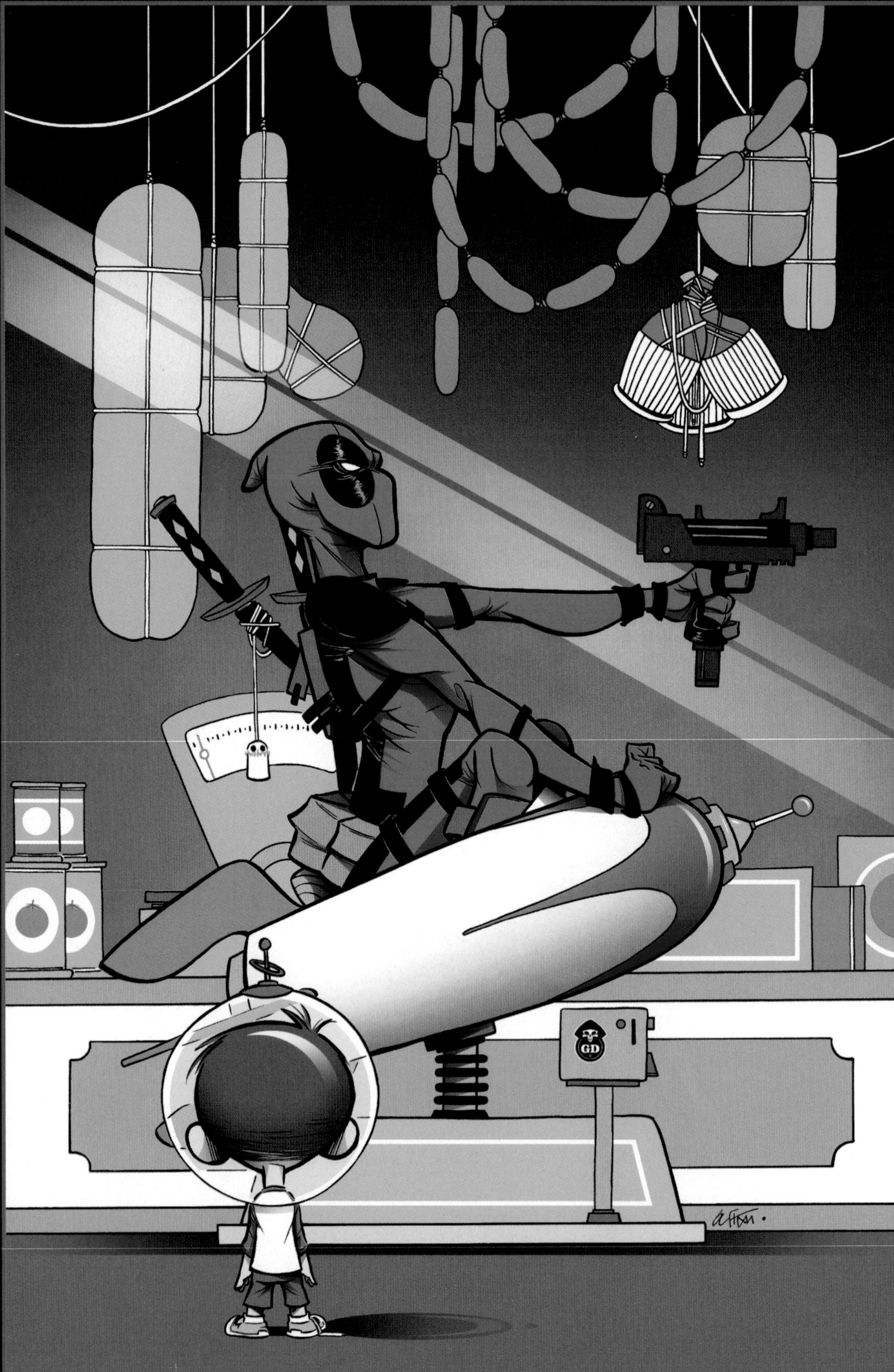

#2 VARIANT BY **GUSTAVO DUARTE**

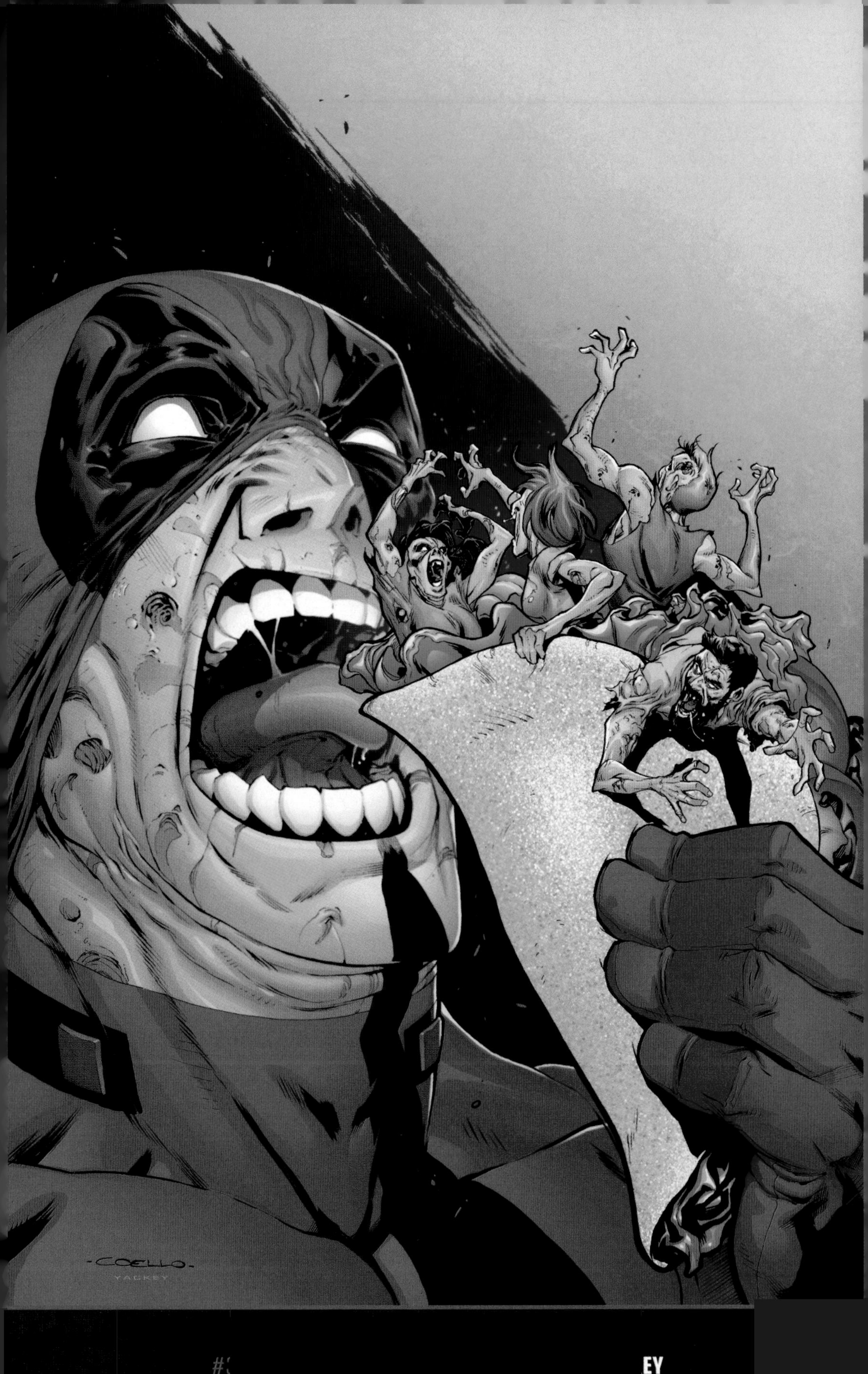
COELLO
YACKEY

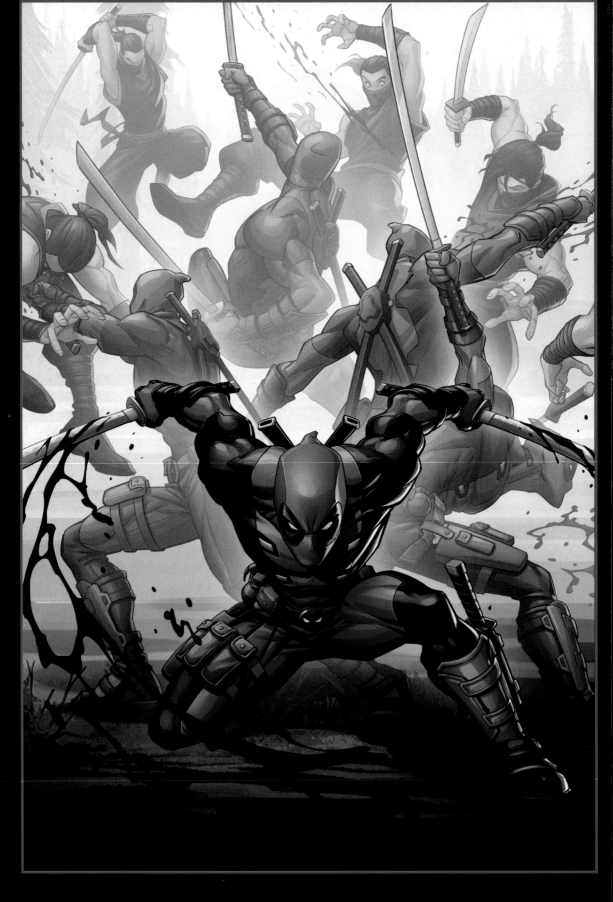

#4 VARIANT BY **PATRICK BROWN**

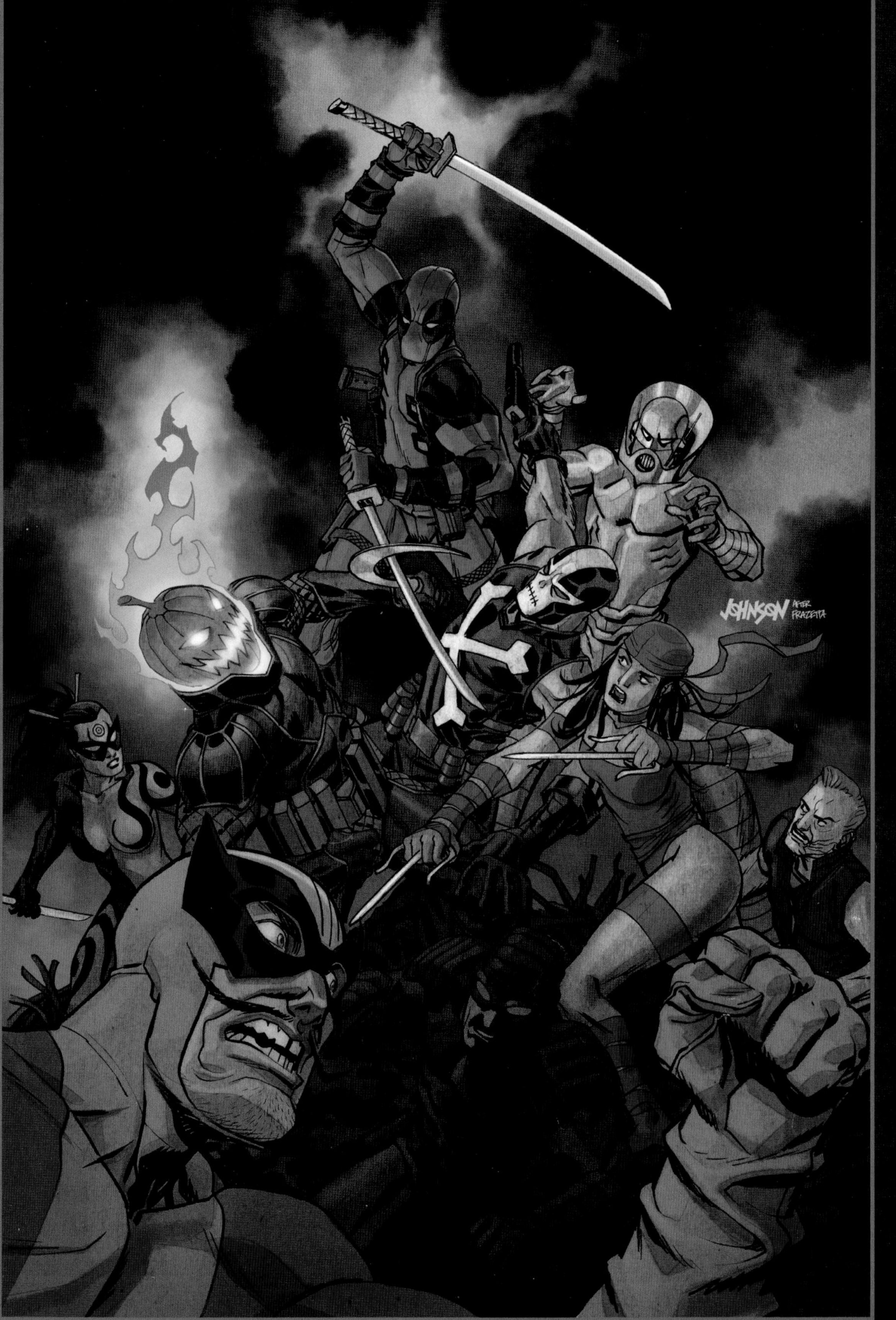
JOHNSON AFTER FRAZETTA

#5 VARIANT BY **DAVE JOHNSON**

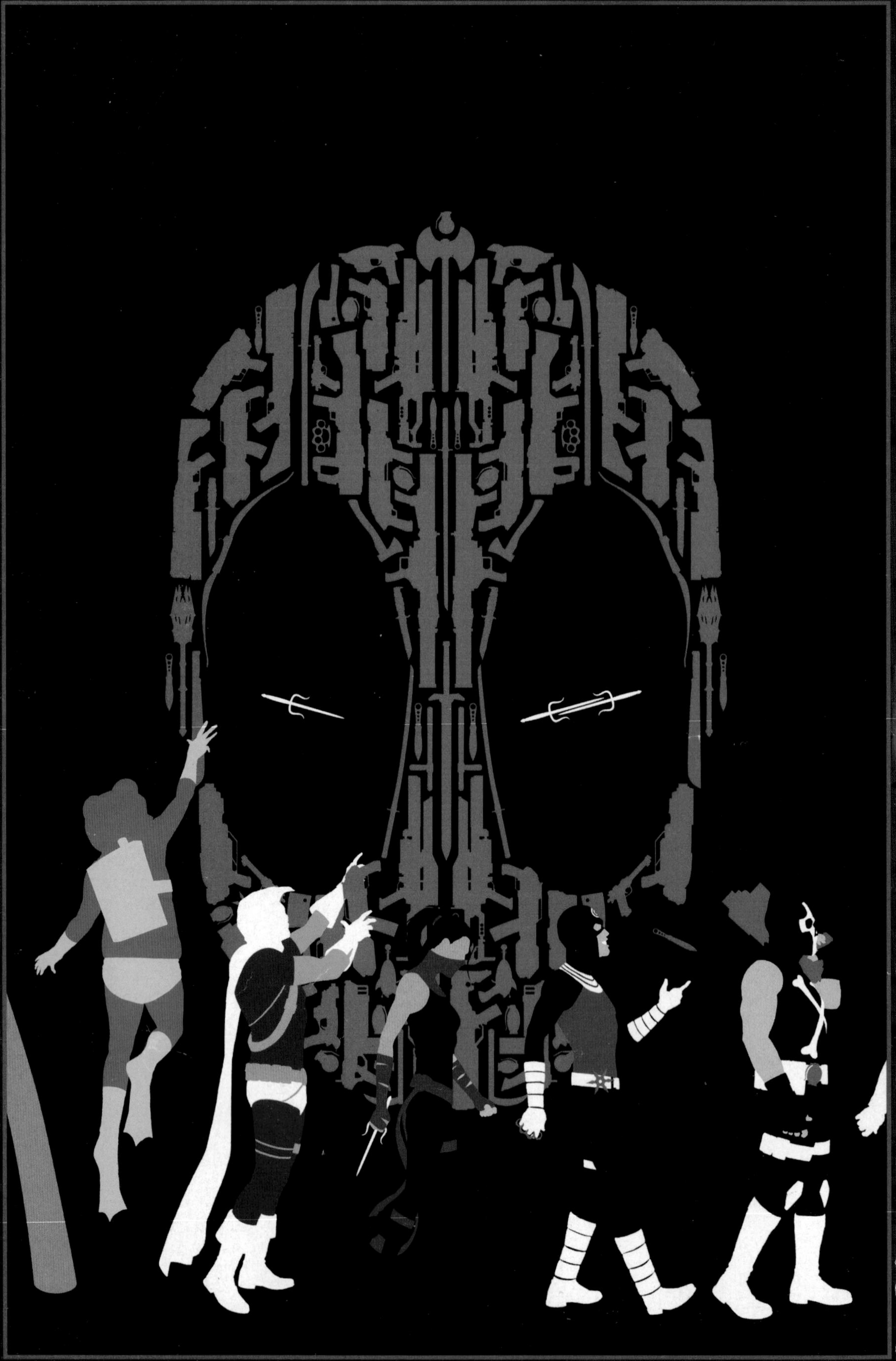

#6 VARIANT BY **JOHN TYLER CHRISTOPHER**